T0229876

Social Engineering in Cybersecurity

In today's digitally interconnected world, the threat landscape has evolved to include not just sophisticated technical exploits but also the art of human manipulation. Social engineering attacks have emerged as a formidable and often underestimated threat to information security. The primary aim of this textbook is to provide a comprehensive and in-depth exploration of social engineering attacks. The book seeks to equip cybersecurity professionals, IT practitioners, students, and anyone concerned with information security with the knowledge and tools needed to recognize, prevent, and mitigate the risks posed by social engineering.

The scope of this textbook is broad and multifaceted. It covers a wide range of social engineering attack vectors, including phishing, vishing, pretexting, baiting, tailgating, impersonation, and more. Each attack vector is dissected, with detailed explanations of how they work, real-world examples, and countermeasures.

Key Features

- **Comprehensive Coverage:** Thorough exploration of various social engineering attack vectors, including phishing, vishing, pretexting, baiting, quid pro quo, tailgating, impersonation, and more.
- **Psychological Insights:** In-depth examination of the psychological principles and cognitive biases that underlie social engineering tactics.
- **Real-World Case Studies:** Analysis of real-world examples and high-profile social engineering incidents to illustrate concepts and techniques.
- **Prevention and Mitigation:** Practical guidance on how to recognize, prevent, and mitigate social engineering attacks, including security best practices.
- **Ethical Considerations:** Discussion of ethical dilemmas and legal aspects related to social engineering that emphasises responsible use of knowledge.

This comprehensive textbook on social engineering attacks provides a deep and practical exploration of this increasingly prevalent threat in cybersecurity. It covers a wide array of attack vectors, including phishing, vishing, pretexting, and more, offering readers an in-depth understanding of how these attacks work. The book delves into the psychology behind social engineering and examines the cognitive biases and emotional triggers that make individuals susceptible. Real-world case studies illustrate concepts and techniques while practical guidance equips readers with the knowledge to recognize, prevent, and mitigate social engineering threats.

Social Engineering in Cybersecurity

Threats and Defenses

Edited by
Dr Gururaj H L, Dr Janhavi V and Ambika V

CRC Press
Taylor & Francis Group
Boca Raton   London   New York

CRC Press is an imprint of the
Taylor & Francis Group, an **informa** business

Designed cover image: www.shutterstock.com/image-photo/internet-network-security-concept-young-man-1931787956

First edition published 2024
by CRC Press
2385 NW Executive Center Drive, Suite 320, Boca Raton FL 33431

and by CRC Press
4 Park Square, Milton Park, Abingdon, Oxon, OX14 4RN

CRC Press is an imprint of Taylor & Francis Group, LLC

ISBN: 978-1-032-52440-5 (hbk)
ISBN: 978-1-032-52442-9 (pbk)
ISBN: 978-1-003-40671-6 (ebk)

DOI: 10.1201/9781003406716

Typeset in Times
by Apex CoVantage, LLC

Contents

SHRUTHI G, AKSHITHA AND KRISHNA RAJ P M

Preface

This book is a descriptive summary of social engineering attacks and their challenges with various case studies from diverse authors across the globe.

The authors of Chapter 1 introduce the concept of social engineering and emphasise its role in hacking. This sets the stage for exploring how human psychology can be exploited for cyberattacks.

Chapter 2 delves into the critical initial phase of social engineering, which is information gathering. It explores the techniques and methods that attackers use to collect data about their targets.

The authors of Chapter 3 discuss the cybersecurity risks and vulnerabilities associated with social engineering. The chapter also presents countermeasures and strategies to prevent and mitigate these types of attacks.

Chapter 4 focuses on packet sniffers and presents a case study that examines the tools, techniques, and tactics employed by attackers to intercept network traffic for malicious purposes.

Chapter 5 explores the broader impact of social engineering attacks on organisations. It delves into the financial, reputational, and operational consequences of successful social engineering attacks.

Chapter 6, "Impacts of Social Engineering in E-Banking", specifically targets e-banking and investigates the unique impacts of social engineering attacks on the financial sector while highlighting the vulnerabilities and potential consequences.

Chapters 7 and 8 unveil the tools and psychological principles behind social engineering, providing insights into how attackers manipulate human behaviour to achieve their goals.

The authors of Chapter 9 focus on machine learning and introduce an algorithm designed to address social engineering attempts within chat messages to enhance security in online communication.

Chapter 10 conducts a survey of security models tailored for the Internet of Things (IoT) and highlights the importance of safeguarding IoT ecosystems from social engineering threats.

In Chapter 11, a study is conducted on image detection and extraction techniques that utilises Convolutional Neural Networks (CNN) and IoT to estimate distracted drivers, emphasising safety and security concerns in the automotive industry. The authors of Chapter 12 focus on cyberattacks, countermeasures, and their conclusions.

Gururaj H L

Editor Biographies

 **Dr. Gururaj H L** Dr. Gururaj H L (Senior Member, IEEE) received his Ph.D. in computer science and engineering from Visvesvaraya Technological University, India in 2019. He has published more than 200 research articles in peer-reviewed and reputed international journals, books for Springer, IET, IGI Global and Taylor & Francis, and presented more than 100 papers at various international conferences. He is a Senior Member of Association for Computing Machinery (ACM). He received a Young Scientist International Travel Support ITS-SERB from the Department of Science and Technology of the Government of India in December 2016. He has also been a recipient of best paper awards at various national and international conferences. He was appointed as ACM Distinguish Speaker (2018–2021) by the ACM U.S. Council. He has been honoured as Keynote Speaker, Session Chair, TPC Member, and Advisory Committee Member at international seminars, workshops, and conferences across the globe. Professor Gururaj's research interests are applications in machine and federated learning, data mining, blockchain, and cybersecurity.

Dr. Janhavi V Dr. Janhavi V received her Ph.D. in computer science and engineering from Visvesvaraya Technological University, India. She is currently working as Associate Professor in the department of Computer Science &Engineering at Vidyavardhaka College of Engineering, Mysuru. She has published many research articles in peer-reviewed and reputed international journals.

Ambika V Ambika V completed her M. Tech in Computer Network Engineering from Visvesvaraya Technological University. She is currently working as Assistant Professor in the Department of Bachelor of Computer Applications at Mysore Institute of Commerce and Arts, Mysuru, Karnataka. She has published various research papers in several reputed international journals and presented them at conferences. Her areas of interest include computer networks, cybersecurity, information security, and cryptography.

Contributors

Akshitha
Ambika N
T N Anitha
Lalitha Bandeppa
Bharath K C
Vishal Bharath
Bhaskar S
Chiranth T S
Joel Deniz D Souza
Santosh L. Deshpande
Girish L
Veda Gupta
Gurushankar H B
Harshitha H
Harshitha K
Chinmaya, Hebbar

Jayasudha K
Prateek Kammakolu
Chethana R Kariger
Krishna Raj P M
Karan Kumar
Colin Lobo
Manjesh R
Kamalakshi Naganna
Najmusher H
Bharati B. Pannayagol
Shruthi G
Soundarya B C
Spoorthi M
Venugeetha Y
Sneha Yadav

1

INTRODUCTION TO SOCIAL ENGINEERING

The Human Element of Hacking

VISHAL BHARATH, GURURAJ H L,
SOUNDARYA B C AND GIRISH L

1.1 Introduction

Take a moment to look around you and observe your surroundings. What do you see? If you reflect on the items around you and think back to how things were just two decades ago, then you will gain insight into the remarkable advancements that have transformed our lives in such a short period.

In the early 2000s, our methods of entertainment and communication were vastly different. We relied on video cassette tapes to watch movies, rotary telephones, 'dumb phones,' or public telephone booths for making calls, and devices such as the famous Sony Walkman or basic MP3 players for music. Photography enthusiasts used Polaroid cameras, while digital cameras were slowly gaining popularity. It was a time when having all of these gadgets was the norm.

Fast forward to the mid-2000s, and a groundbreaking innovation changed everything—the first touchscreen smartphone, LG Prada, was introduced in 2006 [1, 2]. This single device seamlessly replaced the functionality of numerous gadgets. Around the same time, websites such as Facebook, a pioneering social media platform, and YouTube, a revolutionary video streaming and sharing platform, emerged. As we approached the late 2000s, the introduction of Android-powered smartphones and the visionary Steve Jobs unveiling the 'revolutionary product'—the Apple iPhone—marked a turning point in

DOI: 10.1201/9781003406716-1

our technological evolution. These rapid advancements reshaped our world in just a decade.

1.1.1 Why Do We Need to Know about Social Engineering?

Social engineering poses a formidable challenge to network security by transcending the robustness of firewalls, cryptography methods, intrusion detection systems, and antivirus software [3]. As security measures advance, so does the ingenuity of attackers, who constantly seek new avenues to breach these barriers. Remarkably, humans, being naturally inclined to trust fellow humans, often emerge as the weakest link in the security chain.

Malicious activities executed through human interactions manipulate individuals psychologically and coax them into divulging confidential information or bypassing security protocols. Due to the pervasive nature of these human-driven interactions, social engineering attacks emerge as potent threats that can compromise all systems and networks. Traditional software or hardware solutions prove inadequate in preventing these attacks unless individuals are adequately trained to recognize and thwart them.

Notably, cybercriminals turn to social engineering attacks when traditional technical vulnerabilities are absent, which makes social engineering their method of choice. A report from ISACA (formerly the Information Systems Audit and Control Association) underscores the enduring relevance of social engineering, as it continued to top the list of analyzed attack types in 2022 [4]. This resilience is unsurprising, given its effectiveness as a tool in the cybercriminal arsenal.

1.1.2 Open-Source Intelligence (OSINT) and Social Engineering

Many scams succeed because they skillfully convince victims that the scam is not a scam at all but rather a casual and legitimate interaction. This persuasion leads victims to willingly provide their information instead of the information being maliciously stolen from them. Scammers primarily aim to achieve their objectives by convincing individuals to voluntarily surrender their information, as opposed to resorting to forceful intimidation or threats [5].

Using threats and intimidation can be a risky strategy for scammers, as victims may resist such tactics and could opt to report the threats to security authorities. This, in turn, could expose the scammer to legal consequences. As a result, scammers often rely on the power of persuasion and social engineering to deceive individuals by fostering a false sense of trust and credibility in their interactions.

Open-source intelligence (OSINT) has emerged as a prevalent and growing tactic employed by attackers in their efforts to target organizations and their personnel. OSINT involves the collection of data from publicly accessible sources, including social media, news articles, government reports, and academic papers. Attackers leverage this wealth of information to craft convincing social engineering campaigns that instantly resonate with their intended targets.

Numerous open-source channels serve as valuable resources for OSINT, encompassing the internet (via search engines), social media platforms, blog posts, online forums, video sharing sites (such as YouTube), magazines, newspapers, radio, TV, and maps. Attackers utilize an array of tools and websites for OSINT gathering, such as Google dorking, namechk.com, and Glassdoor, which we delve into in subsequent sections. Once they amass this information, attackers construct tailored attack vectors aimed at organizations or individual employees. In the sections that follow, we elaborate on the methodologies that attackers employ in OSINT collection and the potential ramifications of this gathered intelligence [5].

It is essential to emphasize that the data amassed through OSINT tools often provide attackers with sufficient information to target individuals effectively. When infiltrating organizations, attackers frequently focus their efforts on employees, as they recognize employees as the most vulnerable entry points in their quest for unauthorized access.

1.1.2.1 Glassdoor   In the context of OSINT operations that target organizations, platforms such as Glassdoor become valuable sources of internal organizational data [6]. These include sensitive information, namely, medical benefit providers, company images, job titles, salary details, and more. Armed with knowledge of medical benefit providers, attackers can construct sophisticated campaigns designed to deceive individuals by posing as representatives from these medical benefit companies. This is just one illustration of how OSINT-derived insights can be exploited by attackers to craft convincing and targeted social engineering attacks.

1.1.2.2 Namechk.com   In OSINT gathering aimed at individuals, platforms such as namechk.com offer a valuable tool. When provided with a specific username, namechk.com conducts a thorough search across various websites and domains to determine if this username is in use elsewhere. Typically, individuals tend to maintain consistency by using the same username across multiple online platforms. This service enables attackers to identify and aggregate information about multiple accounts maintained by the target, potentially yielding new insights such as additional social media profiles, video-sharing accounts, blogs, and more. Consequently, this aids attackers in amassing additional personal information about the target and further enriches their intelligence.

1.1.2.3 Google Dorking   Google dorking, often referred to as Google hacking, is a technique that utilizes advanced search queries to unveil hidden information within Google search results. Google dorks, or Google hacks, involve specific search commands, parameters, and operators entered into the Google search bar to reveal concealed segments of websites.

When Google indexes web pages for its search engine, it gains access to parts of websites that regular internet users cannot see. Google dorks exploit this capability to uncover information that organizations, companies, and website owners may prefer to keep hidden [7, 8]. Malicious hackers can employ Google dorks to gather data on their targets and identify websites with vulnerabilities, flaws, or sensitive information that can be exploited. Beyond information gathering, dorking can potentially provide unauthorized access to servers, cameras, files, and even phone apps. Some dorking techniques may expose files containing failed login attempts, including usernames and passwords, while others may allow hackers to bypass login portals.

What makes dorking particularly concerning is its simplicity; there is no need to learn complex coding. Gathering data can be achieved through straightforward search commands. Combining dorking with

Table 1.1 Google Dork Operators

OPERATOR	FUNCTION
Site	Search specific site
Filetype	Specific files
Intext	Search text of page only
Inurl	Search URL
*	Wild card for a single word
" "	Searches for exact phrase
+	Returns common words that might ordinarily be discarded
-	Removes pages that mention a given term

social engineering can yield a wealth of information that can be leveraged for identity theft. As our digital footprint expands, we face an increasing risk of being tracked online and becoming vulnerable to various forms of cyberattacks, including Google search hacks. Some of the common Google dork operators and commands are shown in Table 1.1.

A few of the commands are listed as follows.

1) **Site**: Using 'site:' in a search query will provide results focused on the specific website mentioned.

2) **Intitle**: Using 'intitle:' focuses a Google search to look only for pages with that specific text in their HTML page titles.

3) **Inurl**: Using 'inurl:' searches only for pages with that specific text in their URL.

4) **Filetype** or **ext**: Using 'filetype:' or 'ext:' narrows the search to the specific file type mentioned.

5) **Intext**: Using 'intext:' in a search query will search only for the supplied keywords.

All of these can be combined with other keywords and operators for more precise searches. A search can be enhanced by adding additional parameters or commands and shortening the syntax used. Dorks can also be automated to regularly scan for vulnerabilities and other information. The above commands can also be employed in daily search engine life to obtain more focused results of the query given as an input.

Many more tools are used in the planning and execution of a social engineering attack. This section gives an idea of the tools that are being used. Other tools are discussed in detail in the upcoming chapters.

1.2 Impact of Social Engineering

Social engineering attacks have the following adverse effects.

1.2.1 Financial Losses

Perhaps one of the most widely known consequences of cyberattacks is the direct financial losses that a company faces due to social engineering attacks. Depending on the company's size and the attacker's motives, this figure can vary, from $20,000 to millions of dollars. According to IBM's 2022 Cost of a Data Breach report, the average cost of a data breach with social engineering as the initial attack vector exceeded $4 million [9].

Using masks and guns for bank and financial institution robberies is outdated. Criminals have shifted to more advanced methods to obtain funds and data by transitioning from traditional tactics to social engineering attacks and ransomware scripts. Over recent years, there has been a significant increase in attempted social engineering attacks and hacks within the financial sector.

1.2.2 Loss of Productivity

Any successful cyberattack causes a considerable disruption to regular business operations. For example, the IT team and management-level employees need to postpone their other tasks to deal with the breach, all employees need to be updated about the hack and trained to prevent the same attack in the future, etc.

Most attacks when executed successfully make it impossible for businesses to simply go about their usual working routine. Some level of maintenance, cleanup, and introspection will be important to find out about the attack. However, severe attacks that may have caused widespread chaos in the organization and that require a great deal of investigation can destroy company productivity completely and require a significant amount of time to return to normalcy from the setback [10].

Pretexting, phishing, baiting, and similar attacks all fall into this category. When a particular employee is targeted in such an attack, an investigation becomes necessary. Who clicked the malicious link or opened the deceptive message? How did the attacker acquire information about them, and what was the motive for targeting them? Answers to these questions are essential before normal business operations can resume.

In Phishing and baiting attacks, an employee or group of employees may have been targeted, and they need to be questioned to determine the root cause of the attack, estimate the extent of the damage, and evaluate the systems that have been compromised and the repairs and advancements required to return to normalcy and prevent such attacks in the future. The amount of productive time and finances lost is immense.

1.2.3 Cyberattacks Cause Business Disruption

Another consequence of social engineering is akin to the loss of productivity, but it extends to the impact on customer satisfaction rates and the supply chain. A successful attack disrupts regular business operations, which leads to downtime in product manufacturing, shipping, and other crucial processes. These disruptions can result in the loss of customers and even suppliers due to delays. Furthermore, the aftermath of a breach may involve audits of a company's cybersecurity practices by both its insurance company and bank. Returning to normalcy can be a lengthy process, leading to the wastage of funds, labor, and time.

1.2.4 Loss of Reputation

If you were a customer or supplier of a company that underwent a major cybersecurity breach, would you be inclined to trust this company again? Would you choose to maintain your business relationship with them? Regrettably, for numerous businesses, the response is often 'no.' Many individuals are reluctant to expose themselves and their information to potential risks, resulting in a substantial loss of both customers and suppliers for these affected businesses after a security breach.

As previously mentioned, social engineering attacks can cause significant harm to individuals and organizations. To underscore the severity of cyberattacks, let us examine some statistics. In 2021, cybercrime was projected to cause a staggering $6 trillion USD in global damages.

Table 1.2 Impact Categories Associated with Social Engineering Attacks

IMPACT CATEGORY	DESCRIPTION
Financial loss	Unauthorized fund transfers or theft
	Payment card fraud and unauthorized transactions
	Extortion and ransom demands
	Loss of business revenue and profits
Reputation damage	Public disclosure of sensitive or embarrassing data
	Erosion of trust and confidence among stakeholders
	Negative media coverage and public perception
Data breaches	Unauthorized access to sensitive data
	Theft or exposure of personal or corporate data
	Legal and regulatory consequences
Operational disruption	Disruption of critical systems and processes
	Downtime, loss of productivity, and business impact
Intellectual property loss	Theft of proprietary information or trade secrets
	Loss of competitive advantage
Legal and regulatory risk	Fines and penalties for non-compliance
	Regulatory investigations and audits
Psychological impact	Stress, anxiety, and emotional effects

If treated as an economy, then this figure would position cybercrime as the world's third-largest, following only the United States and China.

Table 1.2 outlines various impact categories associated with social engineering attacks, ranging from financial losses and reputation damage to data breaches and psychological impacts. These impacts underscore the importance of implementing robust security measures and awareness programs to mitigate the risks posed by social engineering.

1.3 Types of Social Engineering Attacks

There are many varieties of social engineering attacks. It is important to know the types of these attacks to counter and report them as each kind of attack has a different countermeasure to be taken. We look at some of the types of social engineering attacks in this section.

1.3.1 Phishing Attacks

Phishing is the most prevalent form of social engineering and a tactic that has seen a staggering tenfold increase in the past three years, according to the FBI [11]. Phishing attacks occur when scammers employ various forms of telecommunication, with emails being the most common, to 'fish' for valuable information. These deceptive messages often mimic trusted sources such as organizations or individuals you know.

The term 'phishing' describes an attempt to steal sensitive information, which typically encompasses usernames, passwords, credit card numbers, bank account details, or other crucial data that can be exploited or sold. In this scheme, attackers disguise themselves as reputable sources and use enticing requests to lure victims, much like a fisherman employs bait to catch a fish.

Successful phishing attacks frequently result in identity theft, credit card fraud, ransomware incidents, data breaches, and substantial financial losses for both individuals and corporations.

Phishing represents a subset of social engineering tactics wherein individuals are deceived, pressured, or manipulated into divulging information or assets to malicious parties. Social engineering attacks exploit human error and leverage psychological pressure tactics to achieve their objectives. Attackers often pose as trusted entities and create a sense of urgency, which compels victims to act hastily and negligently. Hackers and fraudsters favor these techniques because of their cost-effectiveness and ease of execution over direct computer or network hacking. However, these methods come with a heightened risk due to direct interaction with the victim. In 2022, Microsoft claimed the unenviable title of the most impersonated brand, closely followed by Facebook, as depicted in Figure 1.1.

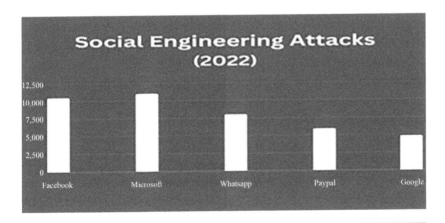

Figure 1.1   Social engineering attacks.

1.3.1.1 Types of Phishing Attacks

1.3.1.1.1 Bulk Phishing Emails   The most prevalent form of phishing attack is bulk email phishing. In this scheme, scammers craft email messages that appear to originate from a reputable and widely recognized business or organization. These messages are then dispatched to millions of recipients. Bulk email phishing operates on a statistical principle: when the entity being impersonated is larger or more prominent, the likelihood that recipients will include customers, subscribers, or members is greater.

Cybercriminals employ various tactics to enhance the authenticity of phishing emails. Typically, they incorporate the logo of the impersonated sender within the email and manipulate the 'from' email address to include the impersonated sender's domain name. In some cases, they may even spoof the sender's domain name—for instance, using 'rnicrosoft.com' instead of 'microsoft.com'—to create the illusion of authenticity.

The subject line plays a pivotal role in phishing emails. It is carefully chosen to address a topic that the impersonated sender could plausibly discuss and is designed to evoke strong emotions in the recipient—such as fear, greed, curiosity, a sense of urgency, or time pressure—to capture their attention. Common subject lines used in these phishing attempts include 'Please update your user profile,' 'Problem with your order,' 'Your closing documents are ready to sign,' and 'Your invoice is attached.'

The content of the email body is strategically crafted to guide the recipient toward taking an action that appears entirely legitimate and aligned with the email's subject. However, this seemingly innocuous action ultimately leads the recipient to disclose sensitive information, such as social security numbers, bank account details, credit card numbers, or login credentials. Alternatively, it may prompt the recipient to download a file that, unbeknownst to them, infects their device or network.

In August 2020, a significant incident of this type of attack came to light when cyberattackers launched phishing emails with the intent of pilfering Microsoft account credentials. These deceptive messages were designed to dupe victims into clicking on a malicious link, which redirected them to a counterfeit Microsoft login page.

1.3.1.1.2 Spear Phishing
Spear phishing is a phishing attack that targets an individual with priv-ileged access to sensitive data or network resources or special authority that the scammer can exploit for fraudulent purposes. A spear-phishing attacker studies the target and gathers information needed to pose as a person or entity that the target truly trusts or to pose as the target itself. Social media and social networking sites have become rich sources of information for spear-phishing research. By gathering data with various open-source channels, the attacker would have enough data to send a personalized message to the target with a specific request. Spear-phishing attacks make up just 0.1% of all email-based attacks but are responsible for two-thirds of all breaches, Barracuda Networks has found.

1.3.1.1.3 Business Email Compromise (BEC)   Business email com-promise (BEC) is a category of spear-phishing attack aimed at illicitly acquiring substantial sums of money or highly valuable information, such as trade secrets, customer data, and financial records, from cor-porations or institutions. BEC attacks manifest in various forms, with two of the most prevalent being the following:

CEO fraud: CEO fraud, a prevalent form of BEC attack, involves the scammer impersonating a high-ranking executive's email account. The attacker either gains unauthorized access to the executive's email or closely mimics their email address. Sub-sequently, the scammer sends a deceptive message to a lower-level employee that directs them to carry out actions such as transferring funds to a fraudulent account, making purchases from bogus vendors, or sharing files with unauthorized parties.
Email account compromise (EAC): EAC involves the scammer gaining unauthorized access to the email account of a lower-level employee, such as a manager in finance, sales, or R&D. The scammer exploits this access to send deceptive invoices to vendors, instruct other employees to make fraudulent payments or deposits, or request access to sensitive and confidential data.

1.3.1.1.4 Whaling   Whaling refers to a specific type of phish-ing attack that sets its sights on high-profile individuals, typically executives, government officials, or celebrities. In the world of cyber-crime, these individuals are considered 'big fish' due to the significant potential they offer scammers, whether in the form of substantial financial gains or access to valuable data. In one scenario, cybercriminals may target celebrities in the hopes of discovering compromising photos that can be used to extort hefty ransoms.

In another example, hackers send spoofed emails to C-level executives, appearing as if the communication originates from within the victim's organization. The sender claims to possess confidential information about a coworker but expresses fear about reporting it in person. Instead, they offer to share their evidence in the form of a spreadsheet, PDF, or slide deck. However, when victims click on the provided link or attempt to open the attachment, they unknowingly expose themselves to malware, which can infect their system and potentially spread throughout their network.

1.3.1.1.5 Smishing and Vishing   Smishing and vishing are forms of phishing attacks that utilize phone communication instead of written messages. Smishing involves sending deceptive SMS messages, while vishing revolves around phone conversations.

In a typical voice phishing (vishing) scam, the attacker impersonates a scam investigator representing a credit card company or bank. They contact victims and claim that their account has been compromised and that urgent action is required. The fraudster then manipulates the victim into providing their credit or debit card information, purportedly for identity verification or to transfer funds to a secure account. In this way, the provided account details are obtained by the attacker.

Vishing scams may also employ automated phone calls from individuals posing as trusted entities who prompt the victim to input personal information by using their phone keypad. These attacks exploit the victim's trust in seemingly legitimate phone interactions to steal sensitive data.

1.3.1.1.6 Angler Phishing   These attacks involve the creation of counterfeit social media accounts that are designed to appear as if they belong to reputable organizations. Attackers use account handles that closely resemble those of legitimate organizations and even adopt the same profile picture as the genuine company account.

The attackers exploit consumers' common practice of reaching out to brands via social media platforms for complaints or assistance. However, instead of contacting the genuine brand, unsuspecting customers engage with the attacker's fraudulent social media account. Upon receiving a customer's request, the attacker may request personal information under the guise of identifying and resolving the issue. In some instances, the attacker may direct the customer to a counterfeit customer support webpage through a provided link. This malicious website serves as a trap designed to compromise the user's security [12].

1.3.2 What Attributes Make Some People More Susceptible to Phishing Attacks than Others

Why do most existing defenses against phishing fail, and what personal and contextual factors render certain individuals more susceptible to phishing attacks than others? Numerous studies have explored these questions by delving into the factors that influence vulnerability to phishing attacks and the underlying reasons for individuals falling victim to them.

Human nature and negligence emerge as key determinants in the phishing process [13]. Phishing attackers capitalize on specific psychological triggers and technical vulnerabilities, which makes virtually everyone susceptible to such attacks [14].

In 2017, a report by PhishMe highlighted curiosity and urgency as the most common triggers prompting victims to respond to phishing attacks. Over time, these triggers evolved, giving way to emotional motivators such as entertainment, social media, and reward/recognition. However, in the context of a phishing attack, these psychological triggers often override individuals' conscious decision making, leading to actions driven by negligence.

Furthermore, individuals working under stress are more prone to making impulsive decisions without considering potential consequences. Prolonged stress can also impact the brain areas responsible for emotional control, further weakening an individual's ability to resist phishing attempts.

Numerous studies have explored the relationship between susceptibility to phishing attacks and various personal factors, aiming to uncover the reasons behind the varying success rates of phishing in different demographic groups. Although it is true that everyone can potentially fall victim to phishing, research has indicated that specific age groups exhibit varying levels of susceptibility to certain phishing tactics.

One noteworthy finding is that individuals aged 18 to 25 years are more prone to phishing attacks than other age cohorts [15]. Younger adults in this age range tend to be more trusting in their online communications, and they are also more inclined to click on emails from unknown sources. This higher level of trust and a greater likelihood to engage with unfamiliar emails contribute to their increased susceptibility to phishing attempts.

A survey conducted by antivirus company Avast revealed that men exhibit a higher susceptibility to smartphone malware attacks than women. The study found that men are generally more vulnerable to such attacks primarily because they tend to be more comfortable and trusting when using mobile online services. Additionally, the research demonstrated a positive correlation between internet addiction and risky cybersecurity behaviors, while individuals with a positive attitude toward cybersecurity in a business context displayed fewer risky cybersecurity behaviors.

Another study [16] highlighted that participants who spend extensive time on personal computers (PCs) tend to more accurately and swiftly identify phishing attempts than their counterparts with lower PC usage. Conversely, scammers and cybercriminals often exploit people's trust in websites and platforms [17], particularly when this trust is based on visual appearances that can deceive users. For example, fraudsters capitalize on users' trust in a website by replacing a letter in a legitimate site's URL with a number, such as 'goog1e.com' instead of 'google.com'.

In a study conducted by [16], phishing attacks were systematically sent to 1,350 randomly selected undergraduate students representing various academic fields, ranging from engineering and mathematics to arts and social sciences. The primary objective of this study was to analyze user click rates when confronted with phishing attempts.

The research uncovered that several factors influenced students' vulnerability to phishing, including their level of phishing awareness, the amount of time spent on computers, their participation in cyber training, age, and academic year. However, the study's most unexpected finding was that individuals with greater knowledge about phishing were paradoxically more susceptible to phishing scams.

To explain this surprising outcome, the authors propose two speculations. First, they suggest that users' awareness of phishing might have increased because of continually falling for phishing scams, which led them to be more cautious. Second, it is possible that the individuals who fell for phishing attempts had less knowledge about phishing than they initially claimed.

Figure 1.2 shows a simplified flowchart-style diagram that represents the general steps involved in a social engineering attack.

This diagram provides a high-level overview of the stages involved in a social engineering attack, from target selection to the final outcome. In practice, attackers may loop back to earlier stages or employ a combination of tactics to achieve their objectives.

1.3.3 Identification of a Social Engineering Attack

It is crucial to identify an attack in its early stages before any information is passed on to the attacker that allows them to progress to subsequent stages. Detecting such attacks becomes considerably challenging

Figure 1.2 Simplified flowchart-style.

once the attacker has breached the initial security layers. Since a significant portion of social engineering attacks takes the form of phishing attacks, we explore methods to recognize these attacks by familiarizing ourselves with common indicators typically present in them.

According to the Cybersecurity and Infrastructure Security Agency (CISA) [14], there are six common indicators of social engineering attacks and ways to spot them.

Suspicious sender's address When sending an email or a message to the target, the attacker will often replicate the address of a legitimate business. The sender's address may closely resemble that of a notable company, but some words might be altered or omitted, which may not immediately catch the target's attention.

Generic greetings and signature Typically, a generic greeting lacking specific identification, coupled with a dearth of contact information, can be indicative of a phishing attack. This is because a genuine email from a trusted organization will likely include its contact information and address you by name or some form of personal identification.

Spoofed hyperlinks and websites Spoofed links can be readily identified. When you hover your cursor over any of the links within the email's content and the displayed link does not match the text that appears during the hover, this is an indication that it might be a spoofed link. Malicious websites can mimic the appearance of the original site, but upon closer inspection, the URL may exhibit subtle variations in spelling or belong to a different domain (e.g., .net instead of .gov). Attackers may also employ URL shortening techniques to conceal the true destination of the link.

Secondary destinations Some phishing attacks involve directing the victim to a document hosting site or attaching a document to the message. In such cases, attackers can embed a link within a seemingly safe document. Clicking on this link can lead victims to a malicious website, where the attacker hosts infected files or implements a credential skimming scam.

Spelling and layout A message characterized by poor grammar, sentence structure, misspellings, and inconsistent formatting is a common indicator of a phishing attempt. This is because reputable institutions typically have dedicated personnel responsible for ensuring error-free customer correspondence.

Suspicious attachments Unsolicited emails that request the user to download and/or open an attachment often indicate a malware attack. Attackers leverage a false sense of urgency or importance to persuade the user to download or open the attachment without proper scrutiny. This exploits the user's casualness and negligence, which enables the attacker to achieve their objectives.

Identification is the initial step in preventing such attacks. If any of the aforementioned indicators are encountered, then it is advisable to contact a cybersecurity expert promptly to disrupt the attacker's efforts. Detailed methods for preventing social engineering attacks are discussed in upcoming chapters. Let us move on to some of the other types of social engineering attacks.

1.3.3.1 Honey Trap   In a honey trap attack, the attacker feigns romantic or sexual interest in the victim, enticing them into an online relationship. Subsequently, the attacker persuades the victim to divulge confidential information or make substantial payments in exchange for sensitive information acquired by the attacker about the victim. This information may encompass private photos, access to social media accounts, or other delicate personal details. This type of attack is a prevalent small-scale scam employed by attackers to exploit individuals who may be longing for affection and are in desperate search of a partner.

1.3.3.2 Scareware   Scareware is a form of attack that initially deceives individuals into thinking their computer has been infected with malware. The attacker subsequently prompts users to download cybersecurity software, which, in reality, is malware created by the attacker. This type of attack exploits pop-ups and employs other social engineering tactics.

1.3.3.3 Baiting   Baiting is one of the most common and straightforward examples of social engineering attacks. Although it shares similarities with phishing, baiting relies on false promises of a reward to pique a victim's curiosity and greed. In this type of attack, perpetrators often lure users into providing their login credentials in exchange for access to supposedly 'free' pirated movies, TV shows, games, or software.

1.3.3.4 Watering Hole Attacks   A watering hole attack is a targeted security exploit in which cyber actors attempt to compromise a specific group of users by infecting websites frequented by the group's members. The attackers' goal is to infect the victims' computers and gain access to their network resources.

1.3.3.5 Quid Pro Quo   Quid pro quo is another prevalent social engineering attack. In this scheme, hackers promise a benefit to entice victims into divulging personal information. For instance, a victim might receive a call from an unfamiliar number, claiming that they have won a lottery. The caller requests sensitive data in exchange for the supposed lottery reward, even though there is no actual lottery and the call is a scam.

1.3.3.6 DNS Spoofing   DNS spoofing, or DNS cache poisoning, is an attack in which hackers manipulate domain names to divert users to a malicious website that appears as the legitimate one. Users are prompted to enter their login credentials, which enables attackers to steal sensitive data.

1.4 Use of AI in Social Engineering Attacks

Artificial intelligence (AI) is advancing exponentially and introducing numerous tools that can accomplish time-consuming tasks in a matter of seconds. AI can generate personalized text, audio, and even video models of individuals through a user-friendly interface—such as a simple text prompt. This rapid progress in AI presents both incredible opportunities and challenges.

In the context of social engineering attacks, AI has become a powerful tool. Tools such as ChatGPT can assist attackers in crafting highly sophisticated emails, complete with proper grammar and spelling, and create the illusion that a specific person composed them effortlessly. AI can also produce deep fakes, synthetic videos, and realistic virtual identities. Attackers can impersonate real individuals, such as senior executives, customers, or partners, using AI-powered chatbots to engage victims in conversations that mimic human interactions. This enables them to social engineer victims into revealing sensitive information, engaging in financial transactions, or spreading misinformation.

The advancement of AI tools has made social engineering attacks more challenging to detect, as these tools can create near-identical replicas of personalized texts and audio by learning to generate descriptive queries that match our requests.

1.4.1 Most Infamous Cases of Social Engineering

In this section, we look at the major real-world social engineering attacks that have made us realize the deadly threat of social engineering.

1.4.1.1 Evaldas Rimasauskas Google Facebook Fraud   A Lithuanian man named Evaldas Rimasauskas stole $99 million from Facebook and $23 million from Google by creating fake invoices and asking for payment for the funds billed in the invoices across two years from 2013 to 2015 in a classic case of a whaling attack. He executed this attack by posing as a high-level executive of a Taiwanese company called Quanta Computer Inc. that supplied servers and various other hardware components to Google and Facebook. Rimasauskas registered and incorporated a company in Latvia that bore the same name as the Taiwanese company, that is, Quanta Computer Inc., and opened, maintained, and controlled various accounts at banks located in Latvia and Cyprus under this name. After setting up the bank accounts, the perpetrator initiated a series of whaling attacks by using a spoofed high-level executive account designed to appear legitimate. These fraudulent messages included attached invoices, contracts, and letters, all bearing false Quanta Computer Inc. stamps.

Reportedly, Google and Facebook accepted these falsified documents and forwarded them to their respective banks, which subsequently processed multimillion-dollar transactions. To access the transferred funds, the fraudster forged the signatures of executives from Facebook and Google on the invoices, contracts, and letters submitted to the banks.

To obscure the money trail, the perpetrator then sought to transfer these ill-gotten funds to bank accounts located in various countries, including Latvia, Cyprus, Slovakia, Hungary, and Hong Kong [16].

Rimasauskas managed to acquire the required information through a deliberate strategy employed by his employees. They routinely contacted the victim companies' customer service numbers with the aim of gathering as much information as possible about these organizations. During these calls, the fraudsters sought details such as the names of key employees and their contact information. Phishing emails were sent to the employees of the target companies through which Rimasauskas' employees were able to gain control of the companies' email systems, which gave them a treasure of data to plan and deploy a full-fledged social engineering attack. The companies notified the FBI of the email intrusions. Investigators froze some of the funds before Rimasauskas and his associates could move the money. Rimasauskas meticulously crafted an extensive paper trail, which included contracts, invoices, and various documents, all in an attempt to lend an appearance of legitimacy to the fraudulent transactions. However, this paper trail ultimately played a significant role in his apprehension.

In March 2017, Lithuanian authorities arrested Rimasauskas, and later, in August 2017, he was extradited to New York to face charges. In addition to a prison sentence, the court ruled that Rimasauskas must serve two years of supervised release. He was also ordered to forfeit $49,738,559.41 and to pay restitution in the amount of $26,479,079.24. Consequently, approximately $60 million in ill-gotten gains were recovered.

Accordingly, two major observations are noted. First, tech giants such as Google and Facebook can also get scammed by social engineering attacks. Second, Rimasauskas was able to carry out such a detailed plan even though he was on the other side of the globe, which suggests that social engineering attacks can be conducted from anywhere and on anyone or any organization, even one as massive as a giant tech company.

1.4.1.2 Bangladesh Bank Heist of 2016   The Bangladesh Bank heist stands out as one of the most significant bank robberies in recent history. Bangladesh Bank, the central bank of Bangladesh, maintains an account with the Federal Reserve Bank of New York to manage and transfer the foreign currency reserves of Bangladesh. In this auda-cious heist, security hackers orchestrated 35 fraudulent instructions via the Society for Worldwide Interbank Financial Telecommunication (SWIFT) network to unlawfully transfer nearly $1 billion USD from the Federal Reserve Bank of New York account belonging to Bangladesh Bank.

To provide context, SWIFT serves as a secure network that facili-tates governments and financial institutions worldwide in sending and receiving information related to financial transactions securely and reliably. The attack started when the central bank's programmed print-ers used to print out real-time transactions connected with SWIFT software were not working. Hence, the transactions were not getting printed, and the bank employees were not able to verify any transaction. After the printer was restored, the printer printed absurdly more trans-actions than expected. They discovered 35 doubtful payment orders for enormous amounts of money that were transferred from the private account of Bangladesh's central bank to many other accounts in sev-eral other nations. None of the payment orders had been approved by any of the employees. Puzzlingly, SWIFT software, a military-grade security software considered to be unhackable, was not working. The 35 money orders had a grand total of a whopping $1 billion. However, Bangladesh's bank got lucky as New York's bank flagged 30 of these transfer requests for manual review, which happened because in one of the SWIFT orders, there was coincidentally the name of a shipping company that had been blacklisted for political reasons between the US and Iran, which was complete luck in favor of Bangladesh. Out of the five transactions, one of them had a typographical error in the name of a foundation as the receiver bank account, and it therefore failed. The four other transactions could not be traced and were said to have been directed to the Philippines, where the money became untraceable as it was laundered into cash and casinos. Although major money orders were not approved, the 4 transactions resulted in a $81 million loss to the bank.

Following an investigation, it was revealed that a month before the theft, an employee at Bangladesh Bank inadvertently triggered a mal-ware program by opening a malicious email. This action initiated the installation of an infected program within the bank's security system. This infected program, unbeknownst to the bank, granted the attackers access to the bank's network and sensitive information. The attackers were able to study the bank's routine and operations, which helped them formulate a foolproof plan. Bangladesh Bank could have avoided the attack or at least controlled the extent of the damage if it had implemented several necessary controls and adopted routine security tests.

Accordingly, $1 billion of Bangladesh citizen's taxpayer money was compromised, which is not a small amount of money for a third-world, developing nation. In a stroke of luck, Bangladesh escaped a deadly financial crisis, but the bank had to face a loss of $81 million. This incident also showed that certain weak links in SWIFT software had to be upgraded to avoid any similar incidents from occurring.

Fast forward to the present day, and the once-novel devices that used to be considered a luxury have now become an indispensable part of our lives. Nearly every individual possesses a smartphone and wields the computing power of a supercomputer right in the palm of their hand.

In this contemporary landscape, Facebook and Apple have ascended to the coveted status of Tech Giants, joining the ranks of industry titans such as Google, Microsoft, and Amazon. Notably, in the early 2000s, Google was primarily engaged in advertising, Microsoft was busy developing new operating systems, and Amazon, primarily an e-commerce platform, experienced fluctuations in its stock prices.

However, today, these five companies collectively reign as the 'Big Five' that dominate not only the tech industry but also global commerce, setting the pace for innovation and reshaping the way that we live, work, and connect to the world. The rapid pace of technological advancement becomes abundantly evident when we compare the modest examples from the 2000s with the bustling landscape of the present day. Technology, it seems, is reshaping our lives at an unprecedented rate.

We originally conceived technology as a means to enhance our lives, but currently, it is continuously and profoundly altering our daily existence. Technology has seamlessly integrated itself into our everyday routines, and as a result, the demand for these advancements only continues to surge. We have become heavily reliant on technology, with nearly all individuals across the globe now having access to essential devices such as smartphones, laptops, and other gadgets because of their growing affordability. Remarkably, these devices are no longer confined to a specific age group; they are understood and embraced by individuals spanning from toddlers to the elderly.

As our smartphones and other devices accompany us constantly, we inadvertently expose ourselves to potential tracking, given the sensitive data that we transmit across various online platforms. The ever-advancing technology landscape brings with it not only convenience in our daily tasks but also heightened security concerns. Threat actors with various motivations seek to exploit these digital systems for their personal gain. Startling cybersecurity statistics reveal that an average of 2,200 cyberattacks occur every day, with a cyberattack transpiring every 39 seconds. This alarming frequency places users at considerable risk of exploitation.

Among the numerous forms of cyberattacks, social engineering stands out as a prevalent threat. It is the most straightforward method for attackers to gain control over a system, as it requires minimal time and technical expertise. The repercussions of a successful social engineering attack can be devastating, impacting both individuals and organizations. Consequently, there is a pressing need for widespread education on this topic to equip people with the knowledge and awareness necessary to protect themselves and their digital environments from such threats.

Social engineering is a deceptive and manipulative approach employed by individuals or groups to exploit human psychology and behavior, with the aim of gaining unauthorized access to information, systems, or physical spaces. Unlike conventional cyberattacks that target technical vulnerabilities, social engineering attacks focus on exploiting the human factor by capitalizing on our inherent tendencies to trust and assist others.

At its core, social engineering is an art of deception. Attackers employ a wide array of psychological tactics and persuasive techniques to manipulate their targets into divulging sensitive information, executing specific actions, or making decisions that ultimately serve the attacker's interests. These tactics frequently involve impersonation, emotional manipulation, and the exploitation of trust, authority, or fear.

Social engineering attacks manifest in various forms, including pretexting, phishing, baiting, tailgating, and impersonation, each with its own distinctive approach and objectives. Although the methods may differ, they all share the common thread of targeting human vulnerabilities. In the realm of cybersecurity, understanding social engineering is of paramount importance, as it poses a significant threat to individuals, organizations, and even entire nations. Regardless of the robustness of an organization's technical defenses, a single successful social engineering attack can circumvent these defenses and lead to dire consequences such as data breaches, financial losses, and reputational damage.

To safeguard against social engineering, it is imperative to recognize the tactics employed by attackers, foster awareness, and implement comprehensive security measures that encompass both technology and human behavior. This chapter delves deeper into the various techniques used in social engineering, explores their historical context, and underscores the critical role of education and preparedness in mitigating these pervasive threats.

This chapter covers the basics of social engineering attacks and provides a deep understanding of the deployment of an attack. Some of the most prominent and devastating attacks are covered as case studies in the later part of this book.

1.5 Conclusion

Social engineering stands as a formidable and ever-evolving threat in the realm of cybersecurity. This deceptive and manipulative approach exploits human psychology and behavior to gain unauthorized access to information, systems, or physical spaces. As we have explored throughout this overview, social engineering attacks take various forms, from pretexting and phishing to baiting and impersonation, all with the common goal of exploiting human vulnerabilities.

As cybercriminals continue to adapt and innovate, it is essential for individuals and organizations to remain vigilant, educate themselves on the latest tactics, and implement robust security measures to protect against social engineering attacks. Security awareness, strong authentication, regular updates, and a culture of verification are essential components of an effective defense strategy in this ongoing battle against social engineering.

References

1. What is social engineering and how does it work? *Synopsys.* ©2024 Synopsys, Inc. All Rights Reserved.

2. Alkhalil, Zainab, Chaminda Hewage, Liqaa Nawaf, and Imtiaz Khan. "Phishing attacks: A recent comprehensive study and a new anatomy." *Frontiers in Computer Science 3* (2021): 563060.
3. Albladi, S. M., & Weir, G. R. (2020). Predicting individuals' vulnerability to social engineering in social networks. *Cybersecur, 3*(1), 1–19.
4. Lansley, M., Kapetanakis, S., & Polatidis, N. (2020). SEADer++ v2: Detecting social engineering attacks using natural language processing and machine learning. In *2020 International Conference on Innovations in Intelligent Systems and Applications (INISTA)* (pp. 1–6). IEEE.
5. Rahman, A. M., Al Mamun, A., & Islam, A. (2017, December). Programming challenges of chatbot: Current and future prospective. In *2017 IEEE Region 10 Humanitarian Technology Conference (R10-HTC)* (pp. 75–78). IEEE.
6. Pienta, D., Thatcher, J. B., & Johnston, A. (2020). Protecting a whale in a sea of phish. *Journal of Information Technology, 35*(3), 214–231.
7. Anthony, B. (2019). *Social engineering: The human element of cybersecurity* [Doctoral dissertation, Utica College].
8. Canham, M., Posey, C., Strickland, D., & Constantino, M. (2021). Phishing for long tails: Examining organizational repeat clickers and protective stewards. *SAGE Open, 11*(1), https://doi.org/10.1177/2158244021990656.
9. Mutreja, M., Khandelwal, K., Dham, H., & Chawla, P. (2021, July). Perception of IOT: application and challenges. In *2021 6th International Conference on Communication and Electronics Systems (ICCES)* (pp. 597–603). IEEE.
10. Alkhalil, Z., Hewage, C., Nawaf, L., & Khan, I. (2021). Phishing attacks: A recent comprehensive study and a new anatomy. *Frontiers in Computer Science, 3*, 563060.
11. Mouton, F., Leenen, L., & Venter, H. S. (2016). Social engineering attack examples, templates and scenarios. *Computers & Security, 59*, 186–209.
12. Liu, Z., Zhou, L., & Zhang, D. (2020). Effects of demographic factors on phishing victimization in the workplace. In *PACIS* (p. 75).
13. Thomas, J. (2018). Individual cyber security: Empowering employees to resist spear phishing to prevent identity theft and ransomware attacks. *International Journal of Business Management, 12*(3), 1–23.
14. Yeng, P. K., Fauzi, M. A., Yang, B., & Nimbe, P. (2022). Investigation into phishing risk behaviour among healthcare staff. *Information, 13*(8), 392.
15. O'Leary, D. E. (2019). What phishing e-mails reveal: An exploratory analysis of phishing attempts using text analysis. *Journal of Information Systems, 33*(3), 285–307.
16. Saleem, B. M. (2021). *The p-fryer: Using machine learning and classification to effectively detect phishing emails* [Doctoral dissertation, Marymount University].
17. Sutter, T., Bozkir, A. S., Gehring, B., & Berlich, P. (2022). Avoiding the hook: Influential factors of phishing awareness training on click-rates and a data-driven approach to predict email difficulty perception. *IEEE Access, 10*, 100540–100565, https://doi.org/10.1109/ACCESS.2022.3207272.

2

SOCIAL ENGINEERING

COLIN LOBO, GURURAJ H L, LALITHA
BANDEPPA AND GURUSHANKAR H B

2.1 Introduction

The internet is a boon to modern-day society, with almost every aspect of our daily lives revolving around it. Our lives are becoming increasingly intertwined with technology, and the backbone of this technological integration is the internet. We use social media platforms such as Facebook/Meta, Instagram, Snapchat, WhatsApp, and more to connect with friends and family. Our legal documents are now digitized, and institutions and workplaces track our attendance digitally. We also frequently share our locations with various apps, which results in our entire online presence and to some extent, our offline presence, being traceable.

Social engineering attacks are classified into two broad categories [1]:

- Individual attacks; and
- Organizational attacks.

An individual can be identified by two types of information, namely, personally identifiable information (PII) [2, 3] and sensitive personally identifiable information (SPII) [4]. PII consists of personal information that can be used to identify a person. SPII is a subset of PII; it includes information that, if leaked, could pose a threat to the reputation and image of that person. On an organizational scale, there may be certain details that, if disclosed, could cause harm not only to the company but also to the individuals who work for it or use its services.

Perhaps the most important question on your mind is, 'How do these threat actors acquire this information?' Threat actors typically obtain sensitive information through five major phases [5]. Phase 1 is reconnaissance, where the social engineer approaches the target by

DOI: 10.1201/9781003406716-2

impersonating someone. Phase 2 involves building trust with the victim and convincing the victim that the social engineer is the person they claim to be. Phase 3 is the attack phase during which the social engineer extracts the necessary information. In Phase 4, they either depart with the collected information or use it to launch attacks on more individuals or organizations.

The chapter is structed as follows: section 2 explains the literature; section 3 follows with a detailed methodology; the discussion and results are depicted in section 4; and finally, the conclusion is drawn in section 5.

2.2 Related Work

In social engineering attacks, the threat actor typically targets the 'weaker person,' not in terms of having a weak password but in terms of having a vulnerable psychology or a weaker mindset [6]. The attacker can employ different phases of attacks to gain access to the desired data, but social engineering operates on the premise that the attacker must first gain the trust of the victim. This can be achieved by pretending to be someone close to the victim or by establishing a connection with the victim under a pseudonym. Phase 1 is the research phase, during which the threat actor gathers information about the victim. This can be accomplished through methods such as dumpster diving, targeting websites, physically interacting with the victim's friends and family, or accessing publicly available documents [7].

Phase 2 is the planning phase during which the attacker carefully and meticulously plans the mode and method of attack on the victim. The attacker may plan a single attack or multiple attacks, either to gather more information, such as that shown in Figure 2.1, about the person for more precise targeting or simply to acquire the desired information. This process continues until the attacker can formulate a sufficiently effective plan to execute the attack on the victim.

In Phase 3, the attacker's primary focus is to gain the trust of the victim. The attacker attempts to engage the victim in casual conversation [8]. Throughout this phase, a skilled social engineer will strive to maintain an air of innocence in the conversation. This phase demands

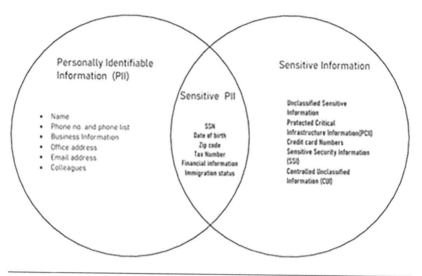

Figure 2.1   Information gathering process.

a great deal of patience, as any misstep could arouse suspicion and jeopardize the entire operation. The threat actor proceeds to gather information by either asking for assistance with minor tasks or offering to help with them [9].

After gaining the trust of the victim, Phase 4 involves exploiting this newly established trust. The information that the victim has provided can now be used to gain access to the victim's PII and SPII [10].

Social engineering can be achieved through various methods, including spear phishing, website attacks, shoulder surfing, water holing, dumpster diving, baiting, and more [11]. These methods can be executed through different channels, such as email, messaging platforms, cloud services, social media, or physical means. Among these methods, one of the most common is the phishing attack.

In Phase 4, the attacker aims to operate with the utmost caution and precision, as they do not want to expose their identity and risk getting caught. The final phase of a social engineering attack is Phase 5, the cleanup or cover-up phase. At this point, the attacker seeks to vanish with the information that they have obtained and to leave no trace of their presence. They may achieve this either by carefully planning their escape and erasing any evidence or by diverting suspicion onto someone else.

2.3 Methodology

In this section, the detailed methodology is explained with schematic diagrams and deep insight of the phases.

Social engineering, despite its various methods of attack and exploitation, generally follows a straightforward process [12, 13]. Initially, the attacker selects a target, typically someone who is vulnerable and easily manipulated. It is often said that 'a person with a weak mind is easy prey for a social engineering attack.' Once a victim is chosen, the attacker utilizes various social networking sites (SNSs) to gather information and understand the victim's vulnerabilities. With this information in hand, the attacker proceeds to plan the attack by employing various socio-psychological techniques to manipulate the victim. The attacker then uses these SNSs to contact the victim while assuming a suitable persona to gain the victim's trust. When the opportune moment arises, the attacker tactfully executes the attack by using the skills and information acquired during this process. These methods can be loosely categorized into five phases as shown in Figure 2.2.

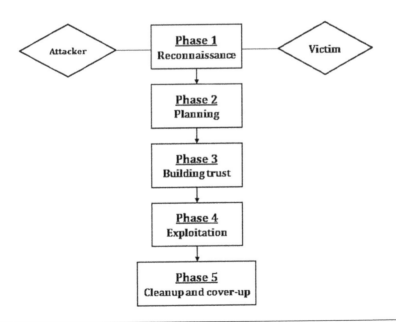

Figure 2.2   Different phases of attacks.

2.3.1 Reconnaissance

Phase 1 is the information-gathering phase, and it stands as one of the most critical stages in the entire process. Inadequate information can lead to errors during the attack, potentially resulting in the attacker being caught or their cover being blown. This risk puts all the time and effort invested in the operation in jeopardy.

Chris Hadnagy, the founder of social-engineer.com, emphasizes that information gathering is the most critical aspect of any engagement. He recommends dedicating more than 50 percent of the time to information gathering, as quality information, including valid names, emails, and phone numbers, significantly enhances the chances of a successful engagement. Moreover, during the information-gathering phase, serious security flaws can often be uncovered without the need for additional testing, which can then confirm these vulnerabilities.

Dave Kennedy, the author of 'The Social-Engineer Toolkit,' echoes this sentiment by emphasizing the importance of understanding the target company for penetration and testing and crafting the attack accordingly. This involves studying how the company and its subsidiaries operate and identifying the path of least resistance. Browsing through the company's website and exploring LinkedIn profiles are valuable methods for gaining insights into the company and its organizational structure. Additionally, extracting metadata from PDFs, Word documents, Excel spreadsheets, and other files found on the website can reveal information about the software versions and operating systems used by the company.

The information collected during this phase often falls under the category of PII. These data are readily available online and can be easily accessed by anyone. For companies and organizations, this information might include details such as the company's history, founder, employment history, and current management team. The attacker can leverage these data to identify vulnerabilities by researching the backgrounds of different employees, understanding their positions, and assessing their mental composure. This enables the attacker to carefully select their targets or the point of entry into the organization they intend to attack.

When an attacker targets an individual, they may delve into the person's email address, parents' names, school, close friends and family members, date of birth, bank details, address, and more. The importance of such information lies in the fact that many individuals use simple passwords related to personal details that they are familiar with, and they often fail to update their passwords regularly. Consequently, this makes it easier for attackers to crack the victim's password.

To achieve social engineering, the attacker may employ various techniques. When attacking from the user's side, the attacker can engage in shoulder surfing by using their observation skills to gain access to the authorization key. Social manipulation is another tactic, where the attacker manipulates the user into sharing their password or key. Alternatively, the attacker may infect the victim's computer with malware and keyloggers to stealthily capture the key right under the victim's nose.

Alternatively, if the attacker attempts to attack from the server side, then they must resort to guessing attacks. In this scenario, the attacker tries to guess the authentication key for multiple people.

Now that we understand how these attacks can occur, we can take appropriate measures to prevent them. Many websites have implemented measures to thwart guessing attacks effectively. To prevent shoulder surfing, individuals should avoid entering their password in public spaces and ensure that they do so in private to maintain secrecy. Furthermore, it is important to exercise caution when plugging in any thumb drives or cables, as attackers might conceal secret keyloggers in these devices.

Preventing server-side guessing attacks can involve the use of CAPTCHA or one-time password (OTP) systems. However, notably, advanced brute force attacks and dictionary attacks have been developed, which can potentially bypass even our most robust prevention systems [14].

One attack that a social engineer may employ is pretexting. In this method, the attacker manipulates the situation to convince the victim to disclose information they should not reveal. Pretexting exploits the lack of reliable identification techniques in voice channels or SNSs [8].

Such strategies used by the attacker are the following [15]:

- The Distraction Principle works on the idea that when people are distracted by something that intrigues them, they will not notice the things happening around them.

- The Social Compliance Principle functions on the theory that people do not question authority.
- The Herd Principle is when people do something because they saw other people do it.
- The Dishonest Principle is that if a person is being dishonest, then this makes them vulnerable.
- The Kindness Principle is that people are fundamentally nice and choose to help others.
- The Need and Greed Principle is that a person's needs and greed make the person vulnerable.
- The Time Principle works on the assumption that when people are under time pressure, they make different choices than if they think things out rationally.

2.3.2 Planning

After gathering information, the next critical phase is the planning phase. This phase is crucial because it outlines the steps that the attacker can take to compromise the victim. The attacker must formulate multiple plans to account for both best-case and worst-case scenarios. The planning phase becomes more straightforward with more information about the victim, as it presents the attacker with multiple vulnerabilities to exploit. Consequently, the attacker can employ various attacks to target the victim, such as the aforementioned phishing attacks or shoulder surfing. Furthermore, they may use other attacks such as the following:

Tailgating attacks: Tailgating attacks involve an attacker following a victim who has access to places that the attacker does not have access to. In this scenario, the attacker tailgates the victim, who possesses a certain level of clearance. The attacker employs manipulation by suggesting that the victim hold the door open because they have forgotten their access card.

Phishing: Phishing is one of the most common social engineering attacks in which attackers obtain the victim's information by sending fraudulent emails or making phone calls. An example of this is when the attacker calls the victim and claims that their credit or debit card has been blocked, and to unblock it,

they need to answer certain questions. Through these questions, the attacker aims to acquire the victim's SPII.

Reverse attacks: Reverse attacks involve the attacker pretending
to solve a network problem that the victim has been facing.
This attack comprises three steps. First, the attacker causes the
problem; second, they advertise themselves as the only person
who can resolve it; and third, they solve the problem. While
addressing the aforementioned issue, the attacker discreetly
acquires the required information and then departs without
leaving a trace.

Trojan horse: Another type of social engineering attack is the Trojan horse. Like the Trojan War story, in this attack, the attacker
sends an email to the victim. Once the victim opens the email,
a malicious attachment is downloaded. After installing itself
on the victim's computer, the Trojan executes its code and can
either slow down the computer or steal information. Trojans
can spread to multiple computers through various means,
including pop-up ads, emails, websites, or links.

One tool in the social engineer's toolkit is quid pro quo. This attack
revolves around the fact that a gullible person would choose to reveal sensitive information if they were to gain some service/incentive from it [16].

2.3.3 Building Trust

After planning how to attack the victim, the attacker is now faced with
the task of positioning themselves so that if an attack were to occur on
the victim, then no suspicion would fall on them. This can be accomplished by the attacker building trust in the victim. This entire phase
focuses on the victim trusting the attacker.

This phase is crucial in a social engineering attack for two main reasons. Firstly, when a person falls prey to the attacker's manipulation,
they become an easy target and can be manipulated to a significant
extent before realizing their mistake. Such individuals are precisely
who social engineering attackers seek out. In general, people tend to
have a 'Lie Detector Bias,' which is an inherent bias in most humans
that makes them believe that most people are telling the truth. This
bias can cloud people's judgment when they are being scammed.

Additionally, when people are asked to identify those who are lying or using deception, they often assume that they are skilled at this and can easily spot liars. Ironically, research shows the opposite to be true. Secondly, if the attacker gets caught in the process of snooping around, fails to obtain the desired information, or leaves behind traces of their activities, then they can use the trust they have built as leverage to divert the victim's suspicion away from them.

Furthermore, the process of deception is a lengthy one. Building trust takes time, but breaking it takes even longer. Therefore, this process requires considerable patience. At times, the wait can be even longer because the attacker may not be able to directly contact the victim immediately; they may have to establish contact through an intermediary, such as a friend or family member. This adds additional waiting time. Despite having multiple methods of attack or manipulation, patience is the most crucial tool in a social engineer's toolbox. The attacker may employ additional socio-psychological manipulation to deceive the victim and coax them into directly providing information. How do they do this? The attacker assumes a specific role, namely, that of a friend or family member, and once the victim develops a sense of safety, they may feel comfortable disclosing some secrets.

During this phase, the attacker appeals to the victims' trust and willingness to help. The attacker manipulates these basic human behaviors in a manner that goes beyond the imagination.

2.3.4 Exploitation

As the title suggests, the attacker now leverages all the information gathered in Phase 1, the reconnaissance phase, and the planning completed in Phase 2 while utilizing the trust acquired in Phase 3 to execute this attack. For this purpose, the attacker uses the toolbox [17] they have acquired over the years of practicing social engineering. Success in this phase is entirely dependent on all previous phases. When the previous phases have gone well, exploitation can be executed more effectively.

Social engineering has two types:

- Human attacks; and
- Automated attacks.

Human-caused attacks are social engineering attacks carried out by humans. For example, when impersonating an employee, the attacker assumes the role of a superior and utilizes self-assumed authoritative powers to command and manipulate the victim. Another scenario occurs in the workplace when the attacker pretends to be an important client to gain access to managers.

Automated social engineering attacks are attacks carried out by computers. One of the major vulnerabilities that an attacker may exploit is the privacy settings of a group or individual. Many people tend to keep default or weaker settings because they are often unaware of changes and updates made to the security and privacy features of the tools they use. The issue here is that attackers are quick to identify vulnerabilities, and they exploit them even faster. To address this, both individuals and companies should be educated about changes in security measures. Additionally, service providers play a role in prevention by continuously providing security updates as soon as a patch for a vulnerability is discovered.

Another vulnerability is when people freely trust random individuals on the internet. This so-called 'friendship' may not actually be genuine. If this 'friend' turns out to be an attacker, then this falls under the building trust phase. Moreover, social engineers can use external tools to spam SNSs to receive more friendship invitations.

A further vulnerability is the improper handling of content. The internet is flooded with various types of content, including short-form content (such as TikTok, Instagram Reels, and YouTube Shorts), long-form content (such as YouTube videos, TV shows, and movies), blogs, photos, notes, or tags. This content can be shared by forwarding a link to the post. When sent by a social engineer with malicious intent, this content may contain an embedded link that leads to an executable file that tricks the victim into downloading it. Additionally, the attacker may simply use the content to manipulate the user or deceive them into revealing certain information.

2.3.5 Exit/Escape

After the completion of the exploitation phase, the next step is the exit phase. This phase involves the least manipulation of all. The most that the attacker might say to deceive the victim one more time is that they are moving somewhere else while maintaining their persona as a friend of the victim. Alternatively, they can simply cut off contact with the victim and disappear. However, the timing of the disappearance may come under scrutiny when the victim realizes that they were attacked. Nevertheless, with proper cover and thorough track-covering, the attacker can easily escape. It is imperative that the attacker covers their tracks and leaves no trace of themselves behind.

2.4 Discussion

Now that we have understood the various phases of a social engineering attack, we can assume the path that a threat actor is planning to take. Therefore, we can make necessary changes to our security policies and defend ourselves from such malicious attacks. One way to defend ourselves from an attack is by accepting the help of machine learning and artificial intelligence [12, 18]. We can use neural language processing (NLP) to identify certain phrases and sentence patterns [19, 20] that lead to a social engineering attack and caution the user beforehand. This method is effective in identifying phishing and spear-phishing attacks but is quite ineffective in identifying the threat actor in SNSs. For SNSs, educating people about social engineering attacks (e.g., not talking to strangers, frequently updating software) is one of the best ways to mitigate the risk of a social engineering attack.

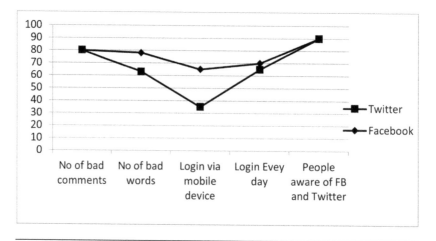

Figure 2.3   Active social media users' comparison.

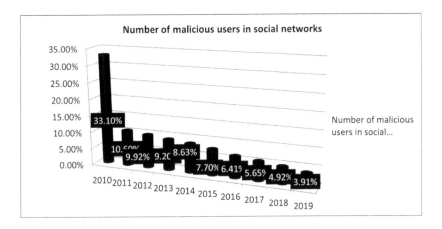

Figure 2.4 Number of malicious users on social media.

Figure 2.3 shows a comparison of active social media users in Facebook and Twitter applications.

The number of malicious users found on social media is shown in Figure 2.4. This graph describes the percentage of malicious users decreasing on social media networks.

2.5 Conclusion

Social engineering is a vast and expansive topic. Attackers can employ many different methods to gather information about individuals and a variety of different ways to carry out attacks. The primary reason for studying the phases of social engineering is to understand the mindset and methodologies of attackers at each stage, which enables us to better predict their actions. This, in turn, allows us to efficiently deal with the threats that they pose. By thwarting their attempts to steal our information, we can prevent their attacks and even catch them in the act.

Social engineering exploits human vulnerabilities, and with technology advancing rapidly, the threat to personal information is ever-present. Therefore, it is crucial to educate individuals who are not technologically proficient. People need to be informed about the ongoing social engineering attacks in today's world and how victims could have prevented these situations. In this way, individuals become aware of the threats they face and may have a plan of action ready for such situations.

Despite our best efforts, threat actors may sometimes breach our defense and cause significant damage. However, our goal should always be to prevent these incidents from occurring.

References

1. UH Rao and U Nayak (2014). "Social Engineering". In: *The InfoSec Handbook*. Apress, Berkeley, CA.
2. S Vandoninck, L d'Haenens, R De Cock and V Donoso (2012). "Social Networking Sites and Contact Risks Among Flemish Youth". *Childhood*, 19(1), 69–85.
3. https://www.techtarget.com/searchsecurity/definition/personally-identifiable-information-PII
4. K Chellappan and MK Jayanthi Kannan (2021). "PII Classification and Applicability in Personal Data Protection Bill 2019." *GIS-Zeitschrift fü Geoinformatik*, 1, 1417–1424.
5. K Michael. "Reconnaissance and Social Engineering Risks as Effects of Social Networking". In: *School of Information Systems and Technology*. University of Wollongong, Wollongong, NSW.
6. S Sharma, JS Sodhi and S Gulati (2016). "Bang of Social Engineering in Social Networking Sites". In: *Proceedings of the International Congress on Information and Communication Technology: ICICT 2015*, vol. 1, pp. 333–341. Springer Singapore.
7. HL Guruaj, BC Soundrya, V Janhavi, H Lakshmi and MJ Prassan Kumar (2022). "Analysis of Cyber Security Attacks using Kali Linux". In: *2022 IEEE International Conference on Distributed Computing and Electrical Circuits and Electronics (ICDCECE)*, pp. 1–6. IEEE.
8. K Njenga. "Social Media Information Security Threats: Anthropomorphic Emoji Analysis on Social Engineering". In: *IT Convergence and Security 2017*, vol. 2, pp. 185–192. Springer Singapore.
9. K Krombholz, H Hobel, M Huber, and E Weippl (2015). "Advanced Social Engineering Attacks". *Journal of Information Security and Applications*, 22, 113–122.
10. K Chetioui, B Bah, AO Alami and A Bahnasse. "Overview of Social Engineering Attacks on Social Networks". https://doi.org/10.1016/j.procs.2021.12.302.
11. N Kashyap, HRK Malali and HL Gururaj (2020). "Cyber Attacks and Security—A Critical Survey". In: M Pant, T Kumar Sharma, R Arya, B Sahana and H Zolfagharinia (eds) *Soft Computing: Theories and Applications. Advances in Intelligent Systems and Computing*, vol. 1154. Springer, Singapore. https://doi.org/10.1007/978-981-15-4032-5_80
12. HL Gururaj, F Flammini, BH Swathi, N Nagaraj and Sunil Kumar B R (2023). "Fault Tolerance of Network Routers Using Machine Learning Techniques". In *Big Data Analytics and Intelligent Systems for Cyber Threat Intelligence*, pp. 253–274. River Publishers.

13. A Algarni and Y Xu (2013). "Social Engineering in Social Networking Sites: Phase-based and Source-based Models". *International Journal of e-Education, e-Business, e-Management and e-Learning*, 3(6), 456–462.
14. N Kumar (2011). "Password in Practice: An Usability Survey". *Journal of Global Research in Computer Science*, 2(5), 107–112.
15. JWH Bullée, L Montoya, W Pieters, M Junger and P Hartel (2018). "On the Anatomy of Social Engineering Attacks—A Literature-Based Dissection of Successful Attacks." *Journal of Investigative Psychology and Offender Profiling*, 15(1), 20–45.
16. *Professional Penetration Testing* (Second Edition). https://doi.org/10.1016/B978-1-59749-993-4.00010-0.
17. F Salahdine and N Kaabouch (2019). "Social Engineering Attacks: A Survey". *Future* Internet, 11(4), 89.
18. HL Gururaj, U Tanuja, V Janhavi and B Ramesh (2021). "Detecting Malicious Users in the Social Networks Using Machine Learning Approach". *International Journal of Social Computing and Cyber-Physical Systems*, 2(3), 229–243.
19. H Lin, P Siarry, HL Gururaj, J Rodrigues and DK Jain (2022). "Special Issue on Deep Learning Methods for Cyberbullying Detection in Multimodal Social Data". *Multimedia Systems*, 28(6), 1873–1875.
20. HL Gururaj, MR Pooja, and PSP Kumar (2022). "Machine Learning (ML) Methods to Identify Data Breaches". In *Methods, Implementation, and Application of Cyber Security Intelligence and Analytics*, pp. 52–64. IGI Global.

3

CYBERSECURITY RISKS, VULNERABILITIES, AND COUNTERMEASURES TO PREVENT SOCIAL ENGINEERING ATTACKS

JOEL DENIZ D SOUZA, GURURAJ H L,
SOUNDARYA B C AND GIRISH L

3.1 Introduction

The threat landscape has expanded to include many risks in our contemporary interconnected society, where technology permeates every aspect of our lives. Social engineering assaults, which exploit human psychology rather than technological flaws, are among the most pernicious threats [1]. Social engineering attacks trick people into disclosing sensitive information, providing unauthorized access, or engaging in actions that compromise security. This chapter investigates social engineering assaults by examining their dangers, vulnerabilities, and potential remedies.

In a rapidly changing digital landscape where technology plays a pivotal role in various aspects of our lives, cybersecurity has become a top priority. Both organizations and individuals are encountering an escalating array of cyber threats, with social engineering attacks proving particularly perilous and detrimental. Social engineering attacks manipulate the human psyche rather than exploiting technical vulnerabilities, which render them a persistent and formidable threat.

Social engineering is a form of cyberattack that leverages human psychology and behavioral tendencies to manipulate individuals into performing actions that compromise security [2]. These attacks exploit the inherent human tendency to trust and engage with others and use

DOI: 10.1201/9781003406716-3

this trust for malicious purposes. Unlike other cyberattacks that target technical vulnerabilities, social engineering focuses on manipulating the 'human element' in the security chain [3]. It encompasses a wide range of tactics, including deception, pretense, seduction, tailing, and mimicry, among many others.

In our interconnected and digitalized world, the increasing reliance on technology not only revolutionizes the way that we live and work but also creates a new set of vulnerabilities that malicious actors seek to exploit. Among these vulnerabilities, the human element emerges as a primary target, serving as a gateway through which cyber adversaries manipulate individuals to breach security defenses [4]. This phenomenon, known as social engineering, has evolved into a complex and formidable threat that challenges conventional notions of cybersecurity. This chapter delves into the intricate field of social engineering, explores its various forms, strategies, and implications while underscoring the urgent need for comprehensive countermeasures.

As technology continues to advance rapidly, so do cyber threats, which often leverage innovations that improve our lives. Although technical vulnerabilities are largely reinforced through security patches and protocols, human vulnerabilities remain an elusive aspect in the cybersecurity landscape. Social engineering exploits these vulnerabilities by taking advantage of psychological, emotional, and social triggers to manipulate individuals into committing security breaches [5].

Phishing is an umbrella term that covers a wide range of tactics for manipulating human behavior to facilitate cyberattacks [6–8]. Unlike traditional cyber threats that exploit technical vulnerabilities, social engineering attacks target the human psyche by exploiting trust, curiosity, fear, and empathy. Attackers use psychological manipulation and deception to trick individuals into revealing sensitive data, performing unauthorized actions, or unknowingly facilitating breaches. The sophistication of these attacks often blurs the line between fact and deception, making them a persistent and confusing challenge.

The chapter is structured as follows: section 2 elaborates on social engineering and its role in cyber-theft; section 3 explains the vulnerabilities; section 4 depicts the risks and challenges of social engineering attacks; and section 5 draws the conclusions.

3.2 Social Engineering and Its Role in Cyber-Theft

In an era where technology is seamlessly integrated into our daily lives, the risk of cyber-theft has grown exponentially. Although we often think of cyber threats as sophisticated pieces of malware or cunning hackers exploiting technical vulnerabilities, there is a more insidious and devious form of cybercrime that does not rely on code or advanced hacking skills—it is called social engineering [9].

Social engineering is the art of manipulating people into revealing confidential information or performing actions that compromise security [5]. It preys on the inherent trust and natural instincts of individuals. Instead of attacking computer systems directly, social engineers exploit the weakest link in the cybersecurity chain: human psychology.

3.2.1 The Role of Social Engineering in Cyber-Theft

1. **Manipulation through Deception:** Social engineers are adept at deception. They can impersonate trusted entities, such as colleagues, IT support, or even friends and family, to gain your trust. Once trust is established, they coax individuals into divulging sensitive information, for example, passwords or financial details [10].

2. **Phishing:** One of the most common social engineering tactics is phishing [10]. Cybercriminals send fraudulent emails or messages that appear to be from legitimate sources to entice recipients to click on malicious links or download malware. This can lead to identity theft, financial loss, or unauthorized access to systems.

3. **Pretexting:** Pretexting involves creating a fabricated scenario to obtain information. For example, a scammer might pose as a bank representative and call an unsuspecting victim while claiming to need account details for a supposed security check. Falling for this ruse can lead to unauthorized access to bank accounts or personal information.

4. **Baiting:** In baiting attacks, malicious actors offer something enticing, such as free software or media downloads, to lure individuals into downloading malware [11]. Once computers are infected, cybercriminals can access sensitive data or hold it hostage for a ransom.

5. **Impersonation:** Impersonation is when attackers masquerade as someone who the victim knows and trusts [12]. This could involve creating a fake social media profile or email account to deceive individuals into revealing personal information or clicking on malicious links.

3.3 Vulnerabilities

Social engineering attacks are sophisticated techniques that exploit human psychology and behavior to defeat security measures. These attacks exploit a variety of vulnerabilities deeply rooted in human nature to manipulate emotions, cognitive biases, and social norms to achieve social engineers' malicious goals. Understanding these vulnerabilities is critical for developing effective countermeasures and strengthening the human element against such fraudulent tactics [13].

Trust and Authority

One of the most basic vulnerabilities that social engineering attacks exploit is the innate human tendency to trust authority figures and established institutions. Attackers often pose as authority figures such as supervisors, IT staff, or law enforcement officers to trick victims into complying with their demands [14, 15]. Awareness of authority blinds victims to possible deception and makes them more likely to divulge sensitive information or take actions they would not normally take. This vulnerability takes advantage of social conditioning to obey orders from those in power.

Curiosity and Novelty

Curiosity is another aspect of human psychology that social engineers manipulate [13]. The lure of the unknown and our natural curiosity drive people to explore links, downloads, or news that they find novel and interesting. Attackers can exploit this curiosity by embedding malicious content in tempting messages or emails and trick victims into clicking links or opening attachments, which can lead to malware downloads. This vulnerability originates from our quest for novelty and new experiences.

Fear and Urgency

Fear is a powerful emotion that defeats rational judgment, and social engineers are well aware of this vulnerability. By creating scenarios that evoke fear and urgency, attackers persuade individuals to act rashly and often evade security protocols. Urgent demands such as password changes, financial transactions, disclosure of confidential information, etc. entice victims to ignore standard procedures. This vulnerability stems from the instinctive human fight-or-flight response and the desire to quickly avoid perceived threats.

Reciprocity and Usefulness

The social norm of reciprocity, namely, the tendency to return one favor for another, is another vulnerability that social engineers exploit. By offering assistance or promising benefits, attackers encourage victims to provide sensitive information or perform requested actions in return. Our innate human desire to be helpful and cooperative often leads us to submit to situations without fully evaluating them, leaving us vulnerable to such manipulation.

Overconfidence and the Illusion of Control

Many people believe that phishing and fraudulent activity can be easily spotted. This overconfidence, combined with the illusion of control, create vulnerabilities that social engineers exploit. Attackers design elaborate scenarios that make victims feel in control to trick them into underestimating risks and ignoring warning signs. Believing that they will not fall prey to such tactics makes individuals blind to manipulation and more vulnerable to such attacks.

Lack of Security Awareness

Perhaps one of the greatest vulnerabilities that social engineers exploit is the lack of security awareness among individuals. Many people are unaware of the different forms of social engineering attacks and the tactics used by attackers [16]. This lack of knowledge makes it easier for attackers to craft compelling scenarios that are difficult for victims to distinguish from legitimate communications. By exploiting this vulnerability, social engineers can easily bypass the skepticism and caution that accompanies informed perception.

Personal and Emotional Ties

Attackers often gather personal information about their targets from social media and other sources and use this information to create emotional ties that can be used for manipulation. By including personal information in communications, attackers create a sense of familiarity and trust, which makes victims more likely to comply with their demands. This vulnerability originates from the human need for social connection and the desire to actively engage with people who we perceive as familiar or relatable.

3.3.1 Risks and Challenges

In this section, various risks faced due to social engineering attacks are discussed, and the mitigation techniques to overcome these challenges are explained.

In the digital age, where technology has penetrated every aspect of our lives, the importance of cybersecurity cannot be overstated. Cybersecurity risks have evolved significantly over the years, posing new challenges to individuals, businesses, and governments. This section explores the multifaceted context of cybersecurity risks by delving deeper into their historical context, current status, and future prospects. With a growing reliance on technology, understanding these risks is paramount to protecting our digital world.

Historical Perspective

To understand the complexity of modern cybersecurity risks, it is essential to trace their evolution from the beginning of computers to the present day.

The Emergence of Cyber Threats

The concept of cybersecurity risk dates to the 1960s, when the first computer viruses were created on a trial basis. However, it was not until the 1980s that cyber threats began to gain popularity. For example, the Morris worm of 1988 was one of the first cases of malware that caused major damage and highlighted the vulnerability of connected computer systems.

Internet Revolution

The 1990s were marked by the rapid expansion of the internet, which fundamentally changed the threat landscape [17]. With the advent of the World Wide Web, cybercriminals now have access to new capabilities to conduct attacks. Phishing attacks, denial of service (DoS) attacks, and malware distribution have become more common.

New Millennium

The Increase in Cybercrime
The 21st century has ushered in a new era of cyber threats. As technology advances, so does the sophistication of cybercriminals. Serious breaches, such as the data breach at TJX Companies in 2007 and at Target in 2013, demonstrate the dire consequences of inadequate cybersecurity measures.

3.4 Current Cybersecurity Risks

In today's connected world, cybersecurity risks are becoming more complex and pervasive. A number of significant threats and challenges dominate the current landscape.

1. Malware and Ransomware

Malware is still a significant concern. Cybercriminals are developing increasingly sophisticated malware variants that can evade traditional antivirus tools. Ransomware attacks, in which data is encrypted and held hostage until a ransom is paid, have increased in recent years, targeting individuals, businesses, and critical infrastructure [18].

2. Scams and Social Engineering

Phishing attacks have evolved from simple email phishing to highly persuasive targeted campaigns. Cybercriminals use social phishing techniques to manipulate individuals into revealing sensitive information, which makes this one of the most common threats.

3. Insider Threats

Insider threats involve trusted employees or individuals that intentionally or unintentionally compromise security. These threats pose a particular challenge because they frequently disrupt traditional perimeter defenses. Insider threats can stem from negligence, dissatisfaction, or malicious intent.

4. Supply Chain Vulnerability

In an increasingly interconnected global economy, supply chains are vulnerable to cyberattacks. Hackers target vendors to gain access to larger organizations' networks, which compromises the integrity and security of products and services.

5. Vulnerabilities of the Internet of Things (IoT)

The proliferation of IoT devices creates new vulnerabilities. Inadequate security measures on smart devices can be exploited by cybercriminals to gain access to the network, infringing on user privacy and data. State-sponsored cyberattacks have increased, with governments using cyber espionage and cyberwarfare as tools of political influence. These attacks can have far-reaching consequences, affecting national security and international relations.

Table 3.1 provides a structured overview of the key aspects related to cybersecurity risks, vulnerabilities, and effective countermeasures aimed at preventing social engineering attacks. Social engineering attacks are a significant threat in the world of cybersecurity, and they often exploit human psychology and trust to breach systems, steal sensitive data, or gain unauthorized access.

Table 3.1   Cybersecurity Risks, Vulnerabilities, and Countermeasures

CATEGORY	DESCRIPTION	EXAMPLES	COUNTERMEASURES
Social engineering	Manipulating human psychology to deceive	Phishing emails, pretexting, impersonation	Employee Training: Educate staff about social engineering tactics. Email Filtering: Implement robust email filtering to catch phishing attempts.
Risks	Unauthorized access	Financial fraud	
Vulnerabilities	Lack of awareness	Gullibility	
Security	Two-factor authentication	Suspicious email reporting	Regular security awareness training
Malware	Malicious software designed to infiltrate	Trojan horses, ransomware, spyware	Endpoint Security: Install antivirus and antimalware software. Software Updates: Keep all software up to date.
Phishing	Fraudulent attempts to obtain sensitive information	Fake emails, websites, phone calls	Email Verification: Always verify requests for sensitive information. URL Inspection: Check website URLs before entering data.

3.4.1 Cybersecurity Challenges

Addressing cybersecurity risks is not without challenges as the threat landscape continues to evolve rapidly.

Lack of Cybersecurity Skills

There is a significant shortage of cybersecurity professionals around the world. The demand for qualified professionals far exceeds the talent pool available, which makes it difficult for organizations to adequately defend against cyber threats.

Rapid Technological Progress

The rapid pace of technological innovation poses a challenge to cybersecurity. When new technologies emerge, they often come with unforeseen vulnerabilities that cybercriminals can exploit.

Compliance and Regulation

Navigating the legal landscape is a complex task for businesses. Compliance with various cybersecurity standards and regulations is essential but can be costly and resource-intensive.

Insider Threats

Identifying and mitigating insider threats requires a delicate balance between security and employee privacy. Finding this balance while maintaining trust within the organization can be difficult.

3.4.2 Mitigating the Threat of Social Engineering

1. Education and Awareness: The first line of defense against social engineering is education. Individuals and organizations must be aware of the various tactics employed by cybercriminals and learn to recognize red flags.
2. Verify Requests: Always verify requests for sensitive information, especially if they come via email, phone calls, or messages. Do not hesitate to double-check with the supposed sender by using official contact information.
3. Use Strong Authentication: Implement strong and unique passwords, enable two-factor authentication, and regularly update software to protect against breaches.
4. Security Training: Organizations should provide cybersecurity training for employees to recognize and respond to social engineering attempts.

3.5 Conclusion

Social engineering plays a pivotal role in cyber-theft by exploiting human psychology and trust. Understanding the tactics used by cybercriminals and taking preventive measures are crucial in defending against these attacks. Cybersecurity is not just about protecting systems and data; it is about safeguarding the human element in the digital age. In the cybersecurity landscape, social engineering attacks are a persistent and evolving danger. Organizations and individuals can better defend themselves against such attacks by understanding the various attack pathways employed, psychological methods used, and vulnerabilities exploited. To combat social engineering effectively, individuals and organizations must utilize a multi-faceted approach. In this chapter, we present a comprehensive framework of countermeasures and best practices. Topics covered include engaging in user education and training, implementing strong authentication mechanisms, creating a security-conscious culture, and using advanced technology solutions.

References

1. Mitnick, K. D., & Simon, W. L. (2002). *The Art of Deception: Controlling the Human Element of Security.* John Wiley & Sons.
2. Hadnagy, C. (2011). *Social Engineering: The Art of Human Hacking.* John Wiley & Sons.
3. Stajano, F., & Paul, W. (2011). Understanding scam victims: seven principles for systems security. *Communications of the ACM, 54*(3), 70–75.
4. Rouse, M. (2017). *Social Engineering.* TechTarget. Retrieved from https://searchsecurity.techtarget.com/definition/social-engineering
5. Anderson, R. (2008). *Security Engineering: A Guide to Building Dependable Distributed Systems.* Wiley.
6. Schneier, B. (2015). *Data and Goliath: The Hidden Battles to Collect Your Data and Control Your World.* WW Norton & Company.
7. Duggal, P. (2020). *Cyberlaw: The Law of the Internet and Information Technology.* Springer.
8. NIST. (2014). *Framework for Improving Critical Infrastructure Cybersecurity.* Retrieved from www.nist.gov/cyberframework
9. Cisco. (2021). *2021 Cisco Annual Cybersecurity Report.* Retrieved from www.cisco.com/c/en/us/products/security/security-reports.html
10. Mitnick, K. D., & Simon, W. L. (2003). *The Art of Deception: Controlling the Human Element of Security.* John Wiley & Sons.
11. Hadnagy, C. (2010). *Social Engineering: The Art of Human Hacking.* John Wiley & Sons.
12. Dhamija, Rachna, J. Doug Tygar, and Marti Hearst. "Why phishing works." In *Proceedings of the SIGCHI conference on Human Factors in computing systems,* pp. 581–590. 2006.
13. Wang, J., Shan, Z., Gupta, M., & Rao, H. R. (2019). A longitudinal study of unauthorized access attempts on information systems: The role of opportunity contexts. *MIS Quarterly, 43*(2), 601–622.
14. Moore, T., Clayton, R., & Anderson, R. (2009). The economics of online crime. *Journal of Economic Perspectives, 23*(3), 3–20.

15. Chaganti, R., Bhushan, B., & Ravi, V. (2022). The role of Blockchain in DDoS attacks mitigation: Techniques, open challenges and future directions. *arXiv preprint arXiv:2202.03617.*
16. Tu, Y. J., & Piramuthu, S. (2023). Security and privacy risks in drone-based last mile delivery. *European Journal of Information Systems*, 1–14.
17. Nield, J., Scanlan, J., & Roehrer, E. (2020). Exploring consumer information-security awareness and preparedness of data-breach events. *Library Trends*, *68*(4), 611–635.
18. Sasse, M. A., Brostoff, S., & Weirich, D. (2001). Transforming the 'weakest link'—a human/computer interaction approach to usable and effective security. *BT Technology Journal*, *19*(3), 122–131.

4

A CASE STUDY ON PACKET SNIFFERS

Tools, Techniques, and Tactics

CHIRANTH T S, MANJESH R, BHARATH K C,
CHINMAYA, HEBBAR AND BHASKAR S

4.1 Introduction

A packet sniffer is a technique for intercepting network packets or a type of spyware that hackers use to track individuals connected to a network. Although packet sniffing technologies are used by network administrators to monitor and verify network traffic, hackers may employ similar tools for unethical objectives [1]. A WIFI adapter with monitor mode and packet sniffing capability is the most crucial item for packet sniffing [2]. It is recommended to use a guest operating system, such as Kali Linux, to carry out packet sniffing [3].

For packet sniffing, a person must be familiar not only with using terminals and sniffer tools such as Wireshark, Ettercap, Driftnet, etc. but also with network layer protocols. There are both ethical and unethical uses for packet sniffing. Network vulnerabilities, for instance, can be found by both monitoring network traffic and detecting network problems.

For unethical purposes, packet sniffing could allow the theft of sensitive data, including login information, the list of websites visited, and the information accessed. A sniffer can be detected on a network by looking for unusual traffic patterns, a high rate of activity, and a network that is unprotected by firewalls or passwords and is located in public areas or by using a straightforward method such as building a Nmap sniffer script for a specific gateway.

DOI: 10.1201/9781003406716-4

4.2 Objective

A packet sniffer's basic function is to simply capture every data packet that passes through a specific network interface. Only required packets are captured by a packet sniffer. A malicious attacker can record and examine all network traffic by installing a packet sniffer in monitor mode on a network. The captured files are in the .Cap file type [4]. Moreover, Wireshark, Ettercap, and other sniffer programmers are utilized [5].

The objectives of the packet sniffer are as follows:

- **Monitoring network traffic:** The person can observe the traffic in the network, the strength of the network, the bandwidth of the network, the channel in which the network is running, and the basic service set identifier (BSSID) of the network.
- **Detecting unusual networks**: The packet sniffer can detect unusual or malicious activity in the network by monitoring the network traffic and can alert the users [6].
- **Retrieve the login credentials of users and the information they are accessing in the browser:** The person using the sniffer can retrieve the user's name and password when the user is trying to login to the browser and can observe the visited browser and the information that the user is trying to access in the browser [7, 8].
- **Problem identification on the network:** As a packet sniffer can analyze the conversation between the network nodes and can identify problems by sending the packets and not getting a response from the nodes, this helps in identifying and correcting problems in the network; a packet sniffer can therefore help in correcting these problems, and the reliability of the network can be improved [9].

Requirements Specification

Software Requirements Specification

Virtual Machine: Basically, every hack will be conducted by using virtual machines. Without fearing that you will destroy your host operating system or its gadgets, you are free to test, hack, and damage the system to any extent. The host system will not be affected if your virtual machine is compromised, and your personal information will be safe [10].

Operating System (OS): Kali Linux is the OS used here because its user interface (UI) and environment make hacking easy. It also provides various sniffer tools such as Wireshark, Ettercap, driftnet, etc. [11]. Figure 4.1 shows the Kali Linux interface used for the sniffing, which has various sniffer tools and different toolkit supports for hacking.

Wireshark: Wireshark is an application that captures packets from a network connection, such as one between your computer and your home office or the internet.

Ettercap: Ettercap is an open-source tool that supports network man-in-the-middle attacks. Ettercap can write captured packets back onto the network. Data can virtually be diverted and changed in real time because of Ettercap.

Hardware Requirements Specification

Network Adapter: Since Kali Linux essentially forbids using the built-in or system WIFI for hacking, it is preferable to utilize

Figure 4.1   The Kali Linux OS.

a network adapter that supports the monitor mode for packet capturing [12, 13].

Personal Computer (PC) or Laptop: The user must have a PC or laptop with the processor configuration of i5 or above and hard disk space of 60 GB.

RAM: At least 2GB is needed for the smooth working of a virtual machine.

Target Devices: These are the devices from which the packets are sniffed with the sniffer tools, and they must be connected to the network for sniffing.

Router or Modem: The sniffer is basically conducted by connecting to a network where there is greater traffic. Hence, a router or modems are preferred for sniffing.

4.3 Sniffing in a Wireless Network

Packet sniffers known as wireless sniffers were developed especially for gathering data via wireless networks. Other frequently used names for wireless sniffers are wireless packet sniffers and wireless network sniffers. Wireless packet sniffers are useful tools for managing wireless networks, but they are also frequently used by hostile actors due to their capabilities. Hackers can use wireless sniffer software to steal data, spy on network activity, and collect information for network attacks. Attackers frequently target logins with wireless sniffer tools (usernames and passwords). Wireless sniffing can be performed in monitor mode or promiscuous mode. A wireless sniffer can gather and read incoming data while operating in monitor mode without sending any data of its own. This makes a wireless sniffer attack in monitor mode very difficult to detect. A sniffer can read any data travelling into and out of a wireless access point when it is in promiscuous mode. However, a wireless sniffer operating in promiscuous mode actually transmits data over the network since it also sniffs outgoing traffic. As a result, promiscuous wireless sniffing attacks are easier to identify. Because promiscuous mode enables attackers to capture all types of data flowing through access points, it is more frequently used by attackers in sniffing attacks [14].

4.4 Types of Sniffing Methods

4.4.1 Sniffing Can Be Done in Two Ways

Passive Sniffing: This type of sniffing often takes place at the hub. In contrast to active sniffing, a sniffer device can be instantaneously injected into the hub to simply capture data packets [9, 15, 16]. Currently, hubs are not often used; therefore, passive sniffing assaults are infrequently observed.

Active Sniffing: Switches, which are sophisticated bits of hardware, are used in active sniffer attacks. Switches transfer data to the specific media access control (MAC) addresses of computers on a network, as opposed to hubs, which send data to all ports even when this is not required. Address Resolution Protocols (ARPs) are frequently used in active sniffing attacks to overload the switch content addressable memory (CAM) table. The attacker can sniff the switch's traffic because it is redirected to other ports [17].

IP-Based Sniffing: All leads are sniffed, limited to a certain Internet Protocol (IP) filter. The data packets are recorded for analysis and diagnosis. IP sniffers record network traffic and send the data in a format that can be read by humans for analysis. They can be used to examine a network's current state, find network vulnerabilities, and gauge network performance by network administrators and hackers of all types [18].

MAC-Based Sniffing: This method works by putting the network card into monitor mode and sniffing all packets matching the MAC address of the target device [18].

ARP-Based Sniffing: ARP poisoning, that is, ARP spoofing, is a typical method used by hackers to send fake ARP packets across networks in which they perform sniffing. The intention of the hacker is that every packet in the network should pass through sniffing device [19].

Password Sniffer: This method collects data from network traffic to gather passwords. To obtain login passwords and other information, hackers target sessions. Without Secure Sockets Layer (SSL) protocol encryption to safeguard them, websites are open to assault and exploitation [20].

Lan Sniffer: This kind of technology, which can inspect all IP addresses, is typically used in internal systems or networks.

Domain Name System (DNS) Poisoning: Another fraudulent technique in which hacker's direct internet traffic to phishing websites is DNS poisoning, which is sometimes referred to as DNS cache poisoning or DNS spoofing. Businesses and individuals are equally in danger of DNS poisoning. One of the most serious problems with DNS poisoning is that, after a device has been infected, it may be impossible to fix the issue because the device may automatically go to the malicious site [21].

4.5 Sniffing Uses

4.5.1 Ethical Uses

With numerous distinct types of packets going in, out, and between networked equipment, networks are incredibly complex. It is easy for things to go wrong because of this complexity. Network administrators have real-time access to information about what is happening in their networks because of packet sniffing technologies. These technologies help them monitor network traffic, check that everything is running smoothly, identify bottlenecks, and provide the information needed to solve issues or identify whether the systems are being attacked maliciously. One of the most popular sniffing tools used for lawful purposes is Wireshark [7].

4.5.2 Unethical Uses

We have discussed how network administrators can use packet sniffing techniques to learn more about their networks, identify issues, and pinpoint dangers. What transpires, however, if a hostile attacker conducts their own packet sniffing on the network traffic of the organization? Packet sniffers can intercept and log a large number of packets that are sent across a network. This creates another weak spot, especially if confidential information is transmitted over the network in an unencrypted fashion. Any packet that crosses the network can be intercepted by an intruder. They may have access to sensitive data about the business or the login credentials of the network users as a result [7].

4.6 Sniffing Procedure

Initial Step for Sniffing: In the OS used for sniffing, the hacker plugs in the network adapter, discovers the target's IP address or MAC address on the network, then uses some sniffing tools to carry out a man in-the-middle attack or ARP poisoning, and captures the packet information.

Selecting the Target Devices: After setting up the sniffing environment, the hacker must select the target device from which they are going to sniff packets. The targets are selected based on their IP addresses by connecting to the network.

ARP Poisoning: Hackers utilize spoofing attacks such as ARP poisoning and ARP spoofing to intercept data. An ARP spoofing attack is when a hacker tricks a device into sending communication to the hacker rather than the intended recipient, wherein the hacker acts as an intermediate [22].

Man-In-The-Middle (MITM) Attack: An MITM attack occurs when a perpetrator inserts himself into a dialogue between a user and an application, either to listen in on the conversation or to pretend to be one of the parties, to create the appearance that information is being shared on a regular basis [6, 23].

Use of Sniffer Tools: Sniffer tools such as Wireshark, Ettercap, etc. are widely available. Ettercap is used to choose targets, carry out ARP poisoning, and launch man-in-the-middle attacks. The victim can use Wireshark's user-friendly graphical UI to capture packets, view source and destination addresses, track the sites that the user has visited, see the information they tried to access and the protocols used, and store the captured packets.

Figure 4.2 shows the diagram of an MITM attack where the hacker acts as an intermediate between PC1 and PC2 and breaks the actual connection between them. Figure 4.3 shows ARP poisoning between PC1 and PC2 in the upper diagram, while the lower diagram shows the normal traffic pattern between PC1 and PC2.

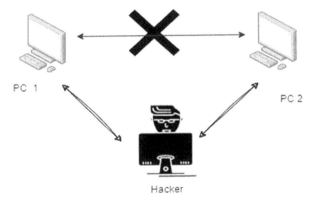

Figure 4.2 An MITM attack.

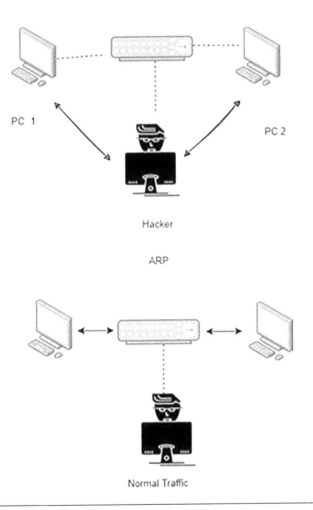

Figure 4.3 ARP poisoning.

4.7 Use of Sniffer Tools

4.7.1 Ettercap Sniffer Tool

The Ettercap sniffer tool is used in sniffing to add targets from the host list and to perform MITM attacks and ARP poisoning so that the sniffing device acts as an intermediate or bridge between the router and the target so that all packets can be intercepted [24, 25].

After scanning for the host in the specific gateway, Figure 4.4 shows the table of selected targets on which the ARP poisoning and MITM attacks are performed.

The Ettercap interface in Figure 4.5 depicts the scanning of hosts for sniffing, MITM attacks, and ARP poisoning.

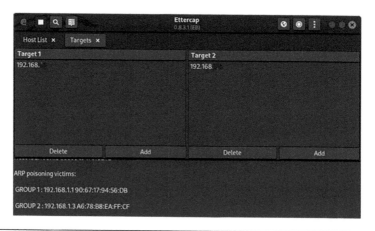

Figure 4.4 Displaying the selected targets.

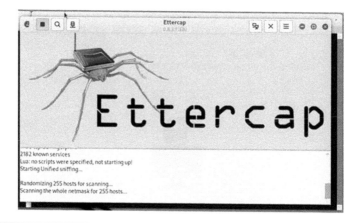

Figure 4.5 Ettercap interface.

4.8 Use of the Wireshark Sniffer Tool

The Wireshark sniffer utilities in Kali Linux feature an excellent UI and options for capturing and storing packets. With Wireshark, packets can also be filtered depending on the IP address of the desired device from the list of all packets [21].

The filtered packets on the target device are shown in Figure 4.6 along with their source, destination IP address, and protocol details over time. In addition, how the user accesses the data on the webpage or in the browser by applying the filter can be observed. The intended device's UDP stream is displayed in Figure 4.7 which can be accessed via the browser [26].

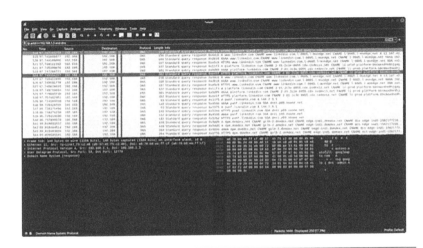

Figure 4.6   Wireshark capturing IP address.

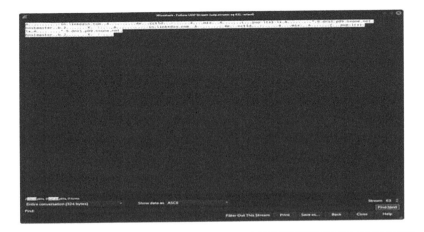

Figure 4.7   Displaying the User Datagram Protocol (UDP) stream

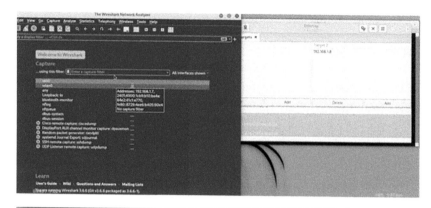

Figure 4.8   Wireshark interface.

Figure 4.8 shows the Wireshark interface in Kali-Linux and the option to capture packets from the list of options including wlan0 (wireless network) or eth0 (ethernet). The graph indicates the strength because the ups and downs can capture more packets and have good signal strength.

Sniffer Detection

There are many ways to detect sniffers in the network. The user can produce packets with erroneous addresses. It can be inferred that a machine (on the network) is running a sniffer if it accepts these packets. Another approach is that the machine's MAC address can be temporarily changed by the user. There should be no acceptance of packets sent to the machine's previous address. If a packet is accepted, then this can identify sniffing. Software instruments such as Anti-Sniff can also be used to detect sniffers, and the remote detection of computers with sniff packets is made possible by Anti-Sniff. Network administrators and security experts can ascertain whether or not a remote machine is listening to all network traffic by running a number of non-intrusive tests with different methods.

By using anti-sniff software, ethernet/IP network segments where data are being voluntarily collected can be found.

Network Tools: Network analysis tools such as Capsa network analyzers are used to scan the network for unusual packets. They facilitate the gathering, aggregation, centralization, and analysis of traffic data from various network resources and technologies. By creating a script for a certain gateway. If the device's name appears in the terminal, then the output must indicate that the device is either a sniffer or an attacker.

Nmap -sn—script = sniffer-detect gateway/24

The sniffer detection test on the gateway is shown in Figure 4.9. The test came back positive, and the sniffer was detected in the gateway, whose identity is highlighted [24, 27].

4.9 Promiscuous Detection Tool: PromqryUI

Another way to detect sniffing is by using the PromqryUI tool. Microsoft's PromqryUI security tool can be used to identify network interfaces that are operating in promiscuous mode. If there are no devices operating in promiscuous mode, then the outcome will be negative [28].

Figure 4.10 shows the results of the sniffer detection test on the gateway that displays the query status as negative, which means that the monitor or promiscuous mode is not detected. If the status was positive, then some devices are in the promiscuous mode.

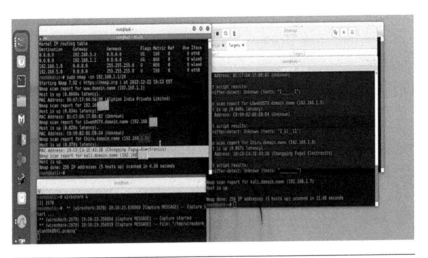

Figure 4.9   Displaying the test result of an Nmap script for sniffer detection.

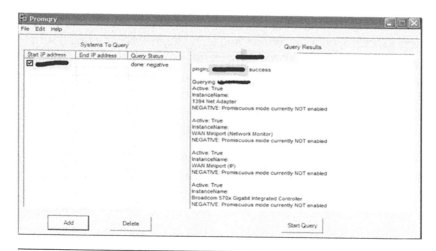

Figure 4.10   Displaying the PromqryUI test.

4.9.1 Ping Method

To find a sniffer, find the system on the network that is operating in promiscuous or monitor mode. The ping approach is helpful in identifying a system that operates in promiscuous mode, which helps identify if network sniffers have been installed. In this method, the ping request with the IP address of the target is sent but not the MAC address. Usually, the packet will be discarded as there is no match of the MAC address, but if a sniffer program is running on the network, then it will accept the packet. However, this method is not very reliable.

4.9.2 Internet Control Message Protocol (ICMP) Test

An ICMP request with an untrue MAC and the proper IP address is sent to the computer under investigation as a sniffer detection technique. Again, the tested host may identify itself by responding to the ping, and the sniffer will be detected if it has an interface in promiscuous mode or monitor mode.

4.9.3 Forged MAC Address Test

A simple and easy method to detect a sniffer on a network is that on a normal network, the ethernet frames are usually dropped when the

MAC address does not match [16]. Here, when the frames or packet is sent using the forged MAC address, the packet must be dropped or discarded. However, when the network card is in monitor mode, the packet will not be discarded.

4.9.4 WIFI Security Alert

When the user's smartphone detects unexpected behavior in the mobile hotspot to which the user is connected, the user may occasionally receive an alert or warning. Only a few cell phones may have access to this feature, and even then, the software must be the current version. The WIFI alert is displayed in Figure 4.11 as the Galaxy F12 mobile hotspot is being sniffed.

4.10 Countermeasures for Sniffing

Encryption: The most popular deterrent against network snooping is encryption. Information can be secured via encryption by being changed from its original form into one that can only be unlocked with the use of an encryption key or password [17].

Firewalls: A network's sensitive data are shielded from unauthorized access via firewalls. In a networked context, firewalls offer security control for networks, host computers, and individual users [17].

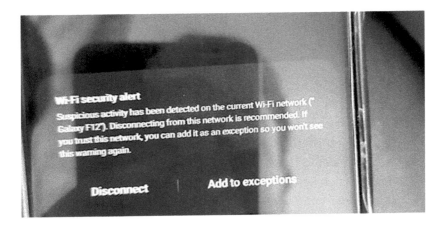

Figure 4.11   Displaying the WIFI alert.

Virtual Private Network (VPN): By encrypting your connection and obscuring your IP address, a VPN protects all the data sent from your computer over the internet. When you use a strong VPN such as AVG Secure VPN, a sniffer watching your traffic would only be able to decipher scrambled information; this keeps your data secret [17].

Secure Protocols: With various methods, for example, authentication, encryption, and authorization, many protocols can be made secure.

Avoid Connecting to Unsecured Networks: Information exchanged over an unprotected network is not encrypted and is readily accessible since the network lacks firewall and antivirus security. Network sniffing attacks are simple to execute when users expose their devices to unsecured WIFI networks. Attackers can install packet sniffers on unsecured networks, which can read and intercept any data sent over the network. By setting up a fake "free" public WIFI network, an attacker can also monitor network activity [17].

To Browse Safely Online, Seek HTTPS Protocols: The term "HTTPS" (hypertext transfer protocol secure) is used in the URL of websites that are encrypted; this signifies that user interaction on certain websites is safe and assures that data are encrypted before they are delivered to a server. Visit websites that start with "HTTPS" to prevent packet sniffing because "HTTP" websites are unable to offer the same level of security [10].

Strengthen Your Endpoint Protections: As endpoints, namely, laptops, desktop computers, and mobile devices, are connected to networks, security risks such as packet sniffers can readily access an organization's network. Robust antivirus software should be utilized to stop malware from infiltrating a system as it identifies anything that should not be on a computer, for example, a sniffer [10, 29].

Install a System to Detect Intrusions: Software called an intrusion detection system (IDS) scans network traffic for any odd activity and notifies of potential intruders. Every potentially dangerous behavior or policy breach is frequently reported to an administrator or consolidated through a security information and event management (SIEM) system. This can scan a network or system for harmful activity or policy breaches [10, 13, 30].

4.11 Conclusion

Packet sniffing has both ethical and unethical purposes. For example, network vulnerabilities can be discovered by monitoring network activity and looking for network issues. It is also important to be aware of how to stop sniffers and how to shield data from attackers and sniffers for immoral objectives that might enable the theft of sensitive data, such as login credentials, browsing history, and accessed information. Sniffers can be found on a network by looking for strange traffic patterns, a high activity level, and a network that is not password- or firewall-protected and is situated in public areas or by utilizing a simple technique such as creating a Nmap sniffer script for a specific gateway. In addition, hackers can sniff data through a wireless connection. Moreover, knowledge of the different types of sniffing and how to stop it must be obtained.

4.12 Future Enhancement

In the future, packet sniffers can be enhanced for both ethical and unethical objectives. They can be utilized as a tool for traffic surveillance for ethical reasons. Meanwhile, configuring high-traffic gateways with additional users may prevent congestion by increasing their capacity. The quantity of devices linked to the network can also be seen. Packet sniffers can occasionally even be used as spyware for ethical reasons at a workplace to monitor workers.

A packet sniffer can also be used for phishing for unethical purposes. By focusing on and keeping track of the user through IP-based sniffing, a hacker can quickly determine the user's susceptibility since the hacker is aware of the often-visited websites and bases their searches on them. Phishing attacks against a person can be carried out simply by hackers. Additionally, by creating some script code for a website that uses the HTTP protocol, a hacker can collect victim credentials.

References

[1] Ryan Spangler, "Packet Sniffing on Layer 2 Switched Local Area Networks", *Packet Watch Research*, pp. 1–5, 2003.

[2] Thomas M. Chen and Lucia Hu, "Internet Performance Monitoring", *Proceedings of the IEEE*, Vol. 90, No. 9, pp. 1592–1603, September 2002.

[3] www.youtube.com/watch?v=D7x4q5SP-wk

[4] https://fileinfo.com/extension/cap

[5] Lanoy, Aaron, and Gordon W. Romney. "A virtual honey net as a teaching resource." In *2006 7th International Conference on Information Technology Based Higher Education and Training*, pp. 666–669. IEEE, 2006.

[6] Jorge Belenguer and Carlos T. Calafate, "A Low-Cost Embedded IDS to Monitor and Prevent Man-in-the-Middle Attacks on Wired LAN Environments", *International Conference on Emerging Security Information, Systems and Technologies*. IEEE, pp. 122–127, October 2007.

[7] A. Meehan, G. Manes, L. Davis, J. Hale and S. Shenoi, "Packet Sniffing for Automated Chat Room Monitoring and Evidence Preservation", *Proceedings of the Second Annual IEEE Systems*. Man and Cybernetics Information Assurance Workshop, New York, pp. 285–288, June 2001.

[8] Sabeel Ansari, S.G. Rajeev and H.S. Chandrashekar, "Packet Sniffing: A Brief Introduction", *IEEE Potentials*, Vol. 21, No. 5, pp. 17–19, December 2003.

[9] Chris Senders, *Practical Packet Analysis, Using Wireshark to Solve Real-World Network Problems*. No Starch Press Inc, San Francisco, 2007.

[10] https://openthread.io/guides/pyspinel/requirements

[11] www.kali.org/downloads

[12] https://nooblinux.com/connecting-a-wireless-adapter-to-kali-linux-virtual-machine/

[13] www.youtube.com/watch?v=JSMw4AHjRAE

[14] www.researchgate.net/publication/267908713_Packet_Sniffing_Network_Wiretapping.

[15] Barnett, Greg, Daniel Lopez, Shana Sult, and Michael Vanderford. "Packet Sniffing: Network Wiretapping." *Group project, INFO* (2002): 3229-001.

[16] Dick Haze Leger, "Packet Sniffing: A Crash Course", Netherlands, 2001. https://clario.co/blog/what-is-sniffing/

[17] https://clario.co/blog/what-is-sniffing/

[18] Ryan Spangler, "Packet Sniffer Detection with Ant Sniff", University of Wisconsin, Department of Computer and Network Administration, May 2003.

[19] Alomoudi, Raed, Long Trinh, and Darleen Spivey. "Protecting Vulnerabilities or Online Intrusion: The Efficacy of Packet Sniffing in the Workplace." *Florida Atlantic University ISM* 4320 (2004).

[20] https://technet.microsoft.com/en-us/library/cc95935 spx

[21] www.wireshark.org/download.html

[22] Cristina L. Abad and Rafael I. Bonilla, "An Analysis on the Schemes for Detecting and Preventing ARP Cache Poisoning Attacks", *27th International Conference on Distributed Computing Systems Workshops (ICDCSW'07)*. IEEE, June 2007.

[23] https://research.utwente.nl/en/publications/on-the-anatomy-of-social-engineering-attacks-a-literature-based-d

[24] https://linuxhint.com/route-add-command-linux/

[25] www.ettercap-project.org/download.html

[26] www.youtube.com/watch?v=k6rx1krSUAo

[27] https://nmap.org/nsedoc/scripts/sniffer-detect.html

[28] www.microsoft.com/en-us/download/details.aspx?id=1851

[29] www.spiceworks.com/it-security/network-security/articles/what-is-packet-sniffing/

[30] https://en.wikipedia.org/wiki/Packet_analyzer

5

UNRAVELING THE IMPACT OF SOCIAL ENGINEERING ON ORGANIZATIONS

DR. JAYASUDHA K AND DR. T N ANITHA

5.1 Introduction

Under the heading of "social engineering," a wide variety of malevolent operations are carried out through interactions among people. Users are psychologically coerced into revealing sensitive information or committing security violations. However, social engineering can lead to positive outcomes including networking, teamwork, and entertainment that offers instant pleasure. Both positive and negative effects of social engineering on an organisation are felt by society. Positive effects include people working together, feeling confident, and networking. With technical developments and social interaction, our lives can be made better. Negative effects include a complete loss of business and public mistrust and may also result in social problems, such as anxiety and incompatibility. Attacks primarily originate from social networks and emails, with phishing and ransomware being the most prevalent. Organizations are required to protect their sensitive data and inform the public about their efforts. According to a study on social engineering, the focus is on business, finance, and automobile entities and their problems [6].

When organisations examine where they spend their money on security, it is evident that the technical aspects of security receive significantly more attention than the human components. These organisations run the risk of having protocols that are inefficient at preventing accidents by focusing solely on technological security issues and ignoring human vulnerabilities. The human element will continue to come up in the conversation about social engineering. A proficient social

DOI: 10.1201/9781003406716-5

engineer will frequently attempt to take advantage of this flaw before devoting time and energy to other ways to break passwords or obtain access to systems.

Because the individuals responsible for protecting an organization's data are extremely susceptible to social engineering attacks, this risk still exists. This chapter provides recommendations for managing the social engineering threat within organisations' risk tolerance.

5.2 Literature Review

Almutairi et al. [1] conducted a study at Shaqra University (Kingdom of Saudi Arabia) with the goals of determining the level of awareness of social engineering, providing appropriate solutions to problems to reduce social engineering risks, and avoiding obstacles that could prevent raising awareness of these risks. Using a survey, 508 employees from various firms were questioned. The aggregate Cronbach's alpha was 0.756, which is very good, and the correlation coefficient between each of the items was statistically significant at the 0.01 level. Overall, 63.4% of the sample had no awareness of social engineering. Of the total sample, 67.3% were not aware of the dangers that social engineering poses. Moreover, 42.1% of the sample had limited knowledge of social engineering, while only 7.5% had a strong understanding.

The article review by Busal et al. [2] explains the stages of social engineering, provides recent research on social engineering attacks, and categorises the numerous forms of attacks into two groups. This study's primary goal was to investigate the numerous social engineering attacks that have been made against people, and it included countermeasures.

The paper by Siddiqi et al. [3] examines the methods used to carry out social engineering-based assaults in great detail. This article discusses the human shortcomings that criminals have exploited in previous security breaches. The report also discusses contemporary countermeasures against cyberattacks based on social engineering, such as machine learning-based methods.

Manyam et al. [4] investigate numerous social engineering assaults and define the basic techniques used by attackers. The main topics of research are the effects of artificial intelligence (AI) on social engineering and how it can be used to identify and stop social engineering attempts. Due to their high effectiveness, efficiency, simplicity, and obscurity, social engineering-based cyberattacks are very challenging to defend against because they do not adhere to any set patterns or methods for carrying out an assault. Properly understanding the assault strategy is crucial for defending against such attacks. Consequently, this study offers a thorough examination of the strategies employed to carry out social engineering-based assaults. Accordingly, the human weaknesses used by criminals in recent security breaches are discussed. The research also covers current defences against social engineering-based cyberattacks, such as machine learning-based approaches.

Basic traits of social engineering and a social engineering activity are presented in a study by Mamedova et al. [5]. In the human-machine interaction system that is used to carry out the unlawful (malicious) modification of human behavioural patterns, the study of social engineering methods is prioritised. Meanwhile, a map of information security hazards brought on by social engineering acts and a matrix of social engineering qualification requirements are developed.

Washo et al. [6] study social engineering from an interdisciplinary perspective. A literature review of the information technology, psychology, and business disciplines explains the subject's interconnections and the necessity to comprehend it from several aspects. Following a review of the literature, social engineering research is examined from philosophical, technological, and ethical perspectives. Researchers might use the recommended framework that promotes a philosophical or practical ethical approach as a flexible model for their research.

Wilcox et al. [7] classify and address security concerns such as organization's information asset availability, confidentiality, and integrity related to social engineering that businesses have when implementing social media for business purposes.

The global pandemic's impact on social engineering attacks is discussed by Venkatesha et al. [8]. The pandemic has caused a significant shift in daily activities to the Internet and online platforms. Although the number of Internet users is growing, there has been a lack of knowledge regarding cybersecurity issues and the numerous types of attacks that Internet users may experience on a daily basis. The authors analysed the processes used by these attackers, from familiarising themselves with a target to successfully carrying out the attack.

A systematic literature review is carried out by W Syafitri et al. [9] by utilising Bryman and Bell's technique. The review reveals a novel approach that employs a protocol in addition to techniques, frameworks, models, and assessments to thwart social engineering attempts. It is also observed that the protocol effectively prevents social engineering attacks, including those involving health campaigns, and the vulnerability of social engineering victims and discusses the co-utile protocol, which can regulate information sharing on social networks. A comprehensive analysis of the literature is conducted to provide recommendations on how to stop social engineering attacks.

Three alternative storylines—"the oblivious employee," "speaking code and social," and "fixing human flaws"—are used by Klimburg et al. [10] to illustrate how ownership of cybersecurity is personalised. The idea of the "stupid user" who is susceptible to social engineering is a common one, and it ties into the idea of shifting responsibility from a collective concern to the individual employee. Finally, the authors suggest starting a conversation about social engineering and the politics of deficit creation and securitization that it is rooted in.

5.3 Conceptual Framework

The conceptual framework shown in Figure 5.1 demonstrates the impact of social engineering on organisations' entire design flow. Starting with numerous social engineering strategies, it moves on to various social engineering consequences on organisations, social engineering prevention methods, social engineering illustration scenarios, a social engineering case study, and ultimately, the conclusion.

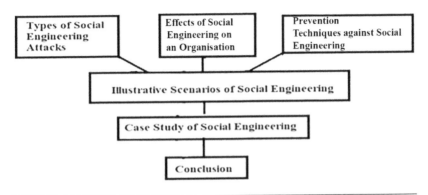

Figure 5.1 Design flow of the impact of social engineering on an organization.

5.4 Types of Social Engineering Attacks

People are the main threat to cybersecurity, and social engineering makes use of a user's incapacity to recognise an assault. The purpose of a social engineering attack is to persuade the victim to do something, such as hand over cash, reveal private customer information, or provide authentication credentials. The 10 social engineering attacks shown in Figure 5.2 are the most common.

i. *Phishing*:

The most frequent form of social engineering assault, specifically, phishing, uses phoney email addresses and links to deceive victims into disclosing their login information, credit card details, or other sensitive information. There are several different types of phishing attacks:
- Using fake customer service accounts on social media or "angler phishing"; and
- Phishing attacks called "spear phishing" target specific companies or individuals.

ii. *Whaling*:

A well-known phishing variant called whaling specifically targets senior business executives and directors of government bodies. The majority of whale attacks involve sending urgent messages about a fabricated emergency or a window of opportunity by using email accounts that are spoofs of

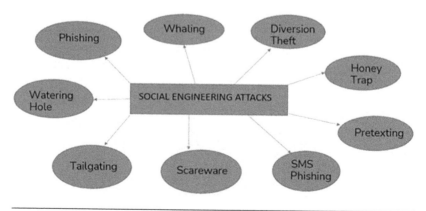

Figure 5.2 Types of social engineering attacks.

other high-ranking individuals within the business or agency. Because senior executives and directors have high-level network access, successful whaling attacks can reveal a lot of sensitive and private information.

iii. *Diversion Theft*:

Tricking a delivery person or courier into going to the wrong location or transferring a package to someone other than the intended receiver is an antiquated diversion stealing tactic. By deceiving the victim into sending sensitive information to the wrong person via email or social media, a thief can steal information via an online diversion theft tactic. Usually, the thief does this by setting up a phoney employee email account with the victim's company, such an accountancy firm or a bank.

iv. *Baiting*:

Baiting is a type of social engineering assault that persuades victims to disclose sensitive information or login credentials by promising them something nice in exchange. An email offering a free gift card, for example, might be sent to the victim, encouraging them to click a link and complete a survey. Users may be taken to a fake Office 365 login page by the link, where a malicious party can obtain their email and password.

v. *Honey Trap*:

When conducting a honey trap attack, the attacker poses as someone who is romantically or sexually interested in the victim in order to seduce them into starting a relationship online. The attacker then demands money as ransom or compels the victim to divulge personal information.

vi. *Pretexting*:

This is an extremely sophisticated form of social engineering where a con artist creates a pretext or imaginary situation— assuming the identity of an IRS auditor, for instance—to trick a victim into divulging personal or delicate information, such as their social security number. This type of assault allows the attacker to physically access your data, for example, by tricking your workers into thinking that the attacker is a vendor, delivery person, or contractor.

vii. *SMS Phishing*:

SMS phishing is becoming a much greater problem as more firms rely mostly on texting for communication. Scammers might send their victims texts that appear to be requests for two-factor authentication and direct them to websites that steal their login information or infect their phones with malware. This is one type of SMS phishing.

viii. *Scareware*:

When con artists insert malicious code into a website to create pop-up windows with flashing lights and terrifying sounds, this is a form of social engineering. A user will receive erroneous notifications from these pop-up windows that a virus has been installed on their computer. When the con artists advise the user to purchase and download their security software, the user's credit card information will be stolen, their machine will actually be infected, or (most likely) both.

ix. *Tailgating*:

The social engineering tactic of tailgating, also known as piggybacking, involves an attacker physically following a victim into a restricted or secure location. To enter the area undetected, the con artist will occasionally claim that they forgot their access card or strike up a lively conversation with a spectator.

x. *Watering Hole*:

A hacker uses a reliable website that their intended victims are known to visit in a "watering hole attack" to spread malware. The hacker then either installs a backdoor Trojan horse to get access to the target's network or they intercept the victims' login information and use it to enter.

xi. *Spear Phishing*:

A spear-phishing attack is more difficult to detect. This is when an attacker sends an email to one or more employees while posing as an organization's IT consultant and forges the signature as the Forzing consultant signature would typically do.

xii. *Receptor Phishing*:

The receptor modifies a user's password and sends them a link that reroutes them to the fraudulent page where the attacker obtains their login information.

5.5 Effects of Social Engineering on Organisations

Understanding the genuine consequences of social engineering attacks can help to pique your employees' interest in better safeguarding your business. Leadership and management must fully comprehend the value of spending money on quality social engineering training (Figure 5.3). Beyond lost information and data theft, social engineering can have other negative impacts. Different attacks could cause interruption, financial loss, and a bad reputation for a company. Because of this, it is crucial that you and your team are knowledgeable in planning, spotting, avoiding, and responding to social engineering attacks. Put procedures, standards, and rules in place to shield your company from social engineering scams. If you do not safeguard your business, then the effects of this neglect on the company's health could be disastrous and the damage from such attacks could be widespread.

The following are some ways that social engineering impacts businesses worldwide.

a) *Interruption of Operations*:
   Social engineers take advantage of employees' trust to lock down systems and demand payment to regain access. They may be "hacktivists" who want to put an end to the operations of a business they believe to be unethical or power-hungry. Whatever their motivation, social engineers can clearly stall or shut down business processes to achieve their objectives.

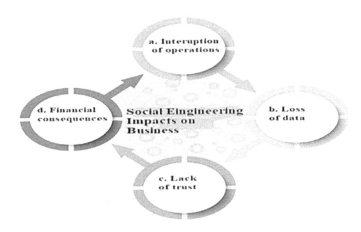

Figure 5.3   Impacts of social engineering on a business.

b) *Loss of Data*:
Social engineers will occasionally utilise their cunning to steal data and sell these data on the dark web for a profit. Sometimes they will do this to expose or humiliate a business. Social engineers can steal confidential information such as bank records, client information, proprietary data, and client information for any cause, including financial gain.

c) *Lack of Trust*:
After a social engineer violates an organisation, people inevitably begin to doubt its dependability. The breached company disappointed customers who relied on them to protect their personal information. Customer names, emails, addresses, credit card numbers, behavioural data, health information, and any other private information can be taken during an attack. A cyber assault can have long-lasting impacts on a company's reputation and can shatter consumers' perceptions of its reliability.

d) *Financial Consequences*:
By posing as a dependable co-worker, manager, or business partner, social engineers can convince workers to wire them money. Bank accounts or authorised user accounts could be broken into, allowing an attacker to steal money. To facilitate future financial attacks or to demand payment in a ransomware exploit, attackers might potentially divulge private information to others on the dark web. Beyond the overt forms of theft, social engineering has hidden costs.

5.6 Prevention Techniques against Social Engineering for Organisations

Despite the prevalence of social engineering methods, it is challenging to recognise and, more importantly, to resist them. Many people are propelled towards a cybercriminal's intended consequence when they react in accordance with human nature. One of the most crucial defences against social engineering initiatives is having good discernment. However, as common sense is a highly subjective concept in the business world, it is crucial that technology analysts share best practises to prevent social engineering, such as the following.

a) Remind staff members not to click on suspicious websites.
b) Never respond to emails from unknown senders or strangers.

c) Never share information with anybody whose approach is doubtful.

d) Do not ever give out any private information about you or the company.

There is nothing you can do to stop social engineers from trying to fool you, but there are things you can do to make it more difficult for them and to prevent attacks (Figure 5.4) through social engineering.

a) *Be aware of potential dangers*:
Learn about the typical forms of social engineering assaults so you can be on the lookout for the current methods.

b) *Enrol your group in cybersecurity education*:
Security experts must give your employees specific instructions on how to identify and prevent cyberattackers. Your employees can stay sharp by attending annual security training.

c) *Establish and enforce transparent security procedures*:
When workers and management do not adhere to the best security practises, social engineers frequently identify back-doors. Clarify your expectations for your team's performance and how they can react successfully in the event of an attack.

d) *Test the security preparedness of your business frequently*:
Your current security architecture may have gaps that can be found via quarterly security assessments and annual penetration tests.

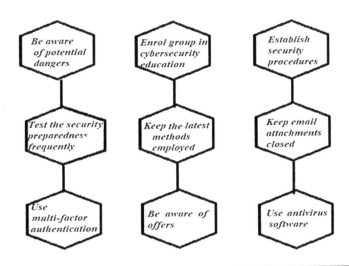

Figure 5.4 Prevention techniques.

e) *Keep up with the latest methods employed*:
Every day, social engineers are coming up with more sophisticated techniques to deceive you. What will happen next is
unknown. Following security-related blogs and often requesting updated training will keep you and your staff informed.

f) *Keep email attachments closed*:
If you are unsure of the sender, then do not open any attachments or emails from dubious sources. Even if you are familiar with them but have doubts about their communications,
you should still double-check and validate the information by
contacting the service provider's website or by calling other
sources. Even emails that appear to be from reliable sources
could have been sent by an attacker.

g) *Multi-factor authentication should be used*:
Using multi-factor authentication increases the security of
your account.

h) *Be aware of offers*:
When an offer seems too good to be true, resist the urge to take
it. Perform a Google search to determine whether the offer is
legitimate.

i) *Use antivirus software*:
Periodically protect your system from attacks by properly
updating the software. Before opening any downloads, scan
them properly.

It is crucial to equip yourself with the appropriate tools and information
to protect yourself from the common social engineering techniques.
The most recent details on social engineering dangers are available on
Cyber Security Hub, which is a comprehensive cybersecurity resource.
Your ability to actively defend yourself and your sensitive data from
hostile cyberattacks depends on your ability to keep informed and be
empowered.

5.7 Illustrative Scenarios for Social Engineering Attacks

Cybercriminals who know what they are doing understand that social
engineering works best when it focuses on risk and human emotion.
Exploiting human emotion is far simpler than hacking a network or
looking for security holes (Figure 5.5).

Figure 5.5   Victims of social engineering.

The following are some well-known emotions that successful social engineering attacks frequently exploit.

a) Panic:
   You receive a message stating that you are under investigation for tax fraud and that you should call immediately to prevent being detained and subject to legal action. A social engineering attack occurs during tax season, when people are already stressed about filing their taxes. Cybercriminals trick consumers into listening to voicemails by using their anxiety and stress over paying taxes.

b) Selfishness:
   Imagine investing $10 and seeing it grow to $10,000 with no effort on your part. By appealing to their fundamental human desires for trust and fulfilment, cybercriminals convince their victims that they might genuinely gain something for nothing. In a well-worded baiting email, victims are told to provide their bank account information so that money can be transferred the same day.

c) Interest:
   Cybercriminals keep an eye out for events that garner a lot of media coverage and then take advantage of people's innate interest to trick their victims into acting. For instance, after the second Boeing MAX8 airliner tragedy, fraudsters sent emails with attachments that claimed to have information that had been leaked about the crash. The attachment installed an Hworm RAT variant on the victim's computer.

d) Cooperation:
   People desire to have mutual trust and assistance. Cybercriminals target two or three employees by using emails that appear

to be from the targets' managers after conducting research about the organisation.

The email emphasises that the manager needs the password to the accounting database to ensure that everyone is paid on time and asks the recipients to provide it. The urgency of the email makes the recipients believe that by acting right now, they are helping their management.

e) Need:

You receive an email from the customer service of an online retailer from whom you frequently make purchases informing you that they must verify your credit card information to protect your account.

The email asks you to respond immediately to stop hackers from stealing your credit card details. You send the information without giving it a second thought, and the recipient ends up exploiting it by committing thousands of dollars' worth of fraud.

5.8 Case Study of Social Engineering

Social engineering is a result of people's propensity to trust. Cybercriminals have learned that a deftly written phone, email, or text message can convince receivers to give money, expose private information, or download a file that infects the office network with malware.

Consider the following spear-phishing incident, which convinced a worker to wire $500,000 to a foreign investor:

The cybercriminal is aware that the CEO of the organisation is travelling because of careful spear-phishing study. A fake CEO-looking email is sent to a staff member of the company. The CEO's name is spelt correctly, but the email address contains a small typo. In the email, the employee is asked to help the CEO by paying $500,000 to a new foreign investor. By using urgent yet cordial language, the email persuades the employee that his assistance will benefit the CEO and the business.

The CEO would normally handle this transfer directly, but she is unable to do this in time to apply for the foreign investment partnership because of her travel. The employee decides to do something without verifying the details. The employee truly believes that by responding to the email, he is helping the CEO, the company, and his co-workers. A few days later, the victimised employee, CEO, and staff members discover that they were duped out of $500,000 through a social engineering scheme.

5.9 Conclusion

The chapter observed several social engineering techniques, and it is evident that the stakeholders' levels of awareness were reflected in their actions as they carried out their jobs. The chapter investigated different social engineering strategies, and it can be inferred that an organisation is at risk if any of the techniques were to be employed by a social engineer and an actual attack took place. The results of these strategies show that despite being a "non-technical" method of infiltration, social engineering should be treated as seriously as any other technical danger. Because social engineering is a topic that is continually evolving due to technological innovation, it is crucial that ongoing study be conducted in this area.

Therefore, organisations are still at risk since the individuals in charge of protecting the data are extremely susceptible to social engineering attacks. The chapter provided advice for managing the social engineering threat within organisations' risk tolerance. As a result, it is critical that ongoing study be conducted in this area because social engineering is a dynamic sector that is changing quickly due to technological innovation.

References

1. Almutairi, Bandar S., and Abdurahman Alghamdi. "The Role of Social Engineering in Cybersecurity and Its Impact." *Journal of Information Security* 13, no. 4 (2022): 363–379.
2. Bhusal, Chandra Sekhar. "Systematic Review on Social Engineering: Hacking by Manipulating Humans." *Journal of Information Security* 12 (2021): 104–114.
3. Siddiqi, Murtaza Ahmed, Wooguil Pak, and Moquddam A. Siddiqi. "A Study on the Psychology of Social Engineering-Based Cyberattacks and Existing Countermeasures." *Applied Sciences* 12, no. 12 (2022): 6042.
4. Manyam, Sowjanya. "Artificial Intelligence's Impact on Social Engineering Attacks." (2022).

5. Mamedova, Natalia, Arkadiy Urintsov, Olga Staroverova, Evgeniy Ivanov, and Dmitriy Galahov. "Social Engineering in the Context of Ensuring Information Security." In *SHS Web of Conferences*, vol. 69, p. 00073. EDP Sciences, 2019.

6. Washo, Amy Hetro. "An Interdisciplinary View of Social Engineering: A Call to Action for Research." *Computers in Human Behavior Reports* 4 (2021): 100126.

7. Wilcox, Heidi, Maumita Bhattacharya, and Rafiqul Islam. "Social Engineering Through Social Media: An Investigation on Enterprise Security." In *Applications and Techniques in Information Security: 5th International Conference, ATIS 2014, Melbourne, VIC, Australia, November 26–28, 2014. Proceedings 5*, pp. 243–255. Springer Berlin Heidelberg, 2014.

8. Venkatesha, Sushruth, K. Rahul Reddy, and B. R. Chandavarkar. "Social Engineering Attacks During the COVID-19 Pandemic." *SN Computer Science* 2 (2021): 1–9.

9. Syafitri, Wenni, Zarina Shukur, Umi Asma'Mokhtar, Rossilawati Sulaiman, and Muhammad Azwan Ibrahim. "Social Engineering Attacks Prevention: A Systematic Literature Review." *IEEE Access* 10 (2022): 39325–39343.

10. Klimburg-Witjes, Nina, and Alexander Wentland. "Hacking Humans? Social Engineering and the Construction of the 'Deficient User' in Cybersecurity Discourses." *Science, Technology, & Human Values* 46, no. 6 (2021): 1316–1339.

6

IMPACTS OF SOCIAL
ENGINEERING ON E-BANKING

SPOORTHI M, GURURAJ H L, AMBIKA V,
JANHAVI V AND NAJMUSHER H

6.1 Introduction

The practise of deceiving others into disclosing private information, carrying out unauthorised activities, or acting in a way that compromises security is known as social engineering. Instead of direct hacking, this method makes use of psychological features and depends on human error. Social engineering assaults in the context of electronic banking (e-banking) can have significant effects on both clients and financial organisations. E-banking has arisen as a breakthrough for people and organisations to manage their funds in the ever-changing world of digital technology. E-banking provides ease, accessibility, and a variety of services that can be used at home or while travelling. However, e-banking has both advantages and possible drawbacks, and one of the most worrisome risks is social engineering. Cybercriminals have plenty of opportunity in the digital world to generate convincing stories and take advantage of trusting e-banking customers. Phishing emails, phone calls pretending to be bank employees, fraudulent websites, and even social media manipulation are all possible methods of assault [1]. These assaults' main objective is to obtain sensitive data, including login passwords, credit card information, personal identification numbers (PINs), and security question and answer sets. Recent advancements in artificial intelligence (AI) have made it easier to utilise sophisticated social engineering methods. The effectiveness of social engineering assaults is facilitated by the capacity of AI algorithms to collect and analyse vast amounts of data from numerous digital channels, which makes it easier to create personalised and

DOI: 10.1201/9781003406716-6

persuasive messages [2]. Further obscuring the distinction between legitimate and fraudulent communication, AI-powered chatbots or voice assistants can mimic human-like interactions. Bank transfers made by individuals using online banking websites or applications are known as authorised push payments (APPs). ACI Worldwide, a provider of payment software, and GlobalData, an analytics company, predict that losses from APP fraud will double across the UK, India, and the US in the next four years, hitting $5.25 billion (£4.44 billion) with a compound annual growth rate of 21% over this time. Particularly in the UK, APP fraud volumes in 2021 reached $789.4 million, with a potential increase to $1.56 billion by 2026. As one of the 21st century's fastest-growing industries, the internet has contributed to the advancement of technical infrastructure. The rapid development of internet-based apps has altered how individuals interact and conduct daily business. Accordingly, there is substantial expansion and use of e-banking services. Figure 6.1 shows some well-known e-banking services provided by banks and other financial organisations.

Everyone wants their transactions to be private, but since everything is accessible online, there is always a chance that someone may obtain the information and use it improperly. Additional sources of e-banking security risk include threats of hacking and unauthorised access to the bank's systems. The reputation of every business is crucial. If a bank fails to complete necessary duties or behaves inconsistently with customer expectations when it comes to e-banking, then it faces the risk of losing its reputation. Eventually, less money is received or less clients are obtained. A major worry is how social engineering can affect online banking. Online banking transaction security is seriously threatened by psychologically manipulative social engineering

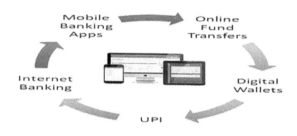

Figure 6.1   E-banking services.

approaches [5, 6]. These strategies have the potential to cause both individuals and organisations to suffer from unauthorised access, identity theft, and financial losses. To reduce the risks posed by social engineering in the context of e-banking, preventive actions are essential. These include education about countermeasures and the adoption of strong security mechanisms. The major objective of e-banking is to expand the geographic reach of both banks and customers. This suggests that the spread can cross international borders, which creates a range of global threats.

Threats from social engineering in e-banking can have serious repercussions as shown in Figure 6.2. Cybercriminals trick victims into disclosing private information, which allows for unauthorised access, fraudulent transactions, and identity theft. Financial losses, reputational harm, and compromised personal data are some of the consequences. Due to manipulation techniques such as phishing emails or impersonation, victims may unintentionally divulge passwords or verification codes. Users must be made aware of possible hazards, encouraged to be wary of unwanted messages, and required to utilise strong security methods, for example, multi-factor authentication, to prevent such attacks. Banks can lessen the impact of social engineering risks on e-banking consumers by boosting cybersecurity knowledge and vigilance [9].

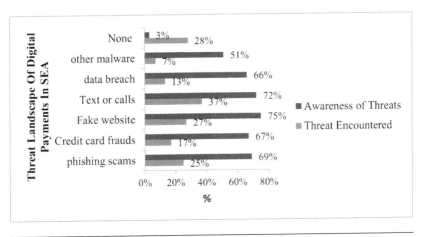

Figure 6.2   The threat landscape of digital payments in South East Asia (SEA).

Globally, the use of digital payment systems is increasing. Although the pandemic is one factor that contributed to its acceleration, the truth is that today's customers prefer digital payments because of their increased flexibility. Digital payment options are now accepted by the majority of companies and services in Southeast Asia. In addition to debit and credit cards, e-wallets are becoming more popular, which makes it easier for customers to handle their financial demands including bill payments and other expenses in addition to making payments. Digital payments are being used more often, but there is also rising worry about the dangers they may pose. Customers are concerned about cyber dangers, for instance, when they make purchases using their mobile devices and e-wallets. Surprisingly, social engineering scams are the most prevalent hazard experienced by most Southeast Asian nations, including Indonesia (40%), Malaysia (45%), the Philippines (42%), Singapore (32%), and Vietnam (38%). The sole exception is Thailand, where bogus websites are the most often encountered danger (31%). Greater awareness may be directly correlated with greater exposure to cyber threats. The most often encountered dangers are social engineering schemes, fraudulent websites, and bogus offers and discounts, with awareness rates of 72%, 75%, and 64%, respectively.

6.2 Literature Survey

Every research field needs literature studies since they provide a description of the information needed for the next research projects, policies, and procedures. A study technique called a systematic literature review (SLR) summarises both qualitative and quantitative data after rigorously evaluating several studies. The research indicates that information security and cybercrime are constantly parallel to one another. Computer criminals continuously attempt to obtain unauthorised access to the data of the commercial and financial sectors to engage in criminal activity. When using online banking and related services, clients are always concerned about the security of their financial information, which undoubtedly has an impact on customers' utilisation of online banking services. Internet banking customers need to be made aware of the available security risks and threats [10–19]. One study examines and evaluates the impacts of online threats when engaging in internet banking services. The study's conclusion is that there is a need to boost customers' knowledge of potential cybercrimes when using internet banking [10].

Today, non-computer experts, such as nurses in the medical arena, soldiers in the military, or firefighters in emergency services, regularly manage critical infrastructure. In such sophisticated systems, protecting against insider attacks is typically not possible or cost-effective, but these risks can be reduced with the appropriate risk management strategies. One type of security technology that aids in protecting computer systems and data assets from unauthorised access is the firewall [13]. The human component of system security, however, is one area that is usually gravely neglected. Social engineering techniques enable malicious attackers to breach organisational security through human interactions. A security awareness training technique can be used to inform operators of critical infrastructure about social engineering security concerns including spear phishing, baiting, and pretexting [3].

The advancement of technology has had an impact on every aspect of society and has made it possible for financial transactions to be made swiftly in an online environment. One of the industries that uses technology the most extensively is the banking sector. To better meet customer demands and increase market share in a competitive economic environment, banks have digitised their services and made them available through online applications [14]. Although this innovation has numerous benefits, it has also produced plenty of victims for deceitful individuals [9]. The goal of phishing assaults is to rapidly and conveniently obtain the needed information from users by using deception, fright, curiosity, or enthusiasm. The majority of phishing websites are built for online banking (e-banking), and with the strategies and discourses that they establish, attackers can obtain financial information from consumers who have been duped. Even if the number of anti-phishing tactics is growing daily, the human element has prevented an effective solution from being discovered for this problem. It is crucial to research and evaluate the attack methods and strategies used by attackers in genuine phishing attempts. In one study, an actual e-banking phishing attempt was detected and examined by utilising a phishing website [4].

The authentication environment designed to secure e-banking applications is presented in this study [5]. The suggested approach is a component of a doctoral dissertation that aims to provide a model for the secure functioning of an internet banking environment, even in the presence of client-side malware. The present internet banking systems will be least affected by the authentication model's easy application. It aims to be immune to more traditional assaults such as man-in-the-middle or social engineering and the all-too-common phishing and pharming methods that occur today [37].

Another study [6] examines the Payment Services Directive (PSD2) compliance of multi-factor authentication schemes based on such techniques. The e-banking assaults taxonomy, which is consistent with authenticator threats from the NIST Digital Identity Guidelines but has a higher degree of detail with respect to the e-banking domain, is introduced to offer an overview. The sources that are readily available in this field often cover a wide range of topics, are geared towards corporate executives, or are more in-depth examinations of a single problem or assault [41]. By offering a comprehensive and complicated tool to aid with orientation in the region, research articles can connect such disparate sources.

People still choose to retain their primary bank accounts with traditional banks, which are financial institutions with a physical presence, but their influence is waning. The non-profit National Community Reinvestment Coalition (NCRC) estimates that between 2017 and 2021, 9% of all branch locations closed, representing a loss of almost 7,500

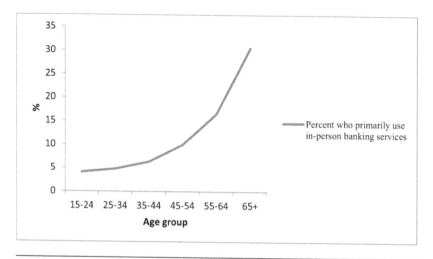

Figure 6.3 Banking trends by age group (years).

branches. One-third of the closures took place in low- to moderate-income or historically marginalised neighbourhoods. The COVID-19 epidemic, during which the pace of branch closures quadrupled, was a major driving force for many of these closures. One feature shared by conventional banks is the provision of in-person services with a bank teller. According to data, older generations are considerably more likely than younger ones to choose chatting with a bank teller as their primary form of account access. These differences by age are based on statistics from the FDIC for 2021 as shown in figure 6.3.

Digital or online banks are characterised by predominantly using web or mobile services. Even if they do not have physical locations, these banks can be a part of large ATM networks that allow clients access to cash. The market for online banks, such as Ally Bank and Discover Bank, has been growing rapidly; by 2021, it is expected that the value of the digital banking industry will reach $4.3 billion. Younger generations are more likely to use digital banking, with over three-quarters of individuals aged 15 to 24 years saying in 2021 FDIC research that mobile banking is their main method of banking. Only 15.3% of people 65 years and older said they primarily used mobile banking. Figure 6.4 shows some differences across age groups in the use of digital banking channels, which include online and mobile banking.

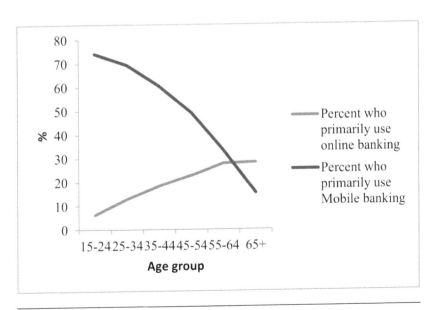

Figure 6.4 Digital banking trends.

6.3 Potential Social Engineering Risks in E-Banking

The term "vulnerability" in the context of social engineering attacks on e-banking refers to the flaws or openings in a person's or an organisation's defences that can be exploited by attackers to coerce them into disclosing sensitive information, carrying out unlawful deeds, or jeopardising their security [15]. These weaknesses are caused by psychological, behavioural, and technological elements that attackers take advantage of to further their objectives. An effective defence against social engineering assaults requires knowledge of and attention given to these weaknesses. The following are some major vulnerabilities:

- Human Psychology and Trust
- Lack of Awareness and Training
- Information Over-Sharing
- Inadequate Verification Processes
- Technological Dependencies
- Fear and Manipulation
- Unsolicited Contact
- Social Engineering Kits and Tools
- Emotional Manipulation
- Lack of Verification and Validation

Through the FBI's Internet Crime Complaint Center (IC3), the American public has a direct line of communication to report cybercrimes to the agency. We examine and assess the information to keep up with the trends and threats that cybercriminals pose. Our colleagues in law enforcement and intelligence are then given access to this information. To prepare our friends for an extensive government response to the cyber threat, the FBI and its partners are aware of how crucial it is to exchange information on cyber activities. This strategy depends on public reporting to IC3. The urgent need for additional cyber incident reporting to the federal government is brought to light by statistics from 2021–2022 as shown in Figure 6.5. Cyberattacks on e-banking are in fact crimes that require investigation and can result in legal consequences for the offenders.

As social engineering scams in online banking flourish, we focus only on the most common scenarios to help identify and avoid them.

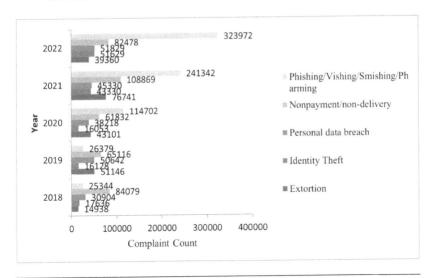

Figure 6.5 Top 5 crime types in e-banking.

Phishing, when hackers pose as reliable organisations to trick unwary victims via emails, text messages (smishing), or phone calls (vishing), is the most damaging and common social engineering assault. Phishing attacks can be quite convincing, as they may use the official logos, email templates, and verbiage of respected banks or organisations to fool users into disclosing personal information by clicking on a malicious link or responding to a message. Once accessed, these data may be exploited for identity theft, unauthorised access, or fraudulent transactions [16, 18]. In e-banking, social engineering can take advantage of a number of weak points in the system to trick customers into disclosing private information or taking security-compromising acts. Among the weak points that attackers frequently choose to exploit are shown in Table 6.1.

As it relates to e-banking, social engineering poses a number of hazards that might have a considerable impact on people, financial institutions, and the wider cybersecurity environment. APP scams, card fraud, and identity theft were the top three fraud strategies in 2022, according to Applied Communications Inc (ACI)'s 2023 Prime Time for Real-Time research, with APP scams ranking as the top fraud

Table 6.1   Social Engineering Vulnerable Mediums in E-Banking

VULNERABLE MEDIUM	DESCRIPTION
Emails	One of the most popular methods used by attackers to trick victims is through emails. They ask people to click on dangerous links or submit personal information in emails that look to be from trustworthy sources, including banks or financial organisations.
Phone calls	Vishing (voice phishing) is a technique that attackers can use to pretend to be bank tellers or customer care employees while on the phone. They frequently seek private information or point users to a phoney website while claiming there is an urgent problem with the user's account.
Text messages	Attackers send texts that request sensitive information or provide misleading links. Attacks such as smishing take advantage of people' faith in text messages from their banks.
Social media	Attackers may construct fictitious accounts on social networking sites to pose as bank workers or reliable contacts. Over time, they establish a connection with victims to win their confidence and obtain private information.
Instant messaging	Attackers use chat applications to convey nefarious links, files, or information demands. They could pose as friends, relatives, or other reliable people.
Websites and mobile apps	Attackers design phoney websites and mobile applications that closely mimic trustworthy banking websites and apps. Users could unintentionally give these bogus platforms their login credentials or personal information.
Online advertisements	Users may be directed to phishing websites or be prompted to download malicious software by malicious advertisements that appear on websites or social media platforms.
Impersonation of friends and family	Attackers may pose as friends, family members, or co-workers to win the trust of their victims and request money or private information.

strategy. The following are some of the major risk categories linked to social engineering impacts on e-banking.

A. *Financial Losses*: By using psychological manipulation to deceive people into disclosing sensitive information or performing acts that cause financial harm, social engineering in e-banking creates a serious danger of financial losses. Users are forced to provide login information, PINs, and personal information through phishing emails, impersonation, and false calls, giving attackers access to accounts without authorisation. This access makes it possible for unauthorised investments, fund transfers, and transactions, which has an immediate negative financial impact. Investment fraud may lure victims and cost them money while ransomware assaults lock accounts and threaten users with extortion. Fraudulent transfers that deplete accounts only make financial problems worse. To reduce these dangers and protect both individuals and institutions from the negative effects of social engineering in e-banking, it is essential to use multi-factor authentication, education, and continuous monitoring [20].

B. *APP Fraud*: There are several ways for criminals to carry out APP fraud, in which they find a victim, seduce them, and persuade them to pay money to the victim's account voluntarily. The money is then removed from the bank drop account to avoid being discovered, such as by splitting it up into smaller amounts before transferring. Thieves also frequently utilise methods that are often employed in other types of fraud, such as phishing, impersonating email addresses, and placing calls that appear to be from a bank or a company. In essence, APP fraud is a targeted, all-encompassing social engineering attack [21].

C. *Identity Theft*: This is a common strategy that involves coercing victims into disclosing sensitive information including passwords, social security numbers, and account information by taking advantage of their psychological weaknesses. Criminals frequently assume legitimate personas, for example, bank employees or technical support staff, and use compelling justifications to trick people into disclosing their personal information. The victim's identity is subsequently assumed by using this information, which results in fraudulent activities, unauthorised transactions, and potentially enormous financial losses. In the digital era, protecting personal information requires vigilance, uncertainty, and a dedication to confirming the validity of requests [30, 31].

D. *Account Takeover*: This is a deceptive tactic used by hackers to access people's online banking accounts without their permission. Attackers deceive people into disclosing sensitive information such as usernames, passwords, or the answers to security questions by preying on their trust or ignorance. Users are frequently tricked into disclosing their credentials through phishing emails, phoney customer service calls, or convincing impersonations of reputable organisations. Once hackers have the victim's account, they can access it and take control of it, giving them the ability to carry out unauthorised activities, move money, and jeopardise the victim's financial security. To stop such account takeovers and guarantee the security of e-banking transactions, it is crucial to adopt robust security measures, such as multi-factor authentication, be knowledgeable of typical techniques, and use care when responding to unwelcome messages [20].

E. *Data Breaches*: Social engineering techniques are widely used in the world of online banking to plan data breaches, a sinister scheme where thieves persuade people in order to obtain unauthorised access to confidential financial information. These criminals prey on human weaknesses by tricking people into divulging their login, credit card, and personal information through phishing emails or bogus websites [28]. These fraudulent credentials are then used to compromise the security of online banking networks by exposing enormous quantities of financial and personal information. Such breaches can result in identity theft, shady business dealings, and substantial financial losses. User education about the risks, the development of a sceptical mindset towards unsolicited communications, and the adoption of strong security measures to protect personal data and thwart these social engineering attacks in the digital banking environment are all necessary for defending against these breaches.

F. *Reputational Damage*: As hackers utilise psychological tricks to deceive people into compromising their own security, they cause reputational damage to both individuals and institutions [31]. Through strategies such as phishing emails or impersonation, attackers can access accounts and sensitive data without the user's knowledge. Unauthorised transactions, identity theft, and even the public disclosure of private financial information are possible consequences. This not only causes immediate financial impact but also erodes public confidence in the banking industry and damages a person's or organisation's image. Protecting financial assets and the priceless confidence of e-banking customers requires rigorous cybersecurity education, strong authentication procedures, and a proactive strategy to recognise and mitigate social engineering risks [32].

G. *Compliance and Legal Consequences*: Social engineering in e-banking can have major compliance and legal consequences by getting people to do things that are against the rules and law. Cybercriminals take advantage of human weaknesses by using phishing, pretexting, or baiting techniques to trick users into disclosing sensitive information or carrying out unauthorised acts. Data protection rules, privacy legislation, and standards for the financial industry may all be broken because of these acts. As a result, financial institutions might be subject to heavy penalties, legal action, and reputational harm [35]. Users who neglect to protect their account information may be held accountable. Such outcomes can be avoided with a comprehensive strategy that includes ongoing employee training, strong security protocols, vigilant monitoring for suspicious activity, and the prompt reporting of any potential breaches to regulatory authorities to ensure compliance and minimise legal repercussions in the event that they occur.

H. *Customer Attrition*: Cybercriminals utilise psychological tricks to fool consumers and jeopardise their financial security, a practise known as customer attrition. These attackers undermine trust and confidence in online financial systems by tricking people into giving sensitive information or accidentally carrying out unauthorised transactions by using techniques such as phishing or impersonation. Customers who fall prey to such scams may suffer from monetary losses, frustration, and feelings of insecurity. Customers may leave the bank in favour of more secure options because of their displeasure, which might have an adverse effect on the institution's profitability and image. Proactive education, strong security protocols, and prompt incident reactions are all necessary for preventing client attrition in the e-banking industry. These actions show a dedication to safeguarding customers' money and maintaining their loyalty [39].

I. *Insider Threat*: This occurs when employees are persuaded to compromise security for their own advantage or malevolent purposes. Insider threats can involve staff members, subcontractors, or other trustworthy individuals who provide private information to outside harmful actors because of psychological manipulation and deceit. Social engineering-enabled insider threats can lead to fraudulent transactions, data breaches, and compromised customer accounts. Detecting these attacks might be difficult because of the possibility that attackers could use lawful system access as leverage. Financial institutions must put in place strong security protocols, regularly train staff on social engineering techniques, keep an eye out for suspicious activity, and promote a culture of security awareness that encourages the reporting of any unusual behaviour or requests within the e-banking environment to reduce these risks [42–44].

J. *Lack of User Awareness*: Cybercriminals exploit people's ignorance of online security to plan fraudulent acts, and this weakness is known as a lack of user awareness. Attackers take advantage of this vulnerability and utilise strategies such as phishing emails, phoney websites, or impersonations to trick users into disclosing sensitive information or carrying out unauthorised transactions. Users may unwittingly fall prey to these scams due to a lack of understanding, which can result in losing money and compromising personal data [57]. To combat this danger, customers must undergo cybersecurity training that focuses on identifying suspicious communications, understanding typical social engineering techniques, and developing secure online behaviours. Financial institutions can enable customers to properly protect their assets and personal information in the world of e-banking by raising user knowledge and encouraging a proactive attitude towards online security [24].

Similar to traditional banking, e-banking also has risks including credit risk, liquidity risk, interest rate risk, market risk, etc. These hazards are increased with e-banking since it operates entirely online and has no physical borders. All of the aforementioned issues might be caused by poor design, outdated technology, negligent staff personnel, and unapproved system access. Banks must use the proper systems, technology, and access restrictions to provide a secure environment for conducting business [24].

6.4 Ontology Model of Social Engineering Attacks on E-Banking

A structured representation that classifies and arranges various components of social engineering assaults is referred to as an ontology model. In this context, ontology refers to a formal framework that establishes ideas, connections, and attributes inside a domain to offer complete knowledge of this domain. Applying an ontology model to social engineering assaults aids in categorising and analysing diverse attack methods, strategies, and motives and results in a methodical approach [58].

Attackers utilise two main strategies to influence targets and obtain information: active communication and passive communication. In social engineering, active communication entails face-to-face engagement between the attacker and the target. This may be conducted through channels including phone calls, instant messaging, in-person interactions, or any other type of communication where the attacker actively engages the victim to coerce them into disclosing private information or taking particular actions. Social engineering assault techniques that involve active contact include vishing, which is the practise of deceiving a legal company, such a bank, over the phone to obtain personal information. In social engineering, passive communication refers to tactics where the attacker does not interact with the target directly but instead uses traps, bogus websites, or other devices to coerce information or actions from gullible people. Sending phishing emails containing malicious links or attachments that the recipient may inadvertently connect to are examples of passive communication techniques used in social engineering attacks [59]. A purpose, a medium, a social engineer, a target, and compliance rules and procedures are additional elements of the ontological model. An attack's purpose may be to earn money, gain unauthorised access, or disrupt services. The medium is a method of communication, such as email, in-person meetings, phone calls, etc. Both a social engineer and a target might be a single person or a group of people. Compliance principles provide the justification for a target's compliance with an attacker's request.

Assault types, strategies, victim profiles, psychological triggers, and countermeasures are only a few of the levels of classification that this ontology covers. For instance, the category "attack types" defines classes including phishing, vishing, and pretexting, each with its own characteristics including attack vectors, objectives, and techniques

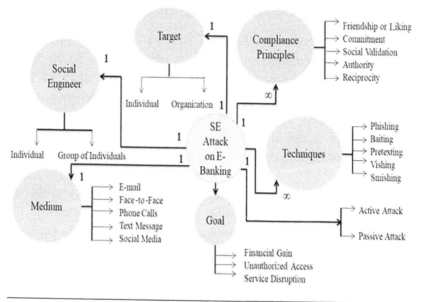

Figure 6.6   Ontology model of social engineering in e-banking.

as shown in figure 6.6. These attack types are associated with particular methods, such as spear phishing or baiting, which are accompanied by vectors, namely, emails or phone calls. The model also investigates the psychological triggers that attackers use, such as authority or familiarity, and it takes into account victim types, specifically, workers or consumers. Relationships between various levels are built by using this ontology, resulting in comprehensive knowledge of how social engineering assaults proceed within the complex environment of e-banking. Relationships within this ontology model in the context of e-banking emphasise the linkages among various elements of social engineering assaults [15]. The "victim profiles" and "psychological triggers" layers, for example, are interwoven because attackers modify their strategies based on the psychological weaknesses of certain targets [55]. The "attack" layer is linked to both "techniques" and "medium" and shows how numerous strategies can be used to carry out a single attack type through a range of communication channels. The model also highlights the significance of "countermeasures," illuminating the preventative measures that e-banking institutions might use to thwart or counteract social engineering attacks. Understanding these connections enables stakeholders to identify potential weak spots and develop stronger defence strategies, such as user education, secure authentication procedures, and ongoing monitoring. This strengthens the security of e-banking platforms against the constantly evolving threat of social engineering attacks.

A "1:1 relationship" between social engineering tactics and attacks suggests that the assailants spend time and resources gathering data on certain people or a chosen set of clients. With this knowledge, they can create attack messages or techniques that are incredibly persuasive. For instance, if an attacker recognises a regular online shopper, then they may send a phishing email imitating a well-known e-commerce site and requesting that the target click on a link for a special deal. The identity, buying habits, and interests of the target might be used by the attacker to make the email seem authentic. The message is tailored to the target's interests and experiences, which considerably improves the likelihood that they will fall for the assault.

Consider the following example of a social engineering assault on a high-net worth user of an e-banking platform.

Medium: The attacker may choose an app or type of email that the victim is known to use regularly as their method of contact.

Target: The attacker's investigation may have included leveraging publicly accessible data or social media profiles to identify the high-net worth client as the target.

Social Engineer: The attacker would customise their strategy depending on their knowledge of the customer's interests, spending patterns, and preferences. The degree of computer savvy of the consumer could also be taken into account.

Goal: The end objective may be to deceive the user into giving private information, moving money to an erroneous account, or clicking on a dangerous link.

The "1:∞" relationship refers to a more generalised strategy where attackers cast a wide net to target a greater number of people or organisations. This strategy entails using a single technique or procedure that may have an impact on several objectives. The "1" stands for a single approach applied to several prospective victims, whereas the "∞" stands for an unlimited number of victims.

Technique: Using a generic attack method that looks to be from the e-banking institution, the attacker asks recipients to click on a link and enter their login information to fix an urgent problem.

Compliance Principle: The difficulty of establishing a strong cybersecurity environment is shown by the "1:∞" relationship. The compliance principle emphasises the value of user knowledge and the necessity for e-banking institutions to employ rigorous security measures and follow compliance guidelines. These precautions could include regular security training, the installation of sophisticated email filtering systems, and the upkeep of stringent authentication procedures [10]. In this way, organisations can use more standardised methods to defend against attacks that target a wider audience, thereby securing consumer data and financial transactions.

Phases: Social engineering assaults on e-payments often involve numerous stages, each of which is carefully planned to influence targets and further the attacker's goals. Phases explore the methical development of fraudulent operations in the field of e-banking and reveal the complex steps by which deceitful actors plan schemes to take advantage of gullible victims as shown in Figure 6.7. These stages demonstrate the sophisticated manipulation strategies used by social engineers to take advantage of psychological vulnerabilities. Understanding these stages can help people see and thwart attacks and encourage a proactive approach to e-banking security and cybersecurity [8].

a. *Preparation*: Attackers acquire data on potential victims during the preparation stage, including personal information, internet habits, and communication preferences. Later, when creating persuasive and customised communications, this knowledge is essential. Attackers can comb through public databases, social media, and other sources to learn more about the victim [12, 17].

b. *Initial Engagement*: The perpetrator makes first contact with the victim during this stage. This may be communicated by a phone call, email, or social media post. The objectives are to form a relationship and develop trust. Attackers may utilise pretexting in which they manufacture a situation to explain their contact or they may mimic a reliable party, such as a bank employee or an IT support staff member.

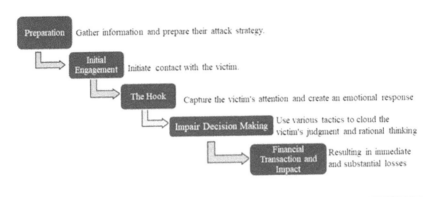

Figure 6.7   Phases in e-banking scams.

c. *The Hook*: After the victim and attacker have established a relationship, the attacker offers a "hook," that is, a motivation for the victim to act. This could entail a sense of necessity, aversion to negative outcomes, or promises of benefits. The goal of the hook is to elicit an emotional response that compels the victim to act as instructed by the assailant without giving the issue any careful thought.

d. *Impair Decision Making*: At this point, the attacker utilises psychological manipulation to compromise the victim's capacity for decision making. They might cause anxiety, tension, or bewilderment, which would impair the victim's judgement. The victim's cognitive defences deteriorate, and this makes them more prone to obediently executing the attacker's orders, even if these orders afterwards appear dubious [22–26].

e. *Financial Transaction and Impact*: The attacker persuades the victim to carry out a certain action in the final stage, frequently one that involves a money transaction. This can entail transferring money or disclosing private information including passwords. Because of the emotional and psychological pressure used during the earlier stages, the victim submits.

6.5 Digital Transaction Scams

According to information provided by the Indian government, there were 84,000 occurrences of Unified Payment Interface (UPI) fraud recorded in 2021–2022 and 77,000 in 2020–2021. The data were made public at a time when internet crimes and UPI-related fraud cases nationwide were on the rise. Indian society is undergoing a digital transition. Online shopping, holiday planning, and even ordering meals or groceries are all made easier by the digital age. The way that we deal with currency has been completely changed by UPI payments, especially regarding online money transactions. However, as online visibility grows, so does the exposure to cyber dangers. Online fraud, such as the WhatsApp scam, part-time work scam, movie scam, etc., are on the rise. Additionally, UPI payments are not exempt from this fraud. India saw around 95,000 UPI transaction fraud instances in 2022–2023, according to the Union Finance Ministry. In one year, the number of cases virtually doubled [33–36].

a. *Fake UPI Money Request*: This occurs when a bad actor uses UPI technology to trick someone into transferring money to them, which is often done by a seemingly genuine payment request. Scammers frequently send money to the victim's UPI account and then telephone the victim to claim that the transfer was made in error as shown in figure 6.8. This is known as a fake UPI money request. In these situations, the con artists phone the victim urgently and demand that the victim refund their money. They also give the victim a UPI link to start the refund procedure,

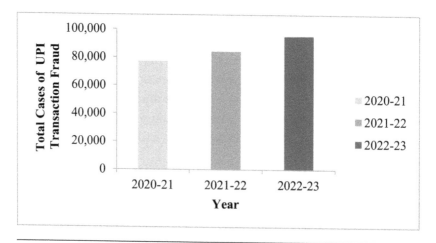

Figure 6.8   Cases of UPI transaction fraud.

which is a bogus or fraudulent link. Additionally, as soon as the victim opens the link, they inadvertently give the scammer remote access to their bank account, phone, or digital wallet. This enables the con artist to hack the victim's account and take their money [11, 38, 40, 43].

b. *Fake Quick Response (QR) Codes*: Malicious actors create phoney UPI QR codes as part of a social engineering attack, which when scanned, result in unauthorised transactions or money transfers to the attacker's account. Money lost is the most noticeable instant effect. Direct financial losses may occur if the victim scans a phoney UPI QR code and inadvertently transfers funds to the attacker's account. People who experience such assaults could be less willing to scan QR codes for payments, even from trustworthy sources [29]. This could make people less confident in the simplicity and security of online payment systems [45]. Attackers can utilise personal information to build convincing phoney QR codes, which might give the impression that the victim's privacy has been invaded.

c. *Emotional Anxiety*: Victims may experience emotional discomfort after learning that they were duped into completing an unauthorised transaction, with emotions of rage, frustration, and helplessness [46–55].

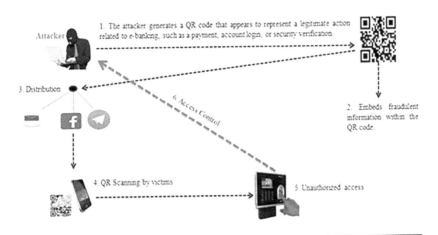

Figure 6.9 Fake QR code request.

6.6 How to Fight Against Social Engineering Attacks on E-Banking

To combat social engineering assaults on e-banking, a complete plan that incorporates technology, education, and preventative measures is required. Users and staff should obtain education on phishing and vishing techniques, with a focus on the significance of request verification. For increased security, multi-factor authentication, strong password guidelines, and real-time transaction monitoring should be used. Software and antivirus products should be updated to prevent vulnerabilities, and email filtering and anti-phishing solutions should be employed to block dangerous communications as shown in figure 6.9 [54]. The use of secure channels for communication should be encouraged, and workers should be given ongoing training in danger recognition. An incident response strategy should be created, security checks should be carried out, and others in the sector should be consulted to gather threat intelligence. Customers should be informed about security precautions, scepticism should be encouraged, and awareness should be raised through educational efforts. Spear phishing is a type of social engineering that can have serious negative repercussions on e-banking. Attackers can access victims' online banking accounts when they trick victims into giving them their login credentials, personal information, or financial information without the victims' knowledge. Unauthorised transactions, money theft, identity theft, or even a full account takeover can be the result. Spear-phishing attacks on e-banking can also reduce client confidence in online banking services, result in financial losses, and harm both banks' and customers' reputations. It takes a mix of strong security measures, user education, and vigilant awareness to resist spear phishing since such attacks frequently utilise social engineering techniques to exploit human vulnerabilities. Attackers modify their messages to make them seem as though they are coming from the recipient's bank or another relevant organisation. To lessen suspicion and maximise the chance of success, these communications frequently include recognisable details including the recipient's name, account information, or the most recent transactions [41, 56].

Website URLs should be verified frequently, mobile banking apps should be protected with robust authentication, and the amount of private information posted on social media should be controlled. To lessen the dangers of social engineering assaults in the world of e-banking,

Table 6.2 Social Engineering (SE) Threats and Their Common Solutions

SE THREATS	COMMON SOLUTIONS
Phishing	Users should be taught to identify signs of phishing, check sender email addresses, stay away from dubious links, and get in touch with the bank immediately if personal information is requested by using the bank's official contact details.
Vishing	Unless you are the one who called, never give out personal information over the phone. Hang up and call the bank immediately at one of the official or personal numbers to get any claims verified.
Smishing	Be aware of unwanted SMS messages. Whenever possible, stay away from links and independently confirm the sender's assertions through legitimate means.
Baiting	Avoid free offers, only download software from legitimate sources, and keep your security software up-to-date.
Pretexting	Before providing any information, confirm the requester's identity. Use the bank's official contact details to contact them directly.
Malware distribution	Use reliable antivirus software, keep your hardware and software updated, and refrain from downloading files from dubious sources.
Spear phishing	Implement multi-factor authentication for additional security layers, enact strict password regulations, utilise cutting-edge email filters, and regularly train users to recognise phishing efforts.

tactics should be adjusted to new threats as they emerge, partnerships with cybersecurity specialists should be formed for advice, and security rules should be updated as necessary. A working group of the Reserve Bank of India (RBI) looks at various e-banking problems and recommends solutions. Several of its suggestions include the following.

- All financial sectors are required to adhere to a standard when considering security issues. Additionally, this standard should be created by the Indian Banks Association.
- To ensure the confidentiality and privacy of data, all banks must implement sufficient security measures. In addition, they need to apply logical access control to put these measures into practise.
- To mitigate the risk of money laundering, banks must develop an Anti-Money Laundering (AML) system for reporting and querying [59].
- Banks need to have a process in place for handling complaints internally if they want to foster a culture of banking free from fraud.

- Every bank has to have a clear, written security plan, and physical access control must also be strictly enforced by banks.
- Banks must set up a wide e-banking network for the benefit of the country's remote and rural areas.

6.7 Detection and Prevention Techniques

In the context of e-banking, detecting social engineering assaults necessitates a mix of technology solutions, user education, and diligent monitoring. Attacks that use social engineering frequently target psychological weaknesses rather than specific technological flaws, making detection more difficult. The bulk of assaults that an information system suffers are thought to be primarily caused by the human component. The most desirable targets for cyberattackers are often banking and other financial services. Currently, one of the main sources of all harmful actions in the e-banking industry is blind phishing or spear phishing. As a result, how security-aware the customers are drives every countermeasure. Attacks are getting smarter, and attackers are looking for techniques where there is no longer any human participation in order to trick these systems. Zero click assaults are one significant step that attackers are making towards an age of unaided attacks by eliminating the need for human interaction in attack initiation. Threats to the payment and banking system's cybersecurity have spread globally [15, 16, 17, 26]. Financial institutions have been compelled by the phenomena to include risk-taking in their business models. Therefore, it is crucial to make purposeful investments in cutting-edge technology and security measures to prevent significant financial losses and data breaches that might result from cyberattacks. Many stakeholders in the banking industry are quite concerned about the rise in cybercrimes. Typically, software systems running on a computer system in cyberspace are used to carry out cyberattacks. As a result, to reduce the danger of cyberattacks on software systems, it is necessary to identify the cyberspace actors and isolate the threats to application security after examining the flaws and creating defences. This chapter looks at many such threats. Although the financial system is designed with conventional procedures and standards, these fail to recognise social engineering assaults, leading to considerable losses.

a. *Machine Learning/AI Algorithms*: By dynamically analysing user behaviours, transaction patterns, and communication subtleties, machine learning and AI algorithms play a crucial role in combating social engineering attacks on e-banking. These systems build thorough user profiles that detect typical behaviour and quickly identify abnormalities or deviations. Machine learning models identify suspicious behaviour including irregular login timings, abnormal transaction behaviour, or strange communication patterns through real-time surveillance and behavioural analysis. AI-driven systems use sentiment analysis to identify deceptive language and natural language processing and examine textual material for phishing signs. Security levels are modified by adaptive authentication techniques under the direction of machine learning when risk variables change. AI-enabled continuous authentication and device fingerprinting also provide user verification. AI can identify phishing attempts in email correspondence and verify URLs to block harmful links. E-banking systems strengthen their defences by incorporating these technologies that help reduce their susceptibility to social engineering assaults and maintain the security and trust of their users' financial interactions [42].

b. *Natural Language Processing (NLP)*: By carefully reading written information for language indications that may point to manipulation or fraud, social engineering attacks on e-banking are prevented. To find the trends related to phishing attempts, impersonation, or urgency, NLP algorithms examine the language used in emails, texts, and other communication channels. These algorithms can identify strange linguistic patterns, undue haste, or requests for private information, and they can flag these as possible social engineering dangers. Additionally, NLP supports sentiment analysis by identifying emotional undertones that can indicate coercion, tension, or manipulation. NLP adds a strong layer of protection against social engineering assaults by automatically removing phishing emails, spotting suspicious attachments, and assessing the veracity of communications. This technique enables e-banking systems to preventatively preserve users' sensitive information by ensuring that only authorised interactions are permitted, which potentially reduces the risk of identity theft [28].

c. *Blockchain Technology*: The intrinsic quality of blockchain is transparency and immutability, and decentralised consensus can be used to identify and reduce social engineering concerns in e-banking. Blockchain improves account activity visibility by storing all transactions and interactions on a common ledger that is impenetrable by outside parties. Any effort at unauthorised access, manipulation, or fraudulent transactions would leave a trace that could be found and recognised instantly, sending alarms to users and system administrators. Smart contracts can be set up to look for unusual patterns or behaviours and to automatically launch replies or freeze accounts when certain criteria are satisfied. Additionally, because blockchain is decentralised, it has fewer single points of failure than other technologies, which makes it more difficult to corrupt user data. Overall, the auditable and tamper-proof record of transactions provided by blockchain's transparent and secure nature increases the identification of social engineering risks and enhances the security and credibility of e-banking systems.

d. *Phishing Detection*: Phishing email detection is an essential tool for identifying and thwarting social engineering attacks on e-banking. This system uses sophisticated algorithms to examine incoming emails and identify traits frequently connected to phishing efforts. It concentrates on different elements such the sender's details, email content, subject lines, and embedded links [24]. It operates with the following steps.
   • Sender Verification
   • URL Analysis
   • Content Analysis
   • Known Threat Databases

e. *User Profiling and Risk Scoring*: This builds thorough user profiles and evaluates the risk involved with each user's activity. E-banking systems create profiles that take a variety of characteristics into account, such as the transaction history, device usage habits, and geographic location, through continuous monitoring and data analysis. For each individual, these profiles create a baseline of typical behaviour. The risk level is then determined by risk scoring algorithms by comparing each transaction or activity to this baseline. Higher risk ratings are triggered by unusual behaviours or deviations, which suggest the necessity for extra verification measures or closer inspection. E-banking systems can identify irregularities with this method, including sudden sizable transactions coming from an unexpected location or irregular login times [10]. User profiling and risk scoring technology supports an adaptive security architecture by dynamically analysing risk and triggering alarms or stronger authentication for potentially problematic behaviours. As a result, normal user actions are completed without incident, and possible risks are investigated further. This multi-layered strategy improves the system's capacity to withstand social engineering assaults and prevent unauthorised access, which protects user accounts and maintains the integrity of e-banking transactions.

f. *Behavioural Biometrics*: By identifying distinctive user behaviours to improve security, behavioural biometrics play a significant role in combating social engineering attacks on e-banking. Based on elements such as typing habits, mouse motions, and touchscreen gestures, these algorithms generate unique biometric profiles. The technology creates a baseline of user interactions by continuously monitoring these distinctive behavioural characteristics. A departure from this norm, such as a sharp increase or decrease in typing speed, a new navigation method, or unusual touch patterns, sets off signals that might indicate unauthorised access or manipulation efforts. Real-time detection provided by behavioural biometrics enables the system to distinguish between trustworthy users and bad actors. By identifying small anomalies and swiftly blocking unauthorised access, this cutting-edge technology strengthens overall cybersecurity and protects users' financial transactions. Accordingly, it strengthens e-banking systems against social engineering assaults [59].

g. *Continuous Authentication*: This is used to stop social engineering attacks on e-banking by maintaining a constant verification procedure during a user's online session. Various user behaviours and biometric indicators, including keystrokes, mouse movements, touchscreen gestures, and face recognition, are continuously monitored by this technology. Any variations or discrepancies can result in rapid alarms after creating a baseline of these patterns during the first verification. This adaptive technique ensures that the authorised user is consistently present and active by dynamically evaluating the user's validity in real time. Because attackers cannot simply get around the continuing verification process, continuous authentication lessens the efficacy of social engineering assaults and lowers the risk of unauthorised access, account breaches, and fraudulent transactions.

h. *Advanced Email Filtering*: To combat social engineering attacks on e-banking, advanced email filtering checks incoming emails for phishing signs, dangerous links, and questionable content, and continuous authentication assures constant user verification. The technology proactively detects potentially hazardous emails by comparing email properties with real-time threat intelligence feeds that specify known phishing sources. By blocking fraudulent communication attempts and concurrently using continuous authentication to confirm their validity, this dual strategy protects users. By prohibiting users from viewing dangerous information and ensuring that only authorised users are involved in transactions, the integration of these technologies improves the security of e-banking and resists social engineering assaults [60].

i. *Multi-Factor Authentication (MFA)*: By providing additional levels of verification for user access, MFA is a critical defence against social engineering concerns in e-banking. Before providing users access to their accounts, MFA demands that they submit at least two or more means of authentication from different categories. These categories often comprise "something you are" (such as a fingerprint or facial recognition), "something you have" (including a smartphone or identification token), and "something you know" (for example, a password). MFA stops social engineers who rely on single-factor weaknesses by demanding multiple factors. Even if an attacker manages to trick or phish their way into a password, they would still need to overcome the other authentication elements to obtain access, which decreases the effectiveness of their strategies. As a consequence, MFA is an effective tool.

j. *Real-Time Alerts*: These notifications are essential for reducing the hazards of social engineering in e-banking systems. When key account activity or changes such as purchases, logins, or profile modifications happen, users are immediately notified via these alerts. Real-time notifications enable users to immediately identify and react to any unauthorised or suspicious activity by instantly notifying them of these actions. With such a quick response, consumers may stop social engineering scams in their tracks before they get out of hand by reporting fraudulent transactions or immediately locking their accounts. Real-time warnings also raise user awareness and educate them of possible hazards, fostering a culture of alertness among clients. This proactive technique encourages users to distinguish between good and bad activities and helps them make educated judgements, which lowers the risk of falling for phishing, impersonation, and other social engineering techniques. Real-time notifications therefore act as a crucial defence mechanism that strengthens the e-banking security environment and protects consumers from monetary losses and personal data breaches.

k. *Collaboration with Law Enforcement*: A key tactic in reducing the risk of social engineering in e-banking is cooperation with law enforcement. Financial institutions may collaborate and create strong partnerships with law enforcement agencies to exchange knowledge, skills, and insights about new risks and attack trends. This cooperation makes it possible to quickly identify and look into suspicious behaviour and bring hackers to justice. Law enforcement organisations can track down and capture these offenders, which interrupts their activities and deters future assailants, by utilising their resources and legal power. Additionally, this collaboration helps to create proactive methods and legislative restrictions that address modern social engineering approaches, improving the e-banking ecosystem's overall cybersecurity posture. Financial institutions secure their clients' funds and private information by collaborating closely with law enforcement. In this way, banks also help fight cybercrime more broadly to make the internet a safer place for both consumers and companies.

6.8 Conclusion

The term "e-banking" refers to the automated delivery of particular banking goods and/or services, whether unique or traditional, directly to consumers by using electronic platforms or other supplemental communication channels. The major threats to e-banking are risks and developments related to social engineering. Whether a cybercriminal wants to directly commit fraud, collect your credentials, or install malware, social engineering assaults are continuously on the rise. Despite the greatest efforts of the general public, cybercriminals still steal millions of dollars from businesses each year through fraud, extortion, and ransomware. As new defences are developed and put into place, technologically skilled and cunning criminals are always looking for new methods to subvert them. To counter this, decision makers who prioritise security have begun to bolster security measures for both physical and cloud-based infrastructure. Your personnel are rapidly becoming the most convenient point of compromise. Users should be made aware of typical social engineering techniques, including how to spot phishing emails, dubious links, and other manipulative methods. Users can become more watchful by attending regular training sessions and awareness campaigns. To see how effectively users can recognise phishing efforts, regularly simulate phishing attacks. Take advantage of these simulations in the learning environment to enhance user comprehension and reaction. To provide an additional layer of protection, use robust MFA techniques, for example, one-time passwords or biometric verification. Even if they know certain user credentials, attackers will find it more challenging to obtain unauthorised access as a result.

References

[1] Ghafir, I., Saleem, J., Hammoudeh, M., et al. "Security Threats to Critical Infrastructure: The Human Factor." *The Journal of Supercomputing* 74 (2018): 4986–5002. https://doi.org/10.1007/s11227-018-2337-2

[2] Aburrous, M., Hossain, M. A., Dahal, K., Thabtah, F. "Experimental Case Studies for Investigating E-Banking Phishing Techniques and Attack Strategies." *Cognitive Computation* 2.3 (2010): 242–253.

[3] Adham, M., Azodi, A., Desmedt, Y., Karaolis, I. "How to Attack Two-Factor Authentication Internet Banking." In *Financial Cryptography and Data Security: 17th International Conference, FC 2013, Okinawa, Japan, April 1–5, 2013, Revised Selected Papers 17*, Springer Berlin Heidelberg, 2013: 322–328.

[4] Basit, A., Zafar, M., Liu, X., Javed, A. R., Jalil, Z., Kifayat, K. "A Comprehensive Survey of AI-Enabled Phishing Attacks Detection Techniques." *Telecommunication Systems* (2020): 1–16.

[5] Brand, M., Valli, C., Woodward, A. "Malware Forensics: Discovery of the Intent of Deception." *Journal of Digital Forensics, Security and Law* 5.4 (2010): 1–11.

[6] Sharma, N. "E-Banking: Present Position in India." *EPRA International Journal of Multidisciplinary Research (IJMR)* 8.10 (2022): 324–327.

[7] Alfeel, M. I. "E-Banking Network Security Threats: An Analytic Study." In *2020 International Conference on Computing and Information Technology (ICCIT-1441)*, IEEE, Tabuk, Saudi Arabia, 2020: 1–6. https://doi.org/10.1109/ICCIT-144147971.2020.9213820

[8] İlker, K. A. R. A. "Electronic Banking (e-Banking) Fraud with Phishing Attack Methods." *Avrupa Bilim ve Teknoloji Dergisi* 31: 982–985.

[9] Organization of American States. (September 2018). *State of Cybersecurity in the Banking Sectorin Latin America and the Caribbean*. Accessed: Feb. 15, 2021. www.oas.org/es/sms/cicte/sectorbancarioeng

[10] Ghazi-Tehrani, A. K., Pontell, H. N. "Phishing Evolves: Analyzing the Enduring Cybercrime." *Victims & Offenders* 16.3 (2021): 316–342.

[11] Kara, I. "Don't Bite the Bait: Phishing Attack for Internet Banking (e-banking)." *The Journal of Digital Forensics Security and Law* 16.5 (2021): 1–12.

[12] Hajiali, M., Amirmazlaghani, M., Kordestani, H. "Preventing Phishing Attacks Using Text and Image Watermarking." *Concurrency and Computation: Practice and Experience* 31.13 (2019): e5083.

[13] Kara, İ. "Security Risks and Safeguard Measures in Social Media Usage." *Avrupa Bilim ve Teknoloji Dergisi* (2020): 10–15.

[14] Kara, I. "A Basic Malware Analysis Method." *Computer Fraud & Security* 2019.6 (2019): 11–19.

[15] Subasi, A., Kremic, E. "Comparison of Adaboost with Multiboosting for Phishing Website Detection." *Procedia Computer Science* 168 (2020): 272–278.

[16] Jain, A. K., Gupta, B. B. "Two-Level Authentication Approach to Protect from Phishing Attacks in Real Time." *Journal of Ambient Intelligence and Humanized Computing* 9.6 (2018): 1783–1796.

[17] Kumar, P., Khan, M. "Systems, Methods, and Computer Readable Media for Payment and Nonpayment Virtual Card Transfer Between Mobile Devices." *U.S. Patent* 10,026,076, issued July 17, 2018.

[18] Morán, D. *Analyzing the Risk of Banking Malware in Android vs. iOS*, October 2019. Accessed: Feb. 15, 2021. www.buguroo.com/en/labs/analyzing-the-risk-of-bankingmalware-in-android-vs-ios

[19] Kara, I. "Cyber-Espionage Malware Attacks Detection and Analysis: A Case Study." *Journal of Computer Information Systems* (2021): 1–18.

[20] Al Mutawa, N., Baggili, I., Marrington, A. "Forensic Analysis of Social Networking Applications on Mobile Devices." *Digital investigation* 9 (2012): 24–33.

[21] Arshad Khan, M., Alhumoudi, H. A. "Performance of E-banking and the Mediating Effect of Customer Satisfaction: A Structural Equation Model Approach." *Sustainability* 14.12 (2022): 7224.

[22] Wassan, S., et al. "A Smart Comparative Analysis for Secure Electronic Websites." *Intelligent Automation & Soft Computing* 30.1 (2021).

[23] Nso, M. A. "Impact of Technology on E-Banking; Cameroon Perspectives." *International Journal of Advanced Networking and Applications* 9.6 (2018): 3645–3653.

[24] Ahmad, I., et al. "A Systematic Literature Review of E-banking Frauds: Current Scenario and Security Techniques." *Linguistica Antverpiensia* 2.2 (2021): 3509–3517.

[25] Mridha, M. F., et al. "A New Approach to Enhance Internet Banking Security." *International Journal of Computer Applications* 160.8 (2017).

[26] Chaimaa, B., Najib, E., Rachid, H. "E-banking Overview: Concepts, Challenges and Solutions." *Wireless Personal Communications* 117 (2021): 1059–1078.

[27] Hanees, A. L. "Phishing e-Mail Detection in e-Banking Using Data Mining Techniques." (2019).

[28] Akbar, M. A., Shameem, M., Ahmad, J., Maqbool, A., Abbas, K. (2018). "Investigation of Project Administration related Challenging Factors of Requirements Change Management in Global Software Development: A Systematic Literature Review." In *2018 International Conference on Computing, Electronic and Electrical Engineering (ICE Cube)*, IEEE, 2018: 1–7.

[29] Andreini, D., Bettinelli, C. "Business Model Definition and Boundaries." In *Business Model Innovation*. Springer, 2017: 25–53.

[30] Barker, R. "Knowledge Management to Prevent Fraudulent e-Banking Transactions." *Communitas* 23 (2018): 71–86.

[31] Blut, M. "E-service Quality: Development of a Hierarchical Model." *Journal of Retailing* 92.4 (2016): 500–517.

[32] Bressolles, G., Durrieu, F., Senecal, S. "A Consumer Typology Based on e-Service Quality and e-Satisfaction." *Journal of Retailing and Consumer Services* 21.6 (2014): 889–896.

[33] Liping, M., Bahadorrezda, O., Paul, W., Simon, B. "Detecting Phishing Emails Using Hybrid Features." In *2009 Symposia and Workshops on Ubiquitous, Autonomic and Trusted Computing*, IEEE, 2009: 493–497.

[34] Alsayed, A., Bilgrami, A. "E-banking Security: Internet Hacking, Phishing Attacks, Analysis and Prevention of Fraudulent Activities." *International Journal of Emerging Technology and Advanced Engineering* 7.1 (2017): 109–115.

[35] Alireza, S., Mojtaba, V., Behrouz, B. M. "Learn to Detect Phishing Scams Using Learning and Ensemble Methods." In *2007 IEEE/WIC/ACM International Conferences on Web Intelligence and Intelligent Agent Technology-Workshops*, IEEE, 2007: 311–314.

[36] Hanees, A. L. *Phishing E Mail Detection in E Banking Using Data Mining Techniques.* (2019).

[36a] Berend, D., Kontorovich, A. "Consistency of Weighted Majority Votes." *Advances in Neural Information Processing Systems* 27 (2014).

[37] James, L., Jason, L., Anthony, B. *A Probabilistic Classifier Ensemble Weighting Scheme Based on Cross-Validated Accuracy Estimates.* Springer, 2019: 1674–1709.

[38] Kashif, R., Phaneendra, P. D. "Implementation of Methods for Transaction in Secure Online Banking." *International Journal of Technical Research and Applications* 3.4 (2015): 41–43.

[39] Cortellazzo, L., Bruni, E., Zampieri, R. "The Role of Leadership in a Digitalized World: A Review." *Frontiers in Psychology* 10 (2019): 21. https://doi.org/10.3389/fpsyg.2019.01938

[40] Lenka, S. K., Barik, R. "Has Expansion of Mobile Phone and Internet Use Spurred Financial Inclusion in the SAARC Countries?" *Financial Innovation* 4.1 (2018): 5. https://doi.org/10.1186/s40854-018-0089-x

[41] Daka, C. G., Jackson, P. "Factors Driving the Adoption of E-Banking Services Based on the UTAUT Model." *International Journal of Business and Management* 14.6 (2019): 43–52.

[42] Ali, Liaqat, Faisal Ali, Priyanka Surendran, and Bindhya Thomas. "The effects of cyber threats on customer's behaviour in e-banking services." *International Journal of e-Education, e-Business, e-Management and e-Learning* 7, no. 1 (2017): 70–78.

[43] Martino, A. S., Perramon, X. "A Model for Securing E-Banking Authentication Process: Antiphishing Approach." *2008 IEEE Congress on Services—Part I*, IEEE, Honolulu, HI, 2008: 251–254. https://doi.org/10.1109/SERVICES-1.2008.32.

[44] Tian, M.-W., Wang, L., Yan, S.-R., Tian, X.-X., Liu, Z.-Q., Rodrigues, J. J. P. C. "Research on Financial Technology Innovation and Application Based on 5G Network." *IEEE Access* 7 (2019): 138614–138623. https://doi.org/10.1109/ACCESS.2019.2936860.

[45] Kour, M., Sharma, N. "Security Issues in e-Banking." *2023 2nd International Conference on Applied Artificial Intelligence and Computing (ICAAIC)*, IEEE, Salem, India, 2023: 1291–1294. https://doi.org/10.1109/ICAAIC56838.2023.10140397.

[46] Conti, M., Dragoni, N., Lesyk, V. "A Survey of Man in the Middle Attacks." *IEEE Communications Surveys and Tutorials* 18.3 (2016): 2027–2051.

[47] Android Developers. *Android Keystore System*. https://developer.android. com/training/articles/keystore (hämtad 2020-06-03) 2017.

[48] Malinka, K., Hujňák, O., Hanáček, P., and Hellebrandt, L. "E-Banking Security Study—10 Years Later." *IEEE Access* 10 (2022): 16681–16699. https://home.kpmg/au/en/home/insights/2019/07/future-ofdigital-banking-in-2030.html

[49] Sijan, Md Ahosan Hossain, Arshad Shahoriar, Md Salimullah, Ankan Shahriar Islam, and Razib Hayat Khan. "A review on e-banking security in Bangladesh: An empirical study." In *Proceedings of the 2nd international conference on computing advancements*, pp. 330-336. 2022.

[50] Paltayian, G., Georgiou, A., Gotzamani, K. "A Combined QFD-AHP Decision-Making Tool for the Investigation and Improvement of e-Banking Usage." *International Journal of Quality & Reliability Management*, 41.1 (2023): 150–172. https://doi.org/10.1108/IJQRM-02-2021-0030

[51] Chaimaa, B., Najib, E., Rachid, H. "E-banking Overview: Concepts, Challenges and Solutions." *Wireless Personal Communications* 117 (2021): 1059–1078. https://doi.org/10.1007/s11277-020-07911-0

[52] Haidar, N. S., Al Mustafa, M.-M. "E-banking Information Security Risks Analysis Based on Ontology." *IJESIR International Journal of Science and Innovative Research* 2.8 (2021): 100–108.

[53] Hammouri, Q., et al. "Explore the Relationship Between Security Mechanisms and Trust in e-Banking: A Systematic Review." *Annals of the Romanian Society for Cell Biology* 25.6 (2021): 17083–17093.

[54] Malinka, K., et al. "E-Banking Security Study—10 Years Later." *IEEE Access* 10 (2022): 16681–16699.

[55] Hammouri, Q., et al. "Explore the Relationship Between Security Mechanisms and Trust in e-Banking: A Systematic Review." *Annals of the Romanian Society for Cell Biology* 25.6 (2021): 17083–17093.

[56] Kour, M., Sharma, N. "Security Issues in e-Banking." *2023 2nd International Conference on Applied Artificial Intelligence and Computing (ICAAIC)*. IEEE, 2023: 1291–1294.

[57] Wang, Z., Li, M., Lu, J., Cheng, X. "Business Innovation Based on Artificial Intelligence and Blockchain Technology." *Information Processing and Management* 59 (2022): 102759.

[58] Liu, X., Ahmad, S. F., Anser, M. K., Ke, J., Irshad, M., Ul-Haq, J., et al. "Cyber Security Threats: A Never-Ending Challenge for e-Commerce." *Frontiers in Psychology* 13 (2022): 927398.

[59] Haruna, W., Aremu, T. A., Modupe, Y. A. "Defending Against Cybersecurity Threats to the Payments and Banking System." *arXiv:2212.12307* (2022).

[60] Mouton, F., Leenen, L., Venter, H. S. "Social Engineering Attack Examples, Templates and Scenarios." *Computers & Security* 59 (2016): 186–209.

7

THE ART OF DECEPTION

Unmasking the Tools and Psychological Principles Behind Social Engineering

PRATEEK KAMMAKOLU, VEDA GUPTA, GURURAJ H L AND SOUNDARYA B C

7.1 Introduction

The earliest documented instance of a social engineering attack dates to approximately 1184 BC and is famously recounted in the Greek myth of the Trojan Horse. In this legendary tale, the Trojan Horse was presented as a gift to the City of Troy, seemingly a symbol of victory for the Greeks who had pretended to retreat. Once the city allowed this wooden horse within its walls, Greek soldiers who were concealed within its belly emerged and wreaked havoc upon Troy. This event serves as an early example of the principle of reciprocity in the realm of social engineering, where trust is exploited to gain unauthorized access or inflict harm.

Social engineering is a tactic used by cybercriminals to manipulate individuals into revealing confidential information or engaging in actions that may not be in their best interest. It is a standard method employed by hackers to gain access to sensitive information or systems. These cybercriminals utilize various tools and techniques to execute social engineering attacks. This chapter examines some of the most prevalent tools and methods of social engineering, explains how they operate, and offers insights on safeguarding against them.

In essence, social engineering is a type of cyberattack that targets the human element within any system, and it may or may not involve the use of technology. It capitalizes on the principles of psychology and exploits traits such as trust, empathy, and curiosity to extract sensitive

DOI: 10.1201/9781003406716-7

119

information and persuade individuals to perform actions that jeopardize their security.

The process of social engineering can be broadly divided into four phases as shown in Figure 7.1. These phases represent the attacker's journey in obtaining confidential information from the target.

7.1.1 Information Gathering

A pivotal element of social engineering is the perpetrator's ability to amass the necessary background information about the victim through a comprehensive investigation of the target. This stage involves utilizing open-source intelligence (OSINT) to acquire knowledge about both the public and private information associated with the target. The OSINT tools are provided in Figure 7.2.

Figure 7.1   Phases of social engineering.

OSINT Tools

- XRay – XRay is a tool for recon, mapping and OSINT gathering from public networks.
- Buscador – A Linux Virtual Machine that is pre-configured for online investigators
- Maltego – Proprietary software for open source intelligence and forensics, from Paterva.
- theHarvester – E-mail, subdomain and people names harvester
- creepy – A geolocation OSINT tool
- exiftool.rb – A ruby wrapper of the exiftool, a open-source tool used to extract metadata from files.
- metagoofil – Metadata harvester
- Google Hacking Database – a database of Google dorks; can be used for recon
- Google-Dorks – Common google dorks and others you prolly don't know
- GooDork – Command line go0gle dorking tool
- dork-cli – Command-line Google dork tool.
- Shodan – Shodan is the world's first search engine for Internet-connected devices
- recon-ng – A full-featured Web Reconnaissance framework written in Python
- github-dorks – CLI tool to scan github repos/organizations for potential sensitive information leak
- vcsmap – A plugin-based tool to scan public version control systems for sensitive information
- Spiderfoot – multi-source OSINT automation tool with a Web UI and report visualizations
- DataSploit – OSINT visualizer utilizing Shodan, Censys, Clearbit, EmailHunter, FullContact, and Zoomeye behind the scenes.
- snitch – information gathering via dorks
- Geotweet_GUI – Track geographical locations of tweets and then export to google maps.

Figure 7.2   Architecture of OSINT tools [1].

The following are a few examples of the information that can be extracted from the target by using OSINT techniques.

1. Personal Details:
   * Date of birth
   * Place of birth
   * Full name
   * Residential address
   * Contact numbers
   * Email addresses
   * Social security numbers (if available)
2. Workplace Details:
   * Names of superiors or colleagues
   * Work address
   * Job titles and responsibilities
   * Projects or tasks the target is involved in
   * Work-related email addresses and contact information
3. Technology Usage:
   * Social media activity and profiles
   * Internet search history (publicly available)
   * Preferred communication channels (email, messaging apps, etc.)
   * Device information (computer, smartphone, etc.)
4. Personal and Professional Relationships:
   * Information about colleagues, friends, and family members
   * Close relationships and associations with specific individuals
   * Insights into mutual connections or shared acquaintances
   By gathering this information, the attacker can effectively 'connect the dots' and attempt to establish a connection or relationship with the target. This helps in building trust and credibility during the social engineering process and makes it easier to manipulate the target into divulging sensitive information or performing actions that benefit the attacker. Awareness of these potential vulnerabilities and the impor-tance of safeguarding personal and professional informa-tion are crucial in defending against social engineering attacks.

7.1.2 Establishing the Relationship

Ultimately, the goal of this phase is to create a scenario that appears believable and compelling to the target. In this way, social engineers can establish trust and rapport, which makes it more likely that the target will comply with their requests, whether this involves revealing sensitive information or taking actions that could compromise security. Vigilance and awareness of these tactics are essential for individuals and organizations to defend against social engineering attacks.

7.1.3 Exploitation Phase

In the exploitation phase, the attacker meticulously cultivates a web of trust around the target, rendering the target susceptible to their malicious intentions. By leveraging this vulnerability, the attacker proceeds to compromise the integrity of the target through a range of tactics, including but not limited to phishing, whaling, baiting, pretexting, and more, which exerts pressure on the target.

7.1.4 Execution Phase

In the execution phase, the attacker's objective goes beyond merely infiltrating the target's security and acquiring the necessary information. They must also ensure a successful escape following the breach. Typically, attackers employ the tactic of cutting off communication just before initiating the breach to maximize their chances of a clean getaway.

Social engineering attacks have witnessed a significant surge in recent times, with cybercriminals adopting deceptive personas to defraud millions of unsuspecting individuals. These attacks are on the rise in terms not only of frequency but also of the diversity of techniques employed.

A multitude of tactics have been devised to facilitate social engineering. These methods encompass a wide range of strategies, including phishing, whaling, tailgating, baiting, pretexting, impersonation, quid pro quo, scareware, diversion theft, and more. A more in-depth exploration of these methods is provided later in this chapter.

7.2 Tools and Techniques

Let us explore several common methods that cybercriminals employ to deceive individuals and employees within organizations into disclosing sensitive information or coercing them into performing specific actions. The different types of social engineering attacks are shown in Figures 7.3 and 7.4.

7.2.1 Phishing

Phishing poses a significant threat to both individuals and organizations and is often executed through the redirection of victims to counterfeit websites, ultimately leading to the exposure of confidential data

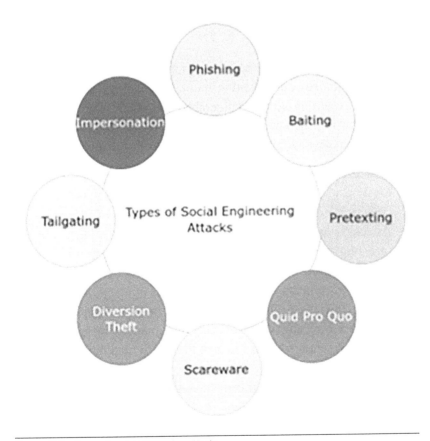

Figure 7.3 Types of social engineering attacks.

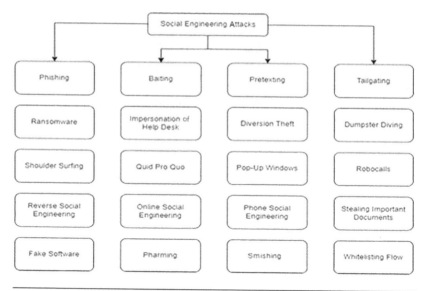

Figure 7.4 Social engineering attacks.

such as passwords and financial information. This deceptive technique primarily capitalizes on exploiting human psychology and emotions rather than exploiting system vulnerabilities, which makes identifying and thwarting such attacks a formidable challenge. The phishing attack process can be broken down into five distinct phases:

1. Attack Planning: During this phase, cybercriminals meticulously plan their phishing campaigns, select targets, and craft convincing messages to maximize their chances of success.
2. Attack Setup: In this stage, attackers establish the infrastructure required to carry out the phishing attack, which may involve setting up fake websites, email accounts, or other deceptive elements.
3. Attack Execution: This phase involves the actual deployment of the phishing attack, where deceptive emails or messages are sent to the chosen targets to lure them into clicking on malicious links or providing sensitive information.
4. Fraud: Once victims fall prey to the phishing scheme, cybercriminals exploit the acquired information for fraudulent activities, which can include unauthorized access to accounts, identity theft, or financial fraud.

5. Post-Attack: After successfully executing the attack and obtaining the desired information, attackers may cover their tracks or continue to exploit the compromised accounts or systems for extended periods.

Understanding these five phases is crucial for organizations and individuals to enhance their defense against phishing attacks and adopt proactive measures to mitigate the risks associated with this pervasive cyber threat [2, 3].

Most phishing attacks are successfully carried out via email, whether they are targeted or random. Other methods include fake websites (i.e., spoofed websites), phone calls, messages, social media scams, intercepting communication (man-in-the-middle attacks), pamphlets, and letters. The fraudulent activity is considered successful when the target is manipulated into revealing sensitive information.

Effective solutions and methods to counter phishing attacks are primarily achieved by raising awareness and educating people about the risks associated with fraudulent calls and messages. Users should be cautioned against clicking on suspicious hyperlinks and disclosing passwords or other confidential information and encouraged to install antivirus software and other security tools [4].

From a technical perspective, web scrapers can be utilized to identify and filter out fake websites. Machine learning is a powerful tool for examining and analyzing various attributes, including the presence of unique characters and IP addresses, to detect patterns indicative of phishing attempts. Fuzzy logic can also be effectively employed to create anti-phishing models that categorize and flag suspicious websites based on nuanced criteria.

Once these suspicious websites have been identified, it is crucial to take swift action. One possible course of action is to notify the internet service provider (ISP) responsible for hosting the fraudulent website. The ISP can then investigate and take appropriate measures, which may include shutting down the website to prevent further victims. This proactive approach can help mitigate the impact of phishing attempts and enhance online security for users.

Moreover, anti-spam software plays a vital role in blocking suspicious emails and often utilizes various techniques such as spell checks to filter out potential threats. Additionally, warning tools integrated into web browsers can provide real-time alerts to users and notify them of potential risks or threats associated with the websites they visit.

To further minimize phishing attacks, authentication and authorization mechanisms are crucial. These measures help establish the legitimacy of the parties involved before sensitive information is exchanged. By verifying the identities of both the sender and the recipient, organizations can significantly reduce the risk of falling victim to phishing schemes and enhance overall cybersecurity [5].

7.2.2 Baiting

Baiting attacks, also known as 'road apples,' rely on exploiting human greed by tempting users with fraudulent offers of free items or exciting opportunities. These schemes create a sense of excitement or curiosity in the user, enticing them to click on a deceptive link, which can lead to the downloading of malware [5].

Baiting attacks can target both individuals and corporations, with specific vulnerabilities often found among young adults, children, and the elderly. In a corporate context, the danger lies in the fact that once malware is installed on one computer, it can potentially gain quick access to other networked devices. To counter this threat, employees should be educated not to trust external devices and should exercise caution when encountering offers on office devices.

Effective education and awareness about baiting attacks can significantly reduce the likelihood of falling victim to such schemes. It is crucial for individuals and employees to adopt a stance of not trusting unknown physical devices including USBs and hard drives, as these are frequently used to distribute malware and viruses [5].

7.2.3 Pretexting

Pretexting is a form of manipulation where the attacker seeks to obtain the victim's credentials and personal information by creating or exploiting a deceptive situation. In pretexting, the attacker typically crafts a scenario that puts the victim in a vulnerable position, which allows the attacker to take advantage. This type of attack often involves impersonation, where the attacker assumes a false identity and deceives the victim with this fabricated identity and scenario. The goal is to trick the victim into divulging sensitive information or taking actions that benefit the attacker.

This method of attack demands a convincing and credible story to avoid arousing suspicion. Thorough research on the target is essential for its success [6]. A distinctive feature of pretexting is the creation of a situation or story, technically referred to as a 'pretext.' This pretext is carefully designed to make the victim believe that the attacker holds a position of authority or can assist the victim within the given scenario. By exploiting this vulnerability in the victim, the attacker aims to extract valuable credentials and information from them.

The following are methods used to protect against a pretexting attack.

1. Domain-Based Message Authentication, Reporting and Conformance (DMARC) is the most prevalent form of protection against email spoofing. It also provides protection against another method of pretexting called spear phishing.
2. Artificial intelligence (AI)-based email analysis. One way that pretexting attacks are carried out is through suspicious and malicious emails. The modern methods used to protect devices and data from attackers are the utilization of AI tools. AI can study user behaviors, analyze the patterns in the received emails, and provide an indication on how to sort the emails into basically 'malicious,' 'potentially malicious,' and 'safe'.

Natural language processing (NLP), a part of AI, examines language and can decipher phrases and words common in spear phishing and pretexting [7].

7.2.4 Quid Pro Quo

Quid pro quo is another form of attack that targets an individual's gullibility; it involves an exchange of information, money, or services. Its name is derived from Latin, meaning 'something for something,' and signifies an asset exchange. Typically, the attacker impersonates a service provider or a member of tech support and entices the victim by offering assistance. They propose services, products, or discounts in exchange for certain information, creating a significant risk of sensitive data and personal information being compromised. Organizations are also vulnerable to these attacks, with criminals often posing as part of the company's IT department to coax victims into divulging sensitive information. Unlike baiting, quid pro quo attacks do not necessitate extensive research or development. These attacks are primarily carried out through calls or other forms of communication. Implementing identity verification procedures for both parties involved can prevent this type of attack before it occurs.

7.2.5 Scareware

Scareware is a term formed by combining two familiar words: 'Scare' and 'Software.' It typically manifests in the form of pop-up notifications [8]. Scareware occurs when the attacker attempts to deceive individuals into believing that their device has a problem or is under threat, when in reality, it is not. If the target falls for the scareware ruse and responds to the pop-up, then there is a chance that the pop-up contains malware or software designed to corrupt the device or extract valuable data for the attacker's use.

In some cases, the attacker may establish a relationship with the victim to gain their trust and then introduce scareware into their device. Subsequently, the attacker may claim that they can resolve the issue and gain control over the victim's device. This can lead to the transfer of necessary data for the attacker to carry out their operations.

To avoid scareware,

- Do not react immediately to pop-ups,
- Think rationally before clicking on any link or suspicious pop-ups,
- Keep your operating system updated because it also helps defend against malware in a few ways, such as firewalls, pop-up blockers, and URL filters, and
- Use legitimate security software [8].

7.2.6 Diversion Theft

Diversion theft, also known as 'corner game' or 'round the corner game,' is a social engineering attack that occurs offline and does not require the use of a computer system. In this type of attack, the perpetrator manipulates and deceives a delivery person to change the delivery destination to the wrong address, which allows the perpetrator to gain access to the package being delivered [9].

There is also the possibility that the attacker may install malware or spyware into a device being delivered, enabling them to access and retrieve sensitive information from the user.

Although this type of attack may seem relatively straightforward, its implications can be significant, depending on the contents of the package. Attackers could be affiliated with terrorist or anti-government organizations, and the package contents may pose high-risk scenarios. The online counterpart of diversion theft can be described as 'spoofing.' Spoofing comes in various forms, including Internet Protocol (IP) spoofing, email spoofing, web spoofing, and more.

- IP spoofing involves impersonating another system to gain the trust of a target system. This attack can be thwarted by disabling source-routed and external packets.
- Email spoofing entails impersonating a legitimate source, taking advantage of the user's trust, and persuading them to click a link that may automatically download a virus or other malware.
- Web spoofing uses JavaScript and plugins to create an artificial website that mimics the original to trick the user into divulging confidential information.
- Domain Name System (DNS) spoofing redirects the client to a fake website by fraudulently altering entries in the DNS server [10].

7.2.7 Tailgating

Tailgating, also known as piggybacking, is a physical social engineering technique that does not involve technical aspects. It involves gaining unauthorized access to restricted areas by sneaking in behind a legitimate individual with access to the area [11].

For example, if an attacker wishes to access a restricted building within an office, then they might impersonate a non-suspicious person, such as an employee or a delivery person, and attempt to enter the restricted area by following closely behind the legitimate entrant. This practice is referred to as piggybacking or tailgating. These restricted areas often employ electronic access control systems, for example, RFID cards, to grant access. In this case, the attacker's target is typically someone who possesses the necessary access card. The attacker may either discreetly follow the target closely or attempt to steal the RFID card from the target, thereby gaining access to the restricted area.

7.3 Social Engineering Toolkit

The Social Engineering Toolkit (SET) is an open-source tool written in Python. Its primary purpose is to facilitate and execute social engineering attacks, which target the human element within a system's security. The toolkit is widely used in the field of penetration testing, where security professionals test the vulnerability of systems by simulating real-world attacks to identify weaknesses and strengthen security measures.

SET is a notable component of the Kali Linux penetration testing toolkit, a popular Linux distribution used by cybersecurity professionals and ethical hackers. SET provides a range of features and methods for carrying out social engineering attacks, including email- and web-based attacks, with the aims of educating organizations and individuals about potential security risks and helping them protect against such threats. It is essential to emphasize that this toolkit should be used only for ethical and legitimate security testing purposes, with proper authorization and consent.

After selecting option 1 in SET, which is Social Engineering Attacks, a menu will typically be displayed that lists various possible social engineering attacks that can be implemented, as shown in Figure 7.5. These menu options may include a range of attack vectors,

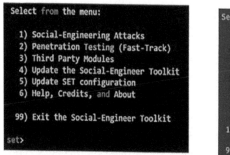

Figure 7.5   Social engineering attack menu.

such as phishing attacks, pretexting, baiting, tailgating, and more. The user can choose from these options to specify the type of social engineering attack they wish to carry out within SET or a similar tool.

7.3.1 Attacks

The attacks that can be performed using SET are listed below.

7.3.1.1 Spear-Phishing Attack Vectors   In a spear-phishing attack, a malicious file is crafted and given a deceptive name designed to capture a user's attention and convince them that it originates from a trustworthy source. This file is then typically attached to an email and sent to the intended victim with the intention of deceiving them. The success of this attack hinges on human gullibility, and the victim may be tricked into revealing sensitive information [12].

Notably, spear-phishing attacks can also be conducted on a larger scale through mass email campaigns, where attackers target a significant number of victims simultaneously. These campaigns can have a widespread impact, which makes it essential for individuals and organizations to remain vigilant and employ robust cybersecurity practices to protect against such threats.

7.3.1.2 Website Attack Vectors   When you select the Website Attack Vectors option, a submenu displaying various attack methods that can be implemented through the browser is presented as in Figure 7.6. The following are some examples of these attack methods.

Credential Harvester Attack Method: This method aims to harvest the victim's username and password by redirecting them to another IP address [13].

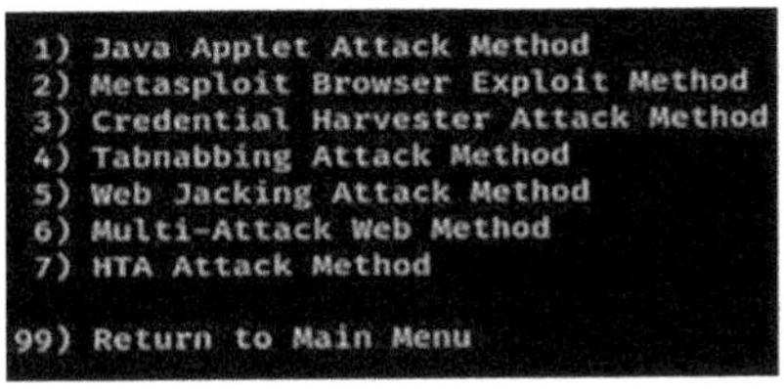

```
1) Java Applet Attack Method
2) Metasploit Browser Exploit Method
3) Credential Harvester Attack Method
4) Tabnabbing Attack Method
5) Web Jacking Attack Method
6) Multi-Attack Web Method
7) HTA Attack Method

99) Return to Main Menu
```

Figure 7.6   Website attack vectors' submenu.

Metasploit Browser Exploit Method: This client-side web exploit relies on prior reconnaissance and specific vulnerabilities to execute a successful attack.

Java Applet Attack Method: This attack uses JavaScript for a DNS lookup and measures the time that it takes to obtain the DNS address. This information helps determine not only if the address appears in the DNS cache but also its last access date [14].

Tabnabbing Attack Method: As the name suggests, tabnabbing takes advantage of the user switching to another browser tab by changing or replacing the content of the original tab.

Web Jacking Attack Method: This method involves cloning a website and replacing the original website as soon as the user clicks on the URL to access the genuine site.

Multi-Attack Web Method: This approach allows the execution of multiple attacks in combination, increasing the likelihood of a successful attack.

These attack vectors demonstrate the various ways in which attackers can exploit vulnerabilities in web browsers and websites to compromise user data and system security. Understanding these methods is essential for cybersecurity professionals to effectively defend against such threats.

7.3.1.3. Infectious Media Generator   The infectious media generator is a concept that involves the creation and encoding of a malicious executable with the objective of evading antivirus detection. This technique is used to generate an infectious USB or DVD by developing a payload using Metasploit, a popular penetration-testing framework. A folder containing this payload is then created, which should be written or burned to a USB/DVD. When the infected device is inserted into a target machine, it will automatically execute and potentially grant the attacker access to the compromised system.

This method leverages the autorun feature, which initiates the execution of the malicious payload as soon as the infected media is connected to the target machine. Notably, such actions are typically carried out for malicious purposes and are illegal without proper authorization and consent.

7.3.1.4. Create a Payload and Listener   The process of creating a payload and listener involves the development of an executable payload and a corresponding listener. This technique often serves as a wrapper around Metasploit.

The following describes how this process typically works.

Payload Creation: A payload is essentially a piece of code or software designed to exploit vulnerabilities on a target system. In this context, the payload is crafted with a specific objective, such as gaining unauthorized access to a victim's device or network. The payload is tailored to exploit known vulnerabilities or weaknesses in the target.

Listener Generation: A listener is a component that waits for incoming connections from the executed payload. It acts as a listening post and is ready to establish a connection with the compromised system once the payload is executed.

Executable Export: Once the payload and listener are configured, an executable file is generated. This executable is often disguised to appear innocuous or as a legitimate file to trick the victim into running it.

Transfer and Execution: The attacker transfers the executable file to the victim's device, often through social engineering tactics or other means of deception. When the victim runs the executable, it establishes a connection with the listener, allowing the attacker to gain access to the compromised system.

Notably, the creation and use of such payloads and listeners for unauthorized or malicious purposes are illegal and unethical. These techniques are typically employed by ethical hackers and security professionals as part of penetration testing or cybersecurity research to identify and rectify security vulnerabilities in systems and networks.

7.3.1.5. Mass Mailer Attack   As the name suggests, the mass mailer attack is a method that allows an attacker to send a large number of emails that they design to multiple recipients simultaneously. These emails are typically sent in bulk, increasing the probability of a successful attack. This type of attack can be used to gather sensitive information from the recipients.

Mass mailer attacks can take various forms, including phishing emails, spam campaigns, or emails that carry malicious attachments or links [15]. The goal is often to deceive recipients into taking specific actions, such as clicking on a link, downloading an attachment, or providing sensitive information.

Notably, although mass mailing itself is not inherently malicious, when used for malicious purposes, it can lead to security breaches, data theft, and other cybercrimes. Organizations and individuals must implement robust email security measures and educate users about the risks associated with unsolicited or suspicious emails to defend against such attacks.

7.3.1.6. Arduino-Based Attack Vector   The Arduino-based attack vector involves the use of an Arduino-based device, such as the Teensy USB device, to execute malicious code on a target system. This attack is designed to bypass system protections and enable autorun functionality, which allows the attacker to deploy a payload.

7.3.1.7. Wireless Access Point Attack Vector   The wireless access point attack vector is a method where an attacker employs DNS spoofing to reroute network traffic packets to their own system. This is achieved by setting up a rogue access point by using a wireless interface card. Several tools and utilities are commonly used to execute this attack successfully, including the following.

AirBase-NG: This tool is utilized to create a rogue wireless access point (AP) that can intercept and redirect network traffic.

AirMon-NG: AirMon-NG is used for monitoring wireless network traffic and can be employed to identify potential targets for an attack.

DNSSpoof: DNSSpoof is a tool that allows the attacker to forge DNS responses, leading to the redirection of network traffic to their system.

dhcpd3: This utility is used to manage Dynamic Host Configuration Protocol (DHCP) settings and IP address assignment within a rogue AP to further enable network manipulation.

By exploiting these tools and techniques, the attacker can intercept and manipulate network traffic, potentially leading to data interception, unauthorized access, or other malicious activities. Organizations and individuals must implement robust security measures to detect and defend against such attacks, including monitoring network traffic and configuring secure DNS settings.

7.3.1.8. QRCode Generator Attack Vector   With the QRCode Generator Attack Vector, an attacker embeds malicious content into a QR code [16]. This attack involves generating a QR code for a URL, which can then be deployed as part of an additional attack vector within a toolkit. The attacker's goal is to trick the victim into scanning the QR code, which may redirect the victim to a malicious website or perform other actions designed to compromise their device or steal confidential information.

This attack leverages the trust that users often place in QR codes, as they are commonly used for legitimate purposes, including quick access to websites or contact information. Attackers take advantage of this trust to deceive victims into engaging with the malicious QR code, which potentially leads to data breaches, unauthorized access, or other cyberattacks.

Users and organizations should exercise caution when scanning QR codes from untrusted sources and regularly update their devices and security measures to protect against such attacks.

7.3.1.9. PowerShell Attack Vectors   PowerShell attack vectors leverage the functionality of Windows PowerShell, a scripting and automation framework available in the Windows operating system. These attacks involve the use of PowerShell to execute specific attack techniques. Some common types of PowerShell-based attacks include the following.

Alphanumeric Shellcode Injector: This attack involves injecting shellcode into a target system by using only alphanumeric characters. It aims to evade detection by security tools that may look for specific patterns or signatures in the code.

Reverse Shell: In a reverse shell attack, a connection is initiated from the target system back to the attacker's system. This allows the attacker to gain control over the compromised system and execute commands remotely.

Bind Shell: In a bind shell attack, a listening service is set up on the target system, and the attacker connects to it. This enables the attacker to gain control over the system and execute commands from their machine.

Dump Security Account Manager (SAM) Database: This attack aims to extract the SAM database from a Windows system. The SAM database contains user account information, including password hashes, which can be used for further attacks such as password cracking.

To execute these PowerShell attack vectors, the attacker typically specifies an IP address and port number. A remote shell session is then created that allows the attacker to interact with the compromised system and carry out malicious activities. Organizations should implement security measures to detect and mitigate PowerShell attacks, as they can pose significant risks to Windows-based environments.

7.3.1.10. Third-Party Modules In this attack scenario, a third-party module called Remote Administration Tool Tommy Edition (RATTE) is utilized. RATTE is a type of HTTP tunnelling payload often used for remote administration and control of compromised systems. The use of third-party modules including RATTE can provide attackers with certain advantages in evading security mechanisms, such as firewalls.

HTTP tunnelling payloads like RATTE are designed to encapsulate malicious traffic within standard HTTP requests and responses, which makes it appear as legitimate web traffic to network security devices. This can help attackers establish covert communication channels with compromised systems and avoid detection by intrusion detection systems (IDS) or firewall rules.

Notably, the use of such third-party modules for malicious purposes is illegal and unethical. Defending against these types of attacks requires robust network monitoring, intrusion detection, and the implementation of security measures to detect and block suspicious traffic.

7.4 Psychological Principles of Social Engineering

To implement social engineering, one must master the principles of influence. These principles assist in the deception of the target. Researchers have proven these principles to be of importance by conducting experiments and surveys.

7.4.1 The Reciprocity Principle

We came across this principle in the introduction to the chapter wherein we discussed the earliest recorded social engineering attack, namely, the Trojan Horse incident during the war between the Greeks and the City of Troy. This particular attack utilizes the psychological principle of reciprocity.

Reciprocity is another term for the word 'gifting'. It works as a principle for social engineering attacks because people feel obliged to repay the favor. That is, when a person receives something in the form of good behavior, a gift, or a service, they feel obliged to repay the same. Researchers found that the custom of servers bringing a small gift with the bill, such as a fortune cookie or mint, effectively increased the chance of tipping [17, 18]. Perpetrators utilize this principle of reciprocity to retrieve confidential or important information from the target.

7.4.2 The Need and Greed Principle

Two emotions that leave humans the most vulnerable are fear and greed. Social engineers take advantage of these particular emotions to obtain valuable information and data.

This principle is also known as the 'scarcity' principle. Specifically, people want more of the things that they feel there may be less of [18].

An attacker can utilize information about what a person is greedy for and take advantage of this.

For example, let us say that the target wants to buy some shoes for cheap prices. The attacker would send directed emails that appeal to the target, and clicking on one of these emails would be dangerous for the target.

7.4.3 The Authority Principle

People tend to follow instructions provided by authorized people. This vulnerability is significant in social engineering attacks because the attacker can impersonate authorized personnel or an entity.

Authority is probably the most apparent principle since authority is something that we all comply with.

There have been numerous cases of perpetrators pretending to be an authorized or legitimate entity and breaching the victim's security.

7.4.4 The Flattery Principle

Social engineering is the art of deception. One of the common ways to deceive someone is by deviating their attention towards something they would like to hear, namely, 'flattery'. There are three important factors in persuasion science: we like people who are similar to us, we like people who compliment us, and we like people who cooperate with us [18]. This principle deals with distracting the target by pretending to be someone who the target would like and stealing information through this façade.

This flattery principle of influence can be dangerous. People tend to give in to flattery when they think that the attacker is being genuine, and the perpetrator will take advantage of them and extract sensitive and confidential information.

7.4.5 The Consistency Principle

People like to behave consistently. As Cialdini states, 'Once we have made a choice or taken a stand, we will encounter personal and inter-personal pressures to behave consistently with that commitment' [19].

Regarding social engineering concerns, people tend to keep connection consistent. That is, people would prefer to keep connections, be it over social media or any other platform, consistent.

This human principle makes it easier for the attacker to build a trusting relationship with the target. Once the relationship is built and the attacker has gained the trust of the target, it will only get more difficult for the target to cut ties with the attacker.

The attacker then utilizes this connection to withdraw information.

7.4.6 The Herd Principle

We prefer to move towards or be around people who are similar to us. For example, we tend to be with and maintain a connection to the people who claim to have something in common with us. For example, if we saw someone at a party who went to the same school as us, then we would instantly feel a connection.

Using this principle, attackers gather data about the target and pretend to be someone who the target has something in common with. The usage of this principle is very common in social engineering. We all have seen people try to scam others for money by claiming to be their classmates or someone who the target had something in common with.

To avoid being a victim of social engineering attacks, the most important advice is not to trust everyone and everything that we come across online. We also should not trust everyone and everything that we see offline. We should always be cautious when it comes to social interactions.

7.5 Conclusion

Accordingly, social engineering is a deceptive art that relies on various psychological tactics, including flattery, to manipulate individuals into divulging sensitive information or taking actions that they would not normally undertake. Understanding the principles of persuasion and psychology that social engineers use is essential for individuals and organizations to defend against such tactics. Maintaining awareness, skepticism, and strong security practices can help protect against the risks posed by social engineering attacks and safeguard sensitive information and assets.

References

[1] Referred the hyperlink: https://github.com/giuliacassara/awesome-social-engineering
[2] Harinahalli Lokesh, G., & BoreGowda, G. (2021). Phishing website detection based on an effective machine learning approach. *Journal of Cyber Security Technology*, 5(1), 1–14.
[3] Aleroud, A., & Zhou, L. (2017). Phishing environments, techniques, and countermeasures: A survey. *Computers & Security*, 68, 160–196. https://doi.org/10.1016/j.cose.2017.04.006
[4] Alkhalil, Z., Hewage, C., Nawaf, L., & Khan, I. (2021). Phishing attacks: A recent comprehensive study and a new anatomy. *Frontiers in Computer Science*, 3, 563060. https://doi.org/10.3389/fcomp.2021.563060

[5] Salahdine, F., & Kaabouch, N. (2019). Social engineering attacks: A survey. *Future Internet*, 11(4), 89. https://doi.org/10.3390/fi11040089 Comprehensive Analysis of Various Cyber Attacks (researchgate.net)

[6] Breda, F., Barbosa, H., & Morais, T. (2017). Social engineering and cyber security. In *INTED2017 Proceedings* (pp. 4204–4211). IATED.

[7] What is pretexting. Article by Imperva. www.imperva.com/learn/application-security/pretexting/

[8] Nadeem, S. M. (2023). Social engineering: What is scareware? *Mailfence Blog*. https://blog.mailfence.com/social-engineering-what-is-scareware/ (Accessed 9 September 2023).

[9] Aldawood, H., & Skinner, G. (2020). An advanced taxonomy for social engineering attacks. *International Journal of Computer Applications*, 177(30), 1–11.

[10] Babu, P. R., Bhaskari, D. L., & Satyanarayana, C. H. (2010). A comprehensive analysis of spoofing. *International Journal of Advanced Computer Science and Applications*, 1(6).

[11] Covic, V. (2023) Social engineering: What is tailgating? *Mailfence Blog*. https://blog.mailfence.com/what-is-tailgating/#:~:text=Tailgating%20or%20piggybacking%20is%20a,otherwise%20not%20allowed%20to%20be.&text=Tailgating%20is%20different%20from%20other,sensitive%20data%2C%20money%2C%20 . . . (Accessed 9 September 2023).

[12] Jeremiah, J. (2019). Awareness case study for understanding and preventing social engineering threats using Kali Linux penetration testing toolkit. *Ech Insig*, 43.

[13] Kavya Rani, S. R., Soundarya, B. C., Gururaj, H. L., & Janhavi, V. (2021). Comprehensive analysis of various cyber attacks. In *2021 IEEE Mysore sub section international conference (MysuruCon)* (pp. 255–262). IEEE.

[14] Felten, Edward W., and Michael A. Schneider. "Timing attacks on web privacy." In *Proceedings of the 7th ACM Conference on Computer and Communications Security*, pp. 25–32. 2000.

[15] Spandan ChowdhurySpandan Chowdhury is a security researcher at Czar Securities. A tech enthusiast (2015). *Social-Engineer Toolkit: An Introduction*. Yaksas Security.

[16] Kali Linux. www.kali.org/

[17] Alfred, R. (2012, April). *April 24, 1184 B.C.: Trojan Horse Defeats State-of-the-Art Security*. Wired. www.wired.com/2012/04/april-24-1184-b-c-trojan-horse-defeats-state-of-theart-security/ (Accessed 5 September 2023).

[18] Coatesworth, B. (2023). The psychology of social engineering. *Cyber Security: A Peer-Reviewed Journal*, 6(3), 261–274.

[19] Cialdini, R. B. (2021), *Influence: The Psychology of Persuasion*. Harper Business, Manhattan, NY.

8

SOCIAL ENGINEERING IN CYBERSECURITY- THREATS AND DEFENSES

SHRUTHI G, AKSHITHA AND KRISHNA RAJ P M

8.1 Introduction

The term "social engineering" encompasses a broad spectrum of malicious actions conducted through interactions with individuals. Users are manipulated into revealing vital information or making security mistakes through psychological tricks. However, a lack of security measures on social media sites and other online platforms might result in the disclosure of private and sensitive data. Even with improvements in cybersecurity and fewer software flaws, people are more vulnerable to online threats in our rapidly developing digital world. Currently, social attacks are more common and effective than technological ones; in fact, social attacks are so effective that human flaws frequently serve a major role in supporting cyberattacks [1].

Humans can now instantly connect with one another around the globe because of advancements in data transmission technologies. Due to a lack of security protocols, private and personal information accessible in online communities and e-services is not safeguarded. As a result, communication networks are more vulnerable and open to social engineering assaults by malicious users. These types of assaults are carried out by duping individuals or groups into performing activities that are advantageous to the assailants or disclosing private information, such as payment codes, user IDs, passwords, social security information, and medical records. Their goal is to obtain these private data or to influence people or groups to engage in actions that will

DOI: 10.1201/9781003406716-8

141

benefit the assailants. Social engineering assaults are becoming more prevalent in today's networks, which makes cybersecurity systems less effective. Hackers strive to advance their own goals by duping people and institutions into giving them crucial and private data [2]. The threat of social engineering hangs over the security of all networks, regardless of the efficacy of firewalls, cryptographic techniques, intrusion detection systems, and antivirus software. People tend to have more faith in one another than they have in computers and other technologies. They become the weakest link in the security chain as a result. Through human interactions, offensive strategies psychologically coerce people into sharing private information or breaking security rules [3]. Attacks using social engineering are particularly dangerous because they affect networks and systems by manipulating people. Software and technology cannot successfully prevent these assaults without training people on how to defend against them. Cybercriminals frequently use these strategies while dealing with systems that are free of technical flaws [4]. Social engineering attacks, which take advantage of people's innate propensity to trust, create a serious security concern. Security breaches caused by social engineering can leave behind vast and difficult-to-find damage. To prevent such attacks, it is imperative for both personnel and their businesses to be knowledgeable about the appropriate precautions. Security awareness training, which informs workers of the risk and teaches them how to secure data, is the greatest line of defense against the growing threat of social engineering assaults [5].

8.2 The Evolution of Social Engineering in the Context of Cybersecurity

This section provides an extensive literature analysis to systematically study the intellectual development process from roughly 1974 to the present to provide sufficient information for discussing social engineering in cyber security.

There are five stages to the development phase, and they are identified by variations and traits over various time periods (Figure 8.1). The progression occurs through these five unique phases: the Phreak Phase (1974–1983), the Phrack Phase (1984–1955), the Professional Hacking Phase (1996–2001), the Multidirectional Evolution Phase

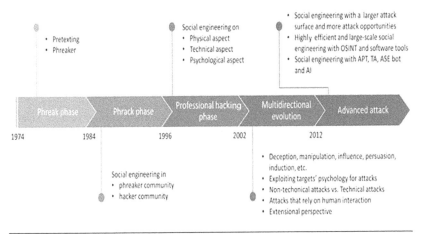

Figure 8.1   Social engineering's development within the context of cybersecurity [6].

(2002–2011), and the Current Phase of Advanced Social Engineering Attacks (since 2012).

Social engineering during the phreak phase (1974–1983) was characterized by using tactics such as pretext, impersonation, and persuasion to obtain information or assistance from telephone switching center personnel. The manipulation of telephone company employees using these strategies in the years that followed, from 1984 to 1995, took on phreaking-like characteristics with the goal of learning more about various phone network systems. From 1996 to 2001, information safety developed significantly. In three crucial dimensions, the development of social engineering is visible over the course of these six years. First, there was a wider variety of social engineering execution techniques, especially in the physical environment. Second, as network information technology developed, social engineering techniques became interconnected, with technically oriented social engineering attacks including email phishing and Trojan horses. Finally, unique aspects of social engineering psychology, including social control, persuasion, and manipulation of trust, began to receive more attention, leading to an increasing understanding of people's vulnerability as the weakest link in the security chain.

This period saw a marked increase in the number of social engineering-related studies, in contrast to the previous phases. Because of this change, the idea of social engineering entered a period of multidirectional evolution, which was characterized by the formation of several conceptual interpretations, some of which are still relevant. Numerous cutting-edge social engineering attack approaches were developed because of improvements in computer technology, network information, and assault strategies. The conceptual realm of social engineering keeps expanding. The execution of highly effective, accurate, and intelligent social engineering attacks has been made possible since 2012 due to the emergence of novel ecosystems driven by cutting-edge technologies, including machine learning, artificial intelligence, etc., and the fusion of innovative threat modalities. In the human, cyber, and physical worlds, this advanced type of social engineering today poses complex, extensive, and serious security challenges [6].

8.3 Phases of Social Engineering

The four phases that define a social engineering engagement are the following.

- Discovery and investigation
- Deception and hook
- Attack
- Retreat

8.3.1 Discovery and Investigation

The first step in committing fraud is choosing the people who have sought-after assets, such as credentials, data, access, money, or personal information. Hackers thus search the internet for potential targets and evaluate online profiles, including people's job, social media activity, and more. With this identification knowledge at their disposal, hackers plan specialized attacks. Furthermore, a person can become less vigilant because of the attacker's extensive understanding of them.

8.3.2 Deception and Hook

As con artists learn more about their intended victims, they actively look for possible ways of entry. Any method that would allow them to get in touch and carry out an assault falls under this category, whether it is through an email address, phone number, or social media account.

A "hook" is then used to contact a target and pique their attention. Consider the scenario where you have received a new work title and announced it on LinkedIn. A con artist may simply pose as an email from a reputable business website and invite you to an interview. Why would you not answer if it seems innocent and commonplace?

8.3.3 Attack

Scam artists will employ one of many social engineering techniques once the hook has a person interested. For example, after you open the link to schedule an online interview, the scammer covertly implants software on the computer that you are using. As soon as you realize it, the entire network of your business has been compromised, and the con artist has taken gigabytes of sensitive data. Small cybersecurity mistakes like this can be quite expensive for enterprises. The average cost of a company data breach is $4.24 million.

8.3.4 Retreat

Criminals will quickly disappear after achieving their goals. Given that it can take an average of 200 days to identify a cyberattack or data breach, you might not even be aware of what has happened until it is too late.

8.4 Social Engineering Threats

Users need to understand the hazards that they face online, the threat actors, and the motivations of online criminals in order to be appropriately trained. Users frequently are unaware of the importance of the data they use daily to perform their jobs. For example, a law firm amasses sensitive information to safeguard the needs of its clients. In accounting firms, the firm has access to its clients' private financial information. Exposure to private health information is available to physicians, hospitals, and insurance providers. To handle insurance and payroll, employers gather personal information from their workers, including social security numbers and other financial and personal data. Moreover, a company must obtain the social security numbers and other personal data of any close friends of a worker if they have any [5,7].

8.4.1 Data Breaches

Data breaches are unfortunately all too common and do not appear to be stopping anytime soon. Some of the largest hacking incidents of the twenty-first century have affected well-known companies, for example, Yahoo, LinkedIn, Facebook, and Marriott International. According to Comparitech, 212.4 million people were affected by security breaches in the United States in 2021 (compared to 174.4 million in 2020). After the United States, Iran had the second-largest number of data breaches that affected 156.1 million users.

8.4.2 Risky Hybrid or Remote Work Environments

Throughout the COVID-19 pandemic, the idea of hybrid and remote work has gained in popularity. According to Gallup, almost 60 million full-time employees in the United States say that "their current job can be done remotely working from home, at least part of the time." Just 8% of employees operated fully online prior to the outbreak; by 2022, this number had risen to 39%. It is now predicted to reach 24% for 2023.

Although working remotely or in a hybrid environment has many benefits for both employees and businesses, there are extra security threats. Using unencrypted file sharing, weak passwords, and personal devices for work constitute a few of the most common security risks connected with working online.

8.4.3 Mobile Attacks

The average American utilized their cell phone for 4 hours and 23 minutes per day in 2021. Due to their widespread use and frequent commercial necessity, smart phones are further susceptible to online attacks. They are employed for social interaction and bonding. Like PCs and laptops, smart phones are susceptible to a number of security issues, such as phishing (especially via text messaging), lax password protection, malware, or malicious software.

8.4.4 Phishing

Phishing attempts are getting increasingly more sophisticated. They entail delivering carefully chosen electronic messages to deceive users into clicking on a link that might download malware or reveal personal information.

Attackers are ramping up their efforts, for instance, by leveraging devices' intelligence to create and disseminate attractive phony communications much more quickly with the expectation that recipients will unintentionally damage the organization's networks and systems. This increased effort is because most workers at companies have become more cognizant of the risks associated with clicking on dubious-looking links or responding to phishing emails. These types of attacks provide hackers access to safe databases and give them control over user logins, credit card numbers, and other types of private monetary information.

8.4.5 Ransomware

Attacks that employ ransomware are anticipated to cost victims thousands of pounds as a consequence of hackers deploying technology that allows them to effectively seize control of a person's business and the company's databases and hold all of the information for ransom. The advent of cryptocurrencies such as Bitcoin has made it possible for inmates to pay their fines in secret, which is assumed to be what has increased the frequency of malware assaults. Although companies keep working to strengthen their virus defenses, some experts expect that hackers will increasingly target other potentially valuable ransomware of those affected, such as rich people's information.

8.4.6 Crypto Jacking

Cybersecurity is being impacted by the bitcoin boom in other ways. With crypto jacking, fraudsters seize control of an individual's home or workplace computers to "mine" for cryptocurrencies. This is referred to as "system hopping" because mining for cryptocurrencies (for example, Bitcoin), which requires a vast amount of computer processing power, enables hackers to generate money covertly by utilizing other people's systems. Systems that have been cryptographically compromised can harm an organization's success and cost it money while IT works to identify and correct the issue.

8.4.7 Cyber-Physical Attacks

The creativity that has allowed us to automate and update essential infrastructure comes with risk. Potential hacking threats against drinking water treatment facilities, transportation, the electrical grid, and other systems present a severe vulnerability. A recent article in The New York Times claims that everything, including defense systems of the United States that cost billions of dollars, is vulnerable to advanced trickery [10].

8.4.8 State-Sponsored Attacks

Western nations are now using their cyber capabilities to compromise other countries and assault crucial networks, going beyond merely obtaining private data to sell. The judiciary, the entire nation, the corporate sector, individuals, and the public are all seriously threatened by cybercrime today. More criminal acts are predicted in 2022, with attacks on critical infrastructure being of particular concern. Although small businesses are also in danger, a majority of these attacks affect government-operated services and buildings. According to a report from Thomson Reuters Labs, "State-sponsored cyberattacks are an emerging and significant risk to private enterprise that will increasingly challenge those sectors of the business world that provide convenient targets for settling geopolitical grievances."

8.4.9 The Internet of Things (IoT) Attacks

IoT, according to Statista.com, is expanding rapidly and predicted to have 75 billion linked devices by 2025. Laptops and tablets are clearly included, but other devices such as routers, webcams, home appliances, smart watches, transportation, medical, industrial, and even home security systems are also covered. These gadgets are convenient for users, and many businesses have begun employing them to cut expenses by gathering vast volumes of analytical data and improving operating procedures. IoT networks are particularly susceptible to malware infestations and other cyberattacks because of the rising risk that comes with more connected devices. IoT devices can be leveraged by malevolent parties to wreak havoc, overwhelm networks, and shut down critical equipment.

8.5 Social Engineering Attacks

Social engineering attacks are currently the greatest danger to cybersecurity and are therefore an important safety concern in the modern world. According to global research of 853 IT specialists conducted in 2011 in the United States, United Kingdom, Canada, Australia, New Zealand, and Germany, social engineering attacks are costly, particularly for large enterprises. The use of social engineering has resulted in damage to 48% of significant businesses (like health care, finance, manufacturing, and banks) and 32% of all businesses over the last two years. Overall, 30% of large businesses cite related expenses above $100,000 [8,9].

Social engineering tactics can be used by hackers in a variety of ways. The following are a few instances of typical social engineering attacks.

Phishing: Phishing is the practice of sending communications intended to deceive or persuade the target into performing a certain action. For instance, attachments that install malware on the user's machine are frequently included in phishing emails, along with links that go to phishing websites. A specific person or small group is the target of a spear-phishing attack.

Business Email Compromise (BEC): A BEC assault involves the attacker disguising themself as an organization executive. The attacker then gives an employee instructions on how to conduct a wire transfer to transmit money to the attacker.

Fraudulent Invoices: In some situations, fraudsters may pose as a supplier or vendor to steal money from a company. A bogus invoice is sent by the assailant, and when it is paid, funds are transferred to the assailant.

Brand Impersonation: A prominent tactic used in social engineering attacks is brand impersonation. For instance, phishers may impersonate a well-known company (such as DHL, LinkedIn, etc.) and coerce the victim into entering their login information on a phishing page, giving the attacker access to the user's password.

Whaling: Attacks that target senior-level personnel within an organization are essentially variants of whaling attacks. Actions that help an attacker can be approved by executives and higher-up management.

Baiting: Baiting attacks utilize a free or appealing excuse to pique the target's curiosity and persuade them to divulge login information or conduct other activities. Providing targets with free music or discounts on expensive software is one strategy.

Vishing: A type of social engineering that is carried out over the phone is known as "voice phishing" or "vishing." Although it uses a different medium, it employs similar tricks and techniques as phishing.

Smishing: Phishing via SMS text messages is known as "smishing." Smishing is becoming a more frequent danger because of the increased use of cellphones and bitly-link shortening services.

Pretexting: Pretexting entails the attacker fabricating an imaginary situation in which it makes sense for the target to pay money or divulge private information to the attacker. For instance, an intruder can pose as a dependable individual who needs details to confirm the victim's identification.

Quid Pro Quo: In a quid pro quo assault, the attacker offers the victim compensation in return for crucial information, such as cash or a service.

Tailgating/Piggybacking: Social engineering methods such as tailgating and piggybacking are used to enter restricted regions. A person is followed by the social engineer through an entrance regardless of the person's awareness. For instance, a worker might hold a door open for a person lifting large cargo.

Torecognize the most common social engineering attacks, verify the identification of anybody you do not know directly, thoroughly review emails for identities, addresses, and copies, and be aware of frequent phishing email headlines. Evaluate any feelings that the contact elicits as you go forward.

8.6 Social Engineering Defenses

8.6.1 Train Everybody in Your Organization

Even though mistakes made by people will always be an issue for safety measures, there are still things you can do to help reduce them. Training and educating your staff about fundamental cybersecurity procedures is one of the most important things that you can do to secure your business. Go through the fundamentals and delve deeper. The protocol is frequently violated accidentally rather than maliciously. The protocol is broken because people do not understand it. To protect yourself from social engineering assaults, ensure that everyone on your team is aware of the problem [5,10]. Some basic topics to cover include the following.

- Before you click, consider. Your staff members need to be aware of the repercussions of visiting broken or hazardous links.
- Avoid downloading any files that you are unsure of. A file poses a risk if it appears unusual.
- Check your sources before you interact. Ascertain the legitimacy and reputation of the website, message, or group that originated it.
- Refuse offers and rewards. If something seems too good to be true, then it probably is. Do not be deceived by it.

8.6.2 Determine Your Company's Valuable Assets

Initially knowing what you are trying to protect is necessary for the best protection against social engineering attacks. Decide what is most important to your business: extremely sensitive papers, data essential to business projects, private files, etc. These types of files should be continually managed very carefully. Employees interacting with them should exercise caution and follow specific processes [11].

8.6.3 Set Up and Enforce Good Security Policies

There is a need for laws and rules. Once you have a plan in place for everything in the global cyber arena, it is hoped that you will not have to worry about unwanted surprises. Policies are pointless, however, if your workforce does not follow the guidelines to the letter. Hold frequent conferences, plan workshops, and develop guidelines for defending against emotional attacks. Make every effort to guarantee that your personnel are fully aware of these guidelines and that they adhere to them exactly as written. It has been demonstrated that there is a simple but effective defense against social engineering attempts. If you can convince your staff to properly follow these procedures, then the possibility of cyberattacks on your company will be greatly reduced [12].

8.6.4 Update Your Software Regularly

The human element of a defense system is its weakest link. This does not mean that technical components cannot be breached, and it is imperative that all defense and security systems remain current at all times. These defenses are continually changing to counter new assault strategies that are regularly discovered. For the highest level of safety for you and your company, keep your technology frequently updated [13].

8.6.5 Do Not Share Private Information with Strangers

Even though it appears like a no-brainer defense against social engineering efforts, this must be emphasized: you and your team should never divulge information to people or groups you do not know. Ensure that each of your employees is completely aware of the official email addresses used by the business so that they will not be duped by copycats. Every member of the team needs to be aware of which information should be kept confidential and which information can be disclosed to other parties. Along with business data, team members' confidential data need to be protected. Even innocuous information about their recent activities, interests, relationships, or role within the organization might be leveraged to obtain valuable business data outside your knowledge [14].

8.6.6 Implement Access Control Within Your Company

Setting restrictions on the amount of system access that everyone on the team has is one of the best ways to protect against fraudulent activity. When only one component of the system is in danger, regulating the entire system is significantly easier. Utilize administration tools and different group managers to restrict access, offer each user authority, and subsequently minimize damages in the event of an attack [15].

8.6.7 Watch Out for Pretexting and Strange Requests

Pretexting is when cybercriminals attempt to establish a minimal amount of fundamental trust with their targets in order to increase these targets' willingness to provide information. A typical pretexting technique is when an attacker impersonates someone who the victim already knows to persuade them to let down their guard. For instance, one strategy is getting emails or texts from your boss that ask for a favor because your boss had to send them from their household phone. A communication from someone claiming to have met you on a recent trip could likewise serve as a justification. Criminals frequently utilize any ambiguous knowledge of your daily life against you to make you more receptive to their requests [16].

8.6.8 Enforcement of Strong Passwords

One relatively quick, simple, and inexpensive strategy that can be quite helpful in preventing data breaches and other cyberattacks is the implementation of passwords that are secure. To reduce interruption while getting ready for new, more robust security architecture, additional methods and procedures can be implemented concurrently with contemporary technologies. One example is zero-trust network architecture (ZTNA), which can be implemented alongside an SSL virtual private network (VPN), that initially acts as an overlay to enhance security and subsequently becomes the security system [17]. Multi-factor authentication (MFA), another social engineering protection, is occasionally offered as an add-on license for current hardware, such as SSL VPN and future-generation firewalls. Cloud-based MFA and even biometrics are also available as possible countermeasures.

8.7 Conclusion

Social engineering involves taking advantage of people to obtain access to limited assets. A variety of approaches are used by social engineers to trick people into disclosing confidential details. Social engineering protections must be a part of organizational safety requirements. Nevertheless, such attacks cannot be prevented solely by technological advances, and a social engineer without a thorough understanding of privacy can easily bypass an effective defense mechanism. Social engineering techniques are growing more prevalent and intense, affecting not only individuals but also organizations both physically and mentally. Businesses need security procedures that defend against social engineering. Therefore, there is considerable demand for new detection methods, countermeasures, and employee training programs.

References

1. Breda, Filipe, Hugo Barbosa, and Telmo Morais. "Social engineering and cyber security." In *INTED 2017 Proceedings*. IATED, 2017, pp. 4204–4211.
2. Kalniņs, R., J. Puriņs, and G. Alksnis. "Security evaluation of wireless network access points." *Applied Computer Systems* 21 (2017): 38–45.
3. Pokrovskaia, N. "Social engineering and digital technologies for the security of the social capital' development." In *Proceedings of the International Conference of Quality Management, Transport and Information Security*. Petersburg, Russia, 24–30 September 2017, pp. 16–19. DOI: 10.1109/ITMIS.2017.8085750
4. Aroyo, A.M., F. Rea, G. Sandini, and A. Sciutti. "Trust and social engineering in human robot interaction: Will a robot make you disclose sensitive information, conform to its recommendations or gamble?" *IEEE Robotics and Automation Letters* 3 (2018): 3701–3708.
5. Gardner, Bill, and Valerie Thomas. *Building an information security awareness program: Defending against social engineering and technical threats*. Elsevier, 2014.
6. Wang, Zuoguang, Limin Sun, and Hongsong Zhu. "Defining social engineering in cybersecurity." *IEEE Access* 8 (2020): 85094–85115.
7. Abass, Islam Abdalla Mohamed. "Social engineering threat and defense: A literature survey." *Journal of Information Security* 9, no. 04 (2018): 257.
8. Salahdine, Fatima, and Naima Kaabouch. "Social engineering attacks: A survey." *Future Internet* 11, no. 4 (2019): 89.
9. Koyun, Arif, and Ehssan Al Janabi. "Social engineering attacks." *Journal of Multidisciplinary Engineering Science and Technology (JMEST)* 4, no. 6 (2017): 7533–7538.
10. Grant, Robert Luther. "Exploring effects of organizational culture upon implementation of information security awareness and training programs within the defense industry located in the Tennessee valley region." PhD diss., 2017. https://www.proquest.com/docview/1941143998
11. Nohlberg, Marcus. "Securing information assets: Understanding, measuring and protecting against social engineering attacks." PhD diss., Institutionen för data-ochsystemvetenskap (tills m KTH), 2008.
12. Abraham, Sherly, and InduShobha Chengalur-Smith. "An overview of social engineering malware: Trends, tactics, and implications." *Technology in Society* 32, no. 3 (2010): 183–196.
13. Aldawood, Hussain, and Geoffrey Skinner. "Contemporary cyber security social engineering solutions, measures, policies, tools and applications: A critical appraisal." *International Journal of Security (IJS)* 10, no. 1 (2019): 1.
14. Hadnagy, Christopher. *Social engineering: The art of human hacking*. John Wiley & Sons, 2010.
15. Peltier, Thomas R. "Social engineering: Concepts and solutions." *Information Security Journal* 15, no. 5 (2006): 13.
16. Ozkaya, Erdal. *Learn Social Engineering: Learn the art of human hacking with an internationally renowned expert*. Packt Publishing Ltd, 2018.
17. Matyokurehwa, Kanos, Norman Rudhumbu, Cross Gombiro, and Colletor Chipfumbu-Kangara. "Enhanced social engineering framework mitigating against social engineering attacks in higher education." *Security and Privacy* 5, no. 5 (2022): e237.

9

A MACHINE LEARNING ALGORITHM TO TACKLE CHAT MESSAGES

DR. AMBIKA N

9.1 Introduction

Chat-based social engineering (Uthus & Aha, 2013) manipulates individuals through online communication channels, such as chat platforms, email, or messaging apps, to deceive them into divulging confidential information, performing actions that they would not normally do, or compromising their security in some way. This technique preys on human psychology and trust and often exploits cognitive biases to achieve the attacker's goals.

9.2 Social Engineering Attacks

Social engineering attacks are manipulative techniques that exploit human psychology and behavior. They gain unauthorized access to information, systems, or physical spaces. These attacks rely on deception, persuasion, and exploiting trust to trick individuals into revealing sensitive information, performing actions, or making decisions. Social engineering attacks often bypass technical security measures by targeting the weakest link in any security system: people.

The following are some common types of social engineering attacks.

1. **Phishing:** Attackers (Aljeaid, Alzhrani, Alrougi, & Almalki, 2020) impersonate legitimate individuals, organizations, or services and send messages containing links or attachments that, when clicked or opened, lead to malicious websites or malware. The goal is to steal sensitive information including passwords or credit card details.

DOI: 10.1201/9781003406716-9

2. **Pretexting:** Attackers (Workman, 2008) create a fabricated scenario or pretext to manipulate the target into providing sensitive information. For example, an attacker might pose as an IT technician and request the target's login credentials under the guise of needing to fix a technical issue.

3. **Baiting:** Attackers (Lawson, Crowson, & Mayhorn, 2019) offer something enticing, such as a free download, in exchange for the target's information or action. This could involve sharing a link that claims to provide a valuable resource but leads to a malicious website or file.

4. **Quid Pro Quo:** Attackers (Koh, Raghunathan, & Nault, 2020) offer a service or benefit in return for the target's information. For instance, an attacker might promise to help the target with a computer problem in exchange for access to their login credentials.

5. **Tailgating or Piggybacking:** Attackers gain unauthorized access to secure areas by closely following an authorized person. In the digital world, this can involve an attacker requesting entry into a secure system or building and leveraging trust to gain access.

6. **Impersonation:** Attackers (Freire & Garcés, 2022) impersonate someone who the target knows and trusts, such as a friend or coworker, to manipulate them into taking action, for example, transferring money or sharing confidential information.

7. **Reverse Social Engineering:** In this method (Irani, Balduzzi, Balzarotti, Kirda, & Pu, 2011), attackers manipulate victims into approaching them for help, often in a technical context. The attacker then exploits this contact to gain access or information.

8. **Scareware:** Attackers (Gautam & Rahimi, 2023) use fear and intimidation to manipulate individuals into taking actions they would not otherwise take. For instance, a pop-up message might claim that the victim's computer is infected and offer a solution (which is malware).

The CSE-PUC architecture (Tsinganos, Mavridis, & Gritzalis, 2022) comprises a convolutional neural network (CNN) and a multilayer perceptron (MLP). This architecture is designed for a specific task to determine whether a given sentence is an influential payload (pp) container and whether it carries a compelling payload. The main objective of the classifier is to generate a probability distribution over different sentence classes. In this case, it determines whether a sentence is a cogent payload container and whether it carries a persuasive payload. The CNN is a feature extractor. It captures relevant features from the input sentences and passes them on to the rest of the architecture for further processing. The features extracted by the CNN integrate with the rest of the architecture. This integration likely involves combining the CNN's extracted characteristics with features from the MLP or other parts of the network. The entire CSE-PUC network undergoes training. It involves optimizing the network's parameters and weights by using a training dataset and making accurate predictions on the given task. The architecture aims to identify informative cues within sentences. These cues are likely patterns or signals indicating a sentence that contains a persuasive payload. The CSE corpus is a dataset that trains the CSE-PUC architecture. It is created by collecting real-world and fictional social engineering attack dialogues from various sources, such as dark social engineering websites, social engineering books, and logs. The CSE corpus undergoes a pre-processing pipeline, which involves several steps as tokenization (splitting text into individual tokens), standardization (converting text to a particular format), and noise removal (eliminating irrelevant or distracting elements). The CSE corpus is labelled for the pp-container prediction task. Each sentence is assigned a label indicating whether it is a persuasive payload container. The CSE corpus contains a specific number of sentences, with a subset of them (3,880 sentences) labelled as pp-containers. The annotation task ensures a balanced dataset, where the number of sentences from each class is roughly equivalent. Overall, the described architecture and approach seem to focus on using neural networks, specifically, a CNN and an MLP, to identify persuasive payload containers in sentences, particularly in the context of social engineering attacks. The dataset used for training, the CSE corpus, appears to be carefully prepared to facilitate this task.

To enhance accuracy and context-awareness in chatbot responses, back propagation and an Apriori algorithm are used. It is essential to consider a combination of techniques that target different aspects of the chatbot's operation. The work improves accuracy by 6.4% and context-awareness by 11.4% compared to previous work.

The study is divided into seven sections. The background is detailed in section two. A literature survey is summarized in segment three.

Previous work is detailed in section four. Proposed work is discussed in segment five. Future of work is explained in division six. Finally, the study is concluded in section seven.

9.3 Background

9.3.1 Backpropagations Algorithm

Backpropagation (Lillicrap, Santoro, Marris, Akerman, & Hinton, 2020) is a supervised learning algorithm (Cunningham, Cord, & Delany, 2008) used to train artificial neural networks. It involves iteratively adjusting the weights and biases of the network's neurons by calculating gradients of the loss function concerning these parameters. It is achieved by propagating the error gradient backward through the network, starting from the output layer and updating the weights and biases by using an optimization method such as gradient descent. Backpropagation enables the network to learn from labeled training data and improves its ability to make accurate predictions by minimizing the difference between predicted and actual outputs.

Step 1: Initialization—Initialize the weights and biases of the neural network with small random values.

Step 2: Forward Pass—Input a training example into the network. For each layer,

- Compute the weighted sum of inputs for each neuron in the layer,
- Apply an activation function to the weighted sum to obtain the output of each neuron, and
- Pass the output of each neuron as an input to the next layer.

Step 3: Compute Loss—Compare the network's output with the actual target values for the training example.

Calculate the loss with a suitable loss function (e.g., mean squared error or cross-entropy).

Step 4: Backward Pass (Backpropagation)—Starting from the output layer,

- Calculate the gradient of the loss concerning the output of each neuron in the output layer,

- Use the chain rule to calculate the gradient of the loss concerning the weighted sum of the inputs for each neuron in the output layer, and
- Calculate the gradient of the loss concerning the weights and biases of the output layer.

For each hidden layer (moving backward),

- Calculate the gradient of the loss concerning the output of each neuron in the current hidden layer by using the gradients from the layer ahead,
- Use the chain rule to calculate the gradient of the loss concerning the weighted sum of inputs for each neuron in the current hidden layer, and
- Calculate the gradient of the loss concerning the weights and biases of the current hidden layer.

Step 5: Update Weights and Biases—Use the calculated gradients to update the weights and biases of each layer in the network:

- New Weight = Old Weight—Learning Rate * Gradient of Weight
- New Bias = Old Bias—Learning Rate * Gradient of Bias (Learning Rate is a hyperparameter controlling the step size of updates.)

Step 6: Iterate—Repeat steps 2 to 5 for multiple training examples and epochs (iterations) until the network's performance converges or reaches a satisfactory level.

Throughout these steps, the backpropagation algorithm enables the network to adjust its parameters based on the gradients of the loss function and thus learns to make better predictions over time.

9.3.2 Apriori Algorithm

The Apriori algorithm (Aflori & Craus, 2007) (Perego, Orlando, & Palmerini, 2001) finds frequent item sets in a dataset, where an entity set is a collection of items that often occur together. It uses the "apriori property," which states that if an item set is frequent, then all of its subsets must also be frequent.

Algorithm Steps:

1. Generate Candidate Item Sets:
- Start by identifying all individual items in the dataset as potential 1-item sets.
- Combine these 1-item sets to generate candidate 2-item sets.
- Continue this process to generate candidate k-item sets.

2. Scan Dataset and Count Frequencies:
- Scan the dataset to count the frequency of occurrence of each candidate item set.
- This involves iterating through the dataset and checking if the candidate item sets are present in each transaction.

3. Prune Infrequent Item Sets:
- Remove candidate item sets that do not meet a minimum support threshold (i.e., are not frequent enough) from the list of candidates.
- This pruning step helps reduce the number of candidates to consider in subsequent iterations.

4. Generate New Candidates:
- Use the frequent (k-1)-item sets from the previous iteration to generate new candidate k-item sets.
- This step ensures only combinations of frequent item sets, which satisfies the apriori property.

5. Repeat Steps 2 to 4:
- Continue iterating through steps 2 to 4.

6. Generate Association Rules:
- Once frequent item sets are identified, association rules are generated from these sets.
- An association rule is in the form of "If A, then B," where A and B are item sets.
- These rules are generated based on confidence and support thresholds.

9.4 Literature Survey

Some research work (Tsinganos & Mavridis, 2021) involves the early-stage automated recognition of CSE attacks. It achieves this by proposing an approach involving building and annotating a specific-purpose corpus. The focus is on developing a method for identifying and categorizing social engineering attacks in their early stages. The proposed approach consists of two main components: a conceptual framework for studying CSE attacks and a methodology for building and annotating a corpus specific to CSE attacks. This indicates that the research provides a structured way to approach the problem and gather relevant data. The application of the proposed approach is within the domain of computer-supported engineering (CSE). CSE uses technology and software tools to facilitate engineering tasks and processes. ISO/IEC 15408–1:2009(E) Standard focuses on protecting assets from threats. It is mentioned in the context of the research work, which likely indicates that the proposed methodology aligns with established standards for information security. The research conducts a thorough analysis of collected raw dialogues. This analysis aims to extract relevant information that can be categorized into three categories of sensitive data, and the text analysis results in the identification of three categories of sensitive data. These categories likely relate to the types of information that attackers aim to extract or manipulate during social engineering attacks. The research involves analyzing a sample of CSE dialogues from a linguistic perspective. This analysis serves as a baseline to ensure the quality of the software tools and libraries used in the research. It is essential to ensure that these tools can effectively process and understand the linguistic nuances in the dialogues.

Another project (Murnion, Buchanan, Smales, & Russell, 2018) involves multiple steps, including data collection, data transformation, player identification, the classification of chat messages, sentiment analysis, and potential applications such as identifying cyber-bullying messages. Data Collection and Extract, Transform, and Load (ETL) use web scraping techniques to gather in-game chat data from World of Tanks match replays. It applies ETL techniques to process and organize the collected chat data. Player Identification and Player Information Retrieval identify players from the collected chat data. It gathers additional player information from the public API services provided by Wargaming.net. Data Storage and Database Creation create a new database to store the collected in-game chat messages. Classification Prototype develops a classification client that allows for the quick classification of chat messages. It evaluates the potential of using this classified data for machine learning analysis and conducts a basic analytical exercise to demonstrate the practicality and value of the collected chat data. Sentiment Analysis explores the application of sentiment analysis, an AI-based technique, to automatically detect the sentiment of chat messages. It considers the use of sentiment analysis in identifying instances of cyber-bullying in the chat data.

A described platform (Tebenkov & Prokhorov, 2021) utilizes microservices, containerization, RabbitMQ, and a dialogue act recognition (DAR) system to create an efficient and scalable chatbot ecosystem. The DAR has a Dialog Act Markup in Several Layers (DAMSL) annotation scheme and a labeled dataset such as Switchboard. This architecture enables the platform to process natural language conversations effectively and respond appropriately in real-time. The platform employs a microservice architecture that breaks down the application into smaller, loosely coupled services. Each chatbot runs within its own container. Containers provide a lightweight and isolated environment for applications to run consistently across different computing environments. The microservice architecture and containerization allow for easy scalability. New instances of chatbot containers handle increased demand without creating bottlenecks or slowing down the system. RabbitMQ is a message broker that enables efficient communication between different components. It manages the distribution of messages between services by preventing message queues from building up and securing smooth processing. RabbitMQ is built on the AMQP standard. It ensures reliable and efficient communication between distributed applications by defining a shared interface for sending and receiving messages. DAR is the process of identifying the purpose of a sentence within a conversation. It is crucial for chatbots to understand and respond appropriately to user inputs. A statistical machine learning model is trained on a labeled dataset to predict the dialogue act of a given sentence. The DAMSL annotation scheme is a framework used to label sentences in conversation datasets. It categorizes sentences based on several dimensions: communicative status (e.g., statement, question), information level (e.g., informative, directive), forward-looking function (e.g., request, offer), and backward-looking function (e.g., agreement, disagreement). The Switchboard dataset is an adaptation of the DAMSL annotation scheme tailored for automated telephone conversations. It provides a labeled corpus of sentences with dialogue act annotations, which serves as training data for building DAR models. A predefined set of tags or labels represent the different functions or purposes of sentences in a conversation. These tags are designed to be general enough to be applicable to various tasks but specific enough to remain relevant to minimize human labeling confusion.

9.5 Previous Work

The CSE-PUC architecture (Tsinganos, Mavridis, & Gritzalis, 2022) comprises a CNN and MLP. This architecture is designed for a specific task to determine whether a given sentence is a pp-container and whether it carries a compelling payload. The main objective of the classifier is to generate a probability distribution over different sentence class. In this case, it determines whether a sentence is a cogent payload container and whether it carries a persuasive payload. The CNN is a feature extractor. It captures relevant features from the input sentences and passes them on to the rest of the architecture for further processing. The features extracted by the CNN integrate with the rest of the architecture. This integration likely involves combining the CNN's extracted characteristics with features from the MLP or other parts of the network. The entire CSE-PUC network undergoes training. It involves optimizing the network's parameters and weights with a training dataset and making accurate predictions on the given task. The architecture aims to identify informative cues within sentences. These cues are likely patterns or signals indicating that a sentence contains a persuasive payload. The CSE corpus is a dataset that trains the CSE-PUC architecture. It is created by collecting real-world and fictional social engineering attack dialogues from various sources, such as dark social engineering websites, social engineering books, and logs. The CSE corpus undergoes a pre-processing pipeline, which involves several steps as tokenization (splitting text into individual tokens), standardization (converting text to a particular format), and noise removal (eliminating irrelevant or distracting elements). The CSE corpus is labelled for the pp-container prediction task. Each sentence is assigned a label indicating whether it is a persuasive payload container. The CSE corpus contains a specific number of sentences, with a subset of them (3,880 sentences) labelled as pp-containers. The annotation task ensures a balanced dataset, where the number of sentences from each class is roughly equivalent. Overall, the described architecture and approach seem to focus on using neural networks, specifically, a CNN and MLP, to identify persuasive payload containers in sentences, particularly in the context of social engineering attacks. The dataset used for training, namely, the CSE corpus, appears to be carefully prepared to facilitate this task.

9.6 Proposed Work

To enhance accuracy and context-awareness in chatbot responses, back propagation and the Apriori algorithm are used. It is essential to consider a combination of techniques that target different aspects of the chatbot's operation. This might include optimizing the microservice architecture, leveraging efficient data structures, utilizing hardware acceleration, and implementing caching mechanisms. Additionally, applying appropriate techniques for natural language processing, such as pre-trained language models or attention mechanisms, can contribute to the chatbot's overall performance.

Backpropagation is a fundamental technique used in training artificial neural networks. This type of machine learning model is often employed in tasks such as natural language processing. It involves adjusting the weights of the network's connections based on the error (the difference between predicted and actual output) during training. This adjustment process is performed iteratively and uses gradient descent to minimize the error and improve the model's predictions. In the context of a chatbot platform, backpropagation could be used if the chatbot employs neural networks for tasks including natural language understanding or generating responses. By fine-tuning the network's weights through backpropagation, the chatbot can learn from its mistakes and improve its accuracy over time. However, notably, although backpropagation can enhance accuracy, it may not directly impact the platform's speed as it primarily concerns the training phase.

The Apriori algorithm is a classic technique in data mining and association rule learning. It is used to discover patterns and associations within a dataset, particularly in the context of market basket analysis. The algorithm works by iteratively finding frequent itemsets (sets of items that often appear together) and then

Table 9.1 Methodology to Improve the System

{creating training dataset}
Step 1—Accept the sample input {use the back propagation algorithm}
Step 2—Analyze different internal states
Step 3—Jolt down the output
Step 4—Create {input, hidden layer}, {hidden layer, output} pairs using the Apriori algorithm.
{Creating testing dataset}
Step 5—Using these pairs, analyze the input

Table 9.2 Parameters Used in the Study

PARAMETERS USED IN THE WORK	DESCRIPTION
Number of inputs created	1069
No of hidden layers	2
No of states in first hidden layers	762
No of states in second hidden layer	516
No of output states derived	872

generating association rules based on these itemsets. In the context of a chatbot platform, the Apriori algorithm may be used to identify patterns in user interactions and conversations. It could potentially help the chatbot better understand user preferences, common queries, or frequently occurring sequences of dialogue acts. By leveraging these patterns, the chatbot can generate more contextually relevant responses.

Table 9.1 is used to create a training dataset and a testing dataset.

The work is simulated using Python. Table 9.2 describes the parameters used in the work.

9.6.1 Accuracy

Backpropagation is primarily used during the training phase of neural networks. The Apriori algorithm can enhance accuracy by identifying patterns and associations in user interactions. It can help the chatbot understand user preferences, generate contextually relevant responses, and anticipate user needs. By leveraging the discovered patterns, the chatbot can understand user behavior more deeply, leading to improved accuracy in generating responses and interacting with users.

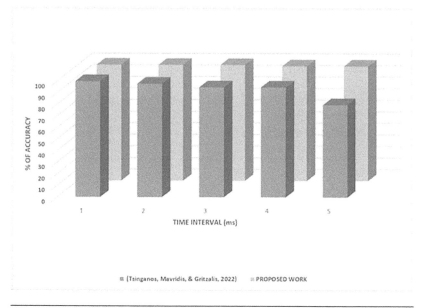

Figure 9.1   Comparison of the accuracy in both works.

Incorporating backpropagation for neural network refinement and the Apriori algorithm for pattern recognition can synergistically enhance a chatbot's accuracy and effectiveness. The work improves accuracy by 6.4% compared to previous work (Tsinganos, Mavridis, & Gritzalis, 2022). This is represented in Figure 9.1.

9.6.2 Context-Awareness

Backpropagation can indirectly contribute to context awareness by enabling the chatbot's neural network models to understand and respond to the nuances of user input. When training the chatbot's neural network for natural language understanding, backpropagation allows the model to learn patterns and associations in language usage. It enables the model to recognize context-dependent meanings, idiomatic expressions, and user intentions. Backpropagation enables the neural network to adjust its weights based on the relationships between words and phrases in different contexts. It allows the chatbot to understand when the meaning of a word changes based on its surrounding words. By training the neural network to capture these context-aware features, the chatbot becomes more skilled at understanding the subtleties of user input, which leads to more contextually relevant responses.

The Apriori algorithm directly contributes to context awareness by identifying patterns and associations in user interactions. It can help the chatbot tailor its responses to the specific context of the conversation. The algorithm can uncover patterns that reveal user preferences, helping the chatbot offer suggestions or recommendations that match the user's interests based on past interactions. By utilizing the Apriori algorithm to recognize these conversation patterns, the chatbot can achieve a higher level of context awareness, which leads to more engaging and personalized interactions. Incorporating both backpropagation for neural network refinement and the Apriori algorithm for pattern recognition equips the chatbot with the ability to understand and respond within the context of ongoing conversations. This results in more accurate, relevant, and context-aware interactions with users. The work improves context-awareness by 11.4% compared to previous work. Figure 9.2 represents this result.

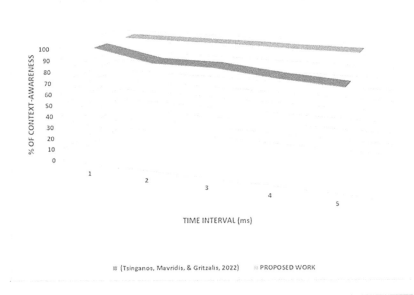

Figure 9.2 Context-awareness.

9.7 Future Scope

Some of the potential developments are discussed as follows.

- **Enhanced Natural Language Understanding**: Future chatbots could understand and respond to natural language with greater accuracy and contextual understanding. This might involve more advanced models that can grasp nuances, idiomatic expressions, and slang in conversations.
- **Personalization**: Chatbots could become more adept at personalizing their responses based on user preferences, historical interactions, and available data. This could lead to more engaging and relevant conversations.
- **Emotion Recognition**: Future chatbots might be equipped with better emotion recognition capabilities. They could detect the user's emotional state based on text input and respond empathetically or appropriately.
- **Multi-Modal Integration**: Chat messages might be based not only on text but also images, videos, and audio. Future chatbots could be trained to analyze and respond to these multi-modal inputs effectively.
- **Continual Learning**: Instead of being trained on a static dataset, chatbots could employ continual learning techniques. This means that they would improve over time through ongoing interactions and adapt to new language trends and user behaviors.
- **Ethical and Bias Considerations**: There will likely be increased emphasis on addressing biases in chatbot interactions and ensuring that AI systems handle sensitive topics ethically and responsibly.
- **Improved Contextual Understanding**: Future chatbots could have better memory and understanding of ongoing conversations, making it easier for them to maintain coherent dialogues over extended periods.
- **Human-Agent Collaboration**: Chatbots might work alongside humans more seamlessly by assisting them in various tasks, such as drafting emails, scheduling appointments, or conducting research.
- **Security and Privacy**: As chatbots become more integrated into our lives, ensuring the security and privacy of conversations

will become even more crucial. Future developments might include better encryption and authentication mechanisms.

- **Advanced Chatbot Architectures**: Future chatbots could utilize more sophisticated architectures that combine different models, for example, a generative pre-trained transformer (GPT) with task-specific networks, to achieve higher levels of performance across a variety of tasks.
- **Conversational Assistants in Various Domains**: Chatbots specialized for specific industries, such as healthcare, finance, education, and customer service, could become more prevalent and offer tailored assistance in these areas.
- **Cultural and Language Adaptation**: Future chatbots might be better equipped to handle a wide range of languages and cultural contexts, which makes them more globally applicable and inclusive.

9.8 Conclusion

The CSE-PUC architecture comprises a CNN and MLP. This architecture is designed for a specific task to determine whether a given sentence is an pp-container and whether it carries a compelling payload. The main objective of the classifier is to generate a probability distribution over different sentence class.

To enhance accuracy and context-awareness in chatbot responses, back propagation and the Apriori algorithm are used. It is essential to consider a combination of techniques that target different aspects of the chatbot's operation. The work improves accuracy by 6.4% and context-awareness by 11.4% compared to previous work.

References

Aflori, C., & Craus, M. (2007). Grid implementation of the Apriori algorithm. *Advances in Engineering Software, 38*(5), 295–300.

Aljeaid, D., Alzhrani, A., Alrougi, M., & Almalki, O. (2020). Assessment of end-user susceptibility to cybersecurity threats in Saudi Arabia by simulating phishing attacks. *Information, 11*(12), 547.

Cunningham, P., Cord, M., & Delany, S. J. (2008). Supervised learning. In *Machine learning techniques for multimedia* (pp. 21–49). Berlin, Heidelberg: Springer.

Freire, J. S., & Garcés, B. (2022). Preparation of a social engineering attack, from scratch to compromise: A USB dropper and impersonation approach. In *Conference on information and communication technologies of Ecuador* (pp. 281–293). Manta, Ecuador: Springer International Publishing.

Gautam, A., & Rahimi, N. (2023). Viability of machine learning in Android scareware detection. *8th International Conference, 91*, 19–26.

Irani, D., Balduzzi, M., Balzarotti, D., Kirda, E., & Pu, C. (2011). Reverse social engineering attacks in online social networks. In *Detection of intrusions and malware, and vulnerability assessment: 8th international conference; DIMVA 2011* (pp. 55–74). Amsterdam, The Netherlands: Springer Berlin Heidelberg.

Koh, B., Raghunathan, S., & Nault, B. R. (2020). An empirical examination of voluntary profiling: Privacy and quid pro quo. *Decision Support Systems, 132*, 113285.

Lawson, P. A., Crowson, A. D., & Mayhorn, C. B. (2019). Baiting the hook: Exploring the interaction of personality and persuasion tactics in email phishing attacks. In *Proceedings of the 20th Congress of the International Ergonomics Association (IEA 2018) Volume V: Human Simulation and Virtual Environments, Work With Computing Systems (WWCS), Process Control* 20, pp. 401–406. Springer International Publishing, 2019.

Lillicrap, T. P., Santoro, A., Marris, L., Akerman, C. J., & Hinton, G. (2020). Backpropagation and the brain. *Nature Reviews Neuroscience, 21*(6), 335–346.

Murnion, S., Buchanan, W. J., Smales, A., & Russell, G. (2018). Machine learning and semantic analysis of in-game chat for cyberbullying. *Computers & Security, 76*, 197–213.

Perego, R., Orlando, S., & Palmerini, P. (2001). Enhancing the apriori algorithm for frequent set counting. In *International conference on data warehousing and knowledge discovery* (pp. 71–82). Munich, Germany: Springer, Berlin, Heidelberg.

Salahdine, F., & Kaabouch, N. (2019). Social engineering attacks: A survey. *Future Internet, 11*, 89.

Tebenkov, E., & Prokhorov, I. (2021). Machine learning algorithms for teaching AI chat bots. *Procedia Computer Science, 190*, 735–744.

Tsinganos, N., & Mavridis, I. (2021). Building and evaluating an annotated corpus for automated recognition of chat-based social engineering attacks. *Applied Sciences, 11*(22), 10871.

Tsinganos, N., Mavridis, I., & Gritzalis, D. (2022). Utilizing convolutional neural networks and word embeddings for early-stage recognition of persuasion in chat-based social engineering attacks. *IEEE Access, 10*, 108517–108529.

Uthus, D. C., & Aha, D. W. (2013). Multiparticipant chat analysis: A survey. *Artificial Intelligence, 199*, 106–121.

Workman, M. (2008). Wisecrackers: A theory-grounded investigation of phishing and pretext social engineering threats to information security. *Journal of the American Society for Information Science and Technology, 59*(4), 662–674.

10
A SURVEY ON A SECURITY MODEL FOR THE INTERNET OF THINGS ENVIRONMENT

BHARATI B. PANNAYAGOL,
DR. SANTOSH L. DESHPANDE
AND SNEHA YADAV

10.1 Introduction

The internet has become a fundamental necessity in our day-to-day lives; in this manner, the administration is provisioned through an internet of things (IoT). However, the safety of the information is ambushed through different strategies of Distributed Denial of Service (DDoS) attacks which are exceptionally risky. Therefore, a few exploratory works have been emphasized for the field of IoT. The usual four types of attacks are U2R, Dos, R2l and probe. The point of any security model is the division of the organization traffic into five classes: R2l, U2R, probe, normal and DoS. When an attacker tries to attack the data, a signal is detected, and using the signal, traffic management can try to protect the data by taking appropriate security measures. Various studies have been conducted for the feature classification and extraction strategies. The Feature extraction strategy is the best technique used for the recognition of the attack; hence, this strategy is known as the selection of the feature process. The selection of the feature process uses the required features from the input data, which has a critical effect on the output data. The feature extraction strategy additionally decreases the information storage size and further increases not only the accuracy of the classifier but also the efficiency of the training in the model. This strategy is good for small-scale algorithms that use large amounts of data for training and testing. For the classification of the network traffic, many machine learning techniques already exist.

DOI: 10.1201/9781003406716-10

Most of the techniques use KNN, SVM, ANN, naïve Bayesian, DTs and fuzzy logic algorithms for the classification of network traffic. On the basis of the selection of the feature, the performance of the previous classifier for attack recognition has been considered. Furthermore, the traditional techniques have considerable challenge when a large network tries to adopt these techniques as they generate a sizable amount of traffic information in a day. The usage of the machine learning classifiers in the large network increases the cost and time required for the calculation because the traffic data constantly increase every day. These machine learning classifiers also help in the detection of an anonymous attack, which boosts the accuracy of the model. When the system is employed, the security of the traffic network is confirmed after some time when it reaches high precision.

Recently, various machine learning techniques, such as the SVM, J48, KNN, random forest, etc., have been used for the detection and identification of malicious packets in the traffic network that have a high accuracy for detection [1]. However, these techniques do not resolve the issue of the concept drift problem in the network traffic. To resolve this issue, the authors of [1] planned a technique in which the information is taken with the help of the unlabelled packets, and the malicious packets are identified. This conquers the issue of malicious packets in the network traffic. The model Lfun has been proposed [1], which shows better performance than [2].

In any case, accomplished precision is not very effective because of variety on schedule. In [2], they proposed a method for the detection of the malicious packets with drift detection by calculating the six statistical features and two non-linear features for the concept drift problem. The statistical feature comprises auto relationship, skewness, kurtosis and variance, whereas the non-linear feature comprises normal data and miscorrelation. These all-features are made with measurements of contribution to obtain the concept vector. After this, the concept vector is coordinated at different time intervals with the help of the total distance [3], cosine distance metrics and histograms consisting of streaming hash [3]. However, a high calculation overhead is presented by the explicit malicious packet drift detection technique. To solve the calculation complexity, in [4], they proposed a technique for the identification of the irregularity in the network traffic by using the KL divergence for the measurement of the distance [5]. however, they effectively presented various procedures that cannot solve the problems of class imbalance and concept drift in the IoT. Hence, a broad survey was performed on various papers to design an efficient method that can detect various cyberattacks in the IoT.

10.2 Literature Survey

The new highlights of the social web, in which clients are the data makers, uncover different issues of information quality (IQ). As an illustration of the IoT, Facebook and its environment are the common micro blogging websites that consist of an ongoing messaging structure. This feature structure helps them not only to be more well-known but also to provide suitable updates about real-time public occasions. However, as Facebook provides the adaptable use of various destinations and there is no limit on the posting of the contents, this leads to an increase of issues in IQ. As the social platforms cannot detect the malicious packets that contain maximum common noise, they cannot be detected by another user who has received this packet. These social malicious packets contain various malicious data such as rubbish content, phishing sites, malicious URLs, pornography and malware. These malicious packets dispatch their garbage and take advantage of the administration's accessibility, reliability, security and other system features when the user opens these messages or URLs. With this advantage, the attacker can reap monetary benefits. For instance, these social malicious packets impact different arrangements of administrations that accommodate dispatching a malicious packets attack over the Hashtag, mention administrations and URLs. To develop the method that recognizes malicious packets, we conducted a literature review on the supervised learning methods of machine learning. The supervised learning methods require a dataset for the training and testing of the model before the model is deployed. Many datasets for the social malicious packets have been in development to distinguish various new examples of how the attacker can attack the user with the social malicious packets. As the training data required for training the supervised learning technique are static, the technique implemented is wasteful. To resolve this problem, in [6], they proposed a scheme for an online group-based malicious bundles arrangement structure, which utilizes the upsides of unaided machine learning methods for giving an explained dataset naturally and occasionally. By utilizing this, the supervised classifying models are refreshed. This model connected bundles of social malicious packets in a brief timeframe to forecast malicious packet conduct.

10.2.1 Supervised Learning-Based Attack Detection Methodologies

Many stages in the IoT environment utilize machine learning strategies for the automatic recognition of malicious packets. However, the element determination is the primary measure that separates them all. Practically all of the strategies provide various elements that are used in machine learning procedures to detect and recognize the malicious packet in the network traffic. These elements differ and change according to different parameters such as packets, detection methods, formula, complexity, manipulation, campaign and effectiveness. Detection of the malicious packets in the online platform with data-driven techniques has been improved and uses different algorithms, such as KNN, SVM, and RF, for the classification, which are also utilized to stabilize the malicious packets in ordinary packets data [6].

The major benefit of data-driven methods is a minimal expense because of the lower labor cost. The data-driven methods help to find the various hidden elements in the malicious packets in the IoT environment [7]. In a similar amount of time, the malicious packets can create and deliver new sorts of malicious packet methods that can deliver colossal malicious packet mail into a framework that can determine whether the message sent is normal or abnormal. When the malicious packets set up bugs in the framework, the subsequent task is quicker. Therefore, models dependent on authentic data, which use the IoT malicious packets for detection, will not work, and most probably will fail in the future. The malicious packets in the IoT environment are considered concept drift because they constantly change with respect to time [8]. In the present situation, to understand the idea of concept drift in a given field or area has become significant [9]. This concept can be used for various applications of the IoT. The applications of the IoT change their distribution and properties with respect to time. To resolve the issue of the drifting of malicious packets, [9] presents a model for both the posting of the language and time.

The models cannot recognize the user that is created by the attacker to send the malicious packets. Moreover, these models can predict whether the user's account is hacked or not, and they also can build the records of the users who were hacked. To resolve the issues in existing methodologies, [9] planned a technique that can obtain the information from non-labelled packets, distinguish the packets that are malicious packets and take care of the malicious packet drifting problem. Generally, various models neglect to resolve the problem of drifting and incorporate additional calculations to resolve other problems [10]. The posterior probability in the drift problem effects the decision of the hyperplane. It is impossible to drift only one part to make changes in the other parts of the drift problem. There are various drift types that constantly change over time. Thus, the drift concept is known as a combination of various drift parts called joint concept drift. Another problem in data mining is known as class imbalance. In this problem, the whole class will not contain the same number of samples, either one of the classes will contain a greater number of samples than the other class [11].

Using the traditional machine learning techniques in various circumstances of class imbalance problems can ignore the sample of the class and can reduce the accuracy of the model. Class imbalance and concept drift build up shared impacts. When the two issues happen at the same time, they affect one another. If the samples of the class are imbalanced, then the identification of the minority class in the concept drift is a very challenging task. Hence, some techniques have been proposed for the identification and detection of the class imbalance and concept drift problems. The answer to these problems was given in [12].

10.2.2 Data Integrity through the Fusion Mechanism

The IoT is a moderately new concept in IT [15]. Numerous data gadgets can be shaped from start to finish and join with a server through appropriate correspondence conventions (e.g., Bluetooth and ZigBee, WIFI and ultra-wideband); in this way, they extend various applications in the areas of home care, industrial monitoring and smart technology. With the help of the combination of the Wireless Sensor Networks (WSNs) and the IoT, a large number of executives can be expanded with the increased use of these technologies. Regardless of whether the IoT or the WSNs, the distributed system has three significant out-comes, namely, independent failures, no global clock and concurrency [14]. This hub can be handily assaulted by an intruder. Therefore, a compelling security algorithm is required. In such a situation, a pow-erful agreement algorithm utilizes the Byzantine algorithm (BA). The BA is a well-known issue-tolerant method. In [15], they cited the historical illustration of agreement among the officers of the Byzan-tine Empire concerning assaulting their foes and applied this idea to develop BA, particularly for a dependable PC system to investigate processor blames successfully.

10.2.3 Ensemble Learning for Concept Drift

On the outfit learning algorithm that addresses idea floats, in [13], they proposed a gathering learning algorithm dependent on variety for diversity with drifts called DDD. At the point when an idea float is identified, the algorithm individually trains the two classifiers, which are dependent on the datasets having low and high varieties, and com-bines the two classifiers with low and high varieties, which adjusts the idea floats. In [16], a model was proposed for a weighted democratic plan in the outfit learning, but this model addressed only the online idea float issues. In [17], they used the idea of gathering learning with a large number of classifiers to resolve the problem of idea floats. The outcome of the model was that the troupe learning method performs well compared with the strategy utilizing just a single classifier intend-ing to ide floats. In [18], an algorithm was proposed that holds the comparability of the cosine to contrast whether two datasets have a place with two distinct ideas.

10.2.4 Ensemble Learning for Imbalance Data

Lately, unevenness information issues have received a lot of consider-ation. For example, [19] and [20] accentuated that the strategies depen-dent on only a single classifier cannot acquire exact outcomes in tending to the information with different classes and much noise; subsequently, embraced troupe learning techniques utilize various classifiers to resolve the imbalance information. In [21], they coordinated various learning techniques to build the general presentation. Troupe learning algorithms dependent on adaptive boosting (AdaBoost) have drawn considerable attention recently. In [22], they proposed a troupe learning strategy dependent on AdaBoost to reduce the figure blunder. In [23], they joined the AdaBoost strategy with a negative relationship to determine how to build a novel AdaBoost, NC conjecture model that performs better than previous techniques in dealing with classification issues.

Certifiable information streams represent a novel test for the implementation of machine learning models and data analysis. An eminent issue that has been presented by the development of IoT organizations across the smart city biological system is that the factual properties of information streams can change over the long run, causing helpless expectation execution and incapable choices. Although idea float discovery strategies intend to fix this issue, arising sensing technologies and emerging communication are creating a considerable amount of information, requiring dispersed conditions to perform calculation errands across smart city authoritative spaces. In [24], they tried various best-in-class dynamic idea float identification algorithms for time series examination inside a conveyed climate. We utilize genuine information streams and conduct a basic investigation of the results recovered. The difficulties of carrying out idea float variation calculations, alongside their applications in smart urban areas, are also discussed.

10.2.5 Software Defined Networking (SDN) of Loading Security

The security in SDN-based systems [25] was characterized to take advantage of SDN's versatility. The further functions provided by SDN innovation empower the coordination of improved security instruments, for example, traffic filtering, routing manipulations and the utilization of a secure organization channel to move the delicate information. Some papers regarding the NFV scope have focused on assessing the plausibility and exhibition of working the virtual security machines on edge utilizing holders [26, 27] such as firewalls and IDS. Although this virtualization innovation demonstrated exceptional productivity, it ended up being tested in relation to the asset-required IoT devices. The convenience of the device is impacted by the high volume of traffic, which can require significant energy and CPU utilization. Employing machine learning techniques is an optional strategy to deal with secure IoT setups. Different arrangements that influence

SDN innovation and machine learning tactics for enhancing network interruption recognition frameworks were recommended in [28]. The work also depicts the challenges identified with the organization interruption of detection systems.

In [29], they proposed a model that predicts urban transport by utilizing the deep-learning method. This model uses an LSTM neural network, which anticipates the data rate and location. The creators in [30] proposed a model using the block chain method for overseeing an adaptable IoT framework. The authors in [31] recommended an answer that recognizes the correspondence between the MEC and IoT devices. This model embraces a technique that can distinguish the possibility for service composition and delivery. The researchers in [32] used ANN to identify a strange traffic network that travels from the doorway to the edge gadgets [33, 34].

10.3 Issues, Challenges and Problem Statement

In this section, various cyberattack methods and their detection in an online platform are discussed.

10.3.1 Time and Memory Constraints

Both "large volume" and "high velocity" show the high scale of IoT streaming data and high generation. The IoT streaming data must be prepared and examined when they arrive at the training model. Nonetheless, in the IoT framework, many IoT gadgets have less cost and less power consumption with less computational resources with restricted computational assets, which limit their information investigation speed [35–37]. The storage imperatives of IoT gadgets additionally reduce the capacity to measure and store considerable data of IoT information and large intricacy learning models.

10.3.2 Class Imbalance

The most common issue in data mining in the IoT climate is class irregularity. In this regularity, all classes do not have the same number of tests, that is, in any one of the class, some extra examples can been seen when contrasted with another class [38]. Using the traditional machine learning strategies in these circumstances will overlook the examples of minority class, as these minority tests influence general precision. Both idea float and class awkwardness support shared impacts. When the two issues happen at a time, they exasperate one another. When the streaming data are imbalanced in the classes, then it is extremely challenging to recognize idea float in the minority classes and determining how to use it. Actually, the status of the class imbalance can be changed by the idea float, as the earlier class is one variable in the idea floating climate thus far; a couple of techniques have been proposed to resolve the problem of idea float with class imbalance.

A related writing survey was found in [39]. The strategies that now exist can be characterized into two methodologies: chunk-based and online. In online methodology [40, 41], for every approaching information test, the prediction model is refreshed and the float identifier is utilized to screen information streams. Assuming that the idea float is recognized, the current model of expectation will be reset, and a new model for the new float idea will be constructed. For instance, consider undersampling based on online bagging and oversampling (OOB) [40], which utilizes a time-postponed plot for acquiring the new proportion of information stream awkwardness. It tends to be employed to join both oversampling and the underdamping in web-based packing. This can be used to connect a float identifier such as DDM-OCI [41].

DDM-OCI gives a warning when required by checking the minority class. It reviews and affirms the location by applying measurable data. However, approaches that depend on indicators suffer from false alarms, identification delays and missed discoveries. In opposite, piece-based methodologies [45, 43], information streams are cushioned for specific examples and accumulated. Then, at this point, the classifiers are assembled depending on the gathered lumps of information. Generally, these methodologies accept that universal idea float will happen in the information stream and will constantly update the current model. Normally, a community-oriented structure is utilized to produce one classifier for each approaching lump of information. The classifier loads are adapted to the new ideas [44, 45].

Simultaneously, the subject of awkwardness will be overwhelmed by gathering the examples of the minority class in past pieces. For instance, significance examining is utilized to gather tests of minority class structure past lumps in DFGW-IS [42]. In addition, the examples of larger part classes are bootstrapped to make a bagging-like collection. This methodology will work if the minority class has a fixed idea in an information stream. However, when the idea float climate is mind boggling, the p(y) float changes the irregularity proportion. In this way, if the minority class is made to shape a greater part class through extension, then the examples of the minority class, which are stored in the past, cannot be utilized to refine the current minority class. Furthermore, it is undeniably challenging to give a legitimate load for singular classifiers that are prepared in various time stamps while limiting the classifier's check not to increment limitlessly.

10.3.3 Concept Drift

When dealing with information streams that are not stationary, idea floats will turn into issues for machine learning models. When the fixed information creating measure is changed, the earlier model will become incorrect or totally pointless [46]. An illustration of idea float is the route framework, which needs to refresh the guide immediately when it is misdirecting the vehicles. Another model is an application site that is utilized for internet shopping, which needs to detect a radical change in the inclinations of clients [47]. The non-versatile model's presentation will fluctuate occasionally when the seasons change [48]. These models are utilized for anticipating the interest and supply of neighborhood heating energy.

The models allude to an obsolete data, which is the reason for their disappointment. It is extremely tedious and in some cases, it is difficult to physically check the floats in an environment. In this way, a technique that naturally distinguishes the floats and embraces them in the models is proposed in [49]. These strategies are sorted into passive approach and active approach [50]. Active methodologies will screen the presentation of models when the presentation is fixed, and it will actuate the variation interaction when it recognizes a float [51]. Here, the primary test is the way to make a floating marker address execution. A good drift indicator is one that is straightforward in strategy for computation and detection. Likewise, it should be exceptionally delicate to distinguish the float. To build the float markers, two strategies are available. One strategy depends on the genuine names in the informational indexes. The other strategy utilizes only unlabeled information. Recently, the comprehension of IoT information with idea floating has acquired importance in the internet learning field. This is because it occurs with a genuine application dependent on machine learning, where the circulation of information changes with time. For instance, attackers will consistently work on the nature of the attack to keep the hindering from the interruption location frameworks. In this manner, highlights and the ideas of assault/malignant bundles on the IoT climate change as often as possible. Thus, for an online algorithm, this interaction information spilling alongside the idea float should maintain a tradeoff between gaining from the past information gathered and embracing the new idea. This is known as the stability-plasticity dilemma. As indicated by the Bayes' hypothesis, idea float happens in four parts, which are as follows: 1) data distribution is a virtual drift where the conveyance of x is changed without altering the decision hyper plane; 2) class conditional probability (likelihood) is a virtual drift that regularly co-happens when preparing information float and testing information float; 3) posterior probability is a genuine float wherein the decision hyperplane will be moved with the progressions in conditional probability; and 4) class prior p(y) is a virtual drift where changes in the irregularity proportion are made dependent on the exchange among the greater part and minority class. The systems present in [52, 53] expect decision hyperplane to be affected only by posterior probability drift.

In any case, it is absurd to expect to change just one drift part by keeping another consistent. Consequently, the four parts of drift happen simultaneously and are associated with one another. These parts can occur in genuine streaming information at any time. One more commonplace issue in data mining is class imbalance. In class imbalance, all the classes do not have the same number of tests, for example, one class can have more examples than another class [52–54]. Straightforwardly applying standard machine learning techniques to these circumstances will overlook the examples in the minority class, as these minority tests influence the overall accuracy.

Class imbalance and concept drift build up mutual impacts. When the two issues happen at the same time, they aggravate one another. On the off chance that the information streams in the classes are imbalanced, it is undeniably challenging to recognize concept drift in the minority class, and furthermore, to take on the internet to figure them out. Actually, class imbalance status can be changed by concept drift, as an earlier class is one variable in the concept drifting climate. Thus far, several techniques have been proposed to deal with the issue of concept drift and class imbalance. Subsequently, the point of the exploration is to resolve this issue in making a proficient interruption location framework for the IoT environment [55–59].

10.4 Cybersecurity and IoT

The countless IoT devices that are used in everyday technologies, such as closed circuit cameras and smart home devices, can be hijacked by malware and used against servers. Hacking into web sites and stealing passwords continue to be hackers' main focus [59]. A default credential was used to exploit thousands of devices in recent assaults such as the Mirai Botnet. The technique of defending systems, networks and programmes from online threats is known as cybersecurity. In [60], they performed automated penetration testing on vulnerabilities in IoT devices. The authors in [61] implemented the productive edge computing group affiliation and update method for the IoT. In [52], the author provided some ideas for preventing social engineering in IoT.

10.5 Conclusion

The most challenging problem in the recent trends of IoT application is providing secure communication. In the IoT environment, numerous data-intensive applications have been emphasized; here, large amount of data are communicated over the internet or wirelessly and are prone to security issues. In this chapter, different security model methods are studied and problems are identified in designing effective authentication models employing machine learning techniques. Furthermore, a possible future research direction is building an effective security model that guarantees confidentiality and data integrity.

References

[1] Chen, Chao, Yu Wang, Jun Zhang, Yang Xiang, Wanlei Zhou, and Geyong Min. "Statistical features-based real-time detection of drifted twitter spam." *IEEE Transactions on Information Forensics and Security* 12, no. 4 (2016): 914–925.

[2] Cavalcante, Rodolfo C., Leandro L. Minku, and Adriano L.I. Oliveira. "Fedd: Feature extraction for explicit concept drift detection in time series." In *2016 International Joint Conference on Neural Networks (IJCNN)*, pp. 740–747. IEEE, 2016.

[3] Webb, Geoffrey I., Loong Kuan Lee, François Petitjean, and Bart Goethals. "Understanding concept drift." *arXiv preprint arXiv:1704.00362* (2017).

[4] Schmidt, Stephan, and P. Stephan Heyns. "Localised gear anomaly detection without historical data for reference density estimation." *Mechanical Systems and Signal Processing* 121 (2019): 615–635.

[5] Inuwa-Dutse, Isa, Mark Liptrott, and Ioannis Korkontzelos. "Detection of spam-posting accounts on Twitter." *Neurocomputing* 315 (2018): 496–511.

[6] Washha, Mahdi, Aziz Qaroush, Manel Mezghani, and Florence Sedes. "Unsupervised collective-based framework for dynamic retraining of supervised real-time spam tweets detection model." *Expert systems with Applications* 135 (2019): 129–152.

[7] Liu, Bo, Zeyang Ni, Junzhou Luo, Jiuxin Cao, Xudong Ni, Benyuan Liu, and Xinwen Fu. "Analysis of and defense against crowd-retweeting based spam in social networks." *World Wide Web* 22 (2019): 2953–2975.

[8] Alrubaian, Majed, Muhammad Al-Qurishi, Atif Alamri, Mabrook Al-Rakhami, Mohammad Mehedi Hassan, and Giancarlo Fortino. "Credibility in online social networks: A survey." *IEEE Access* 7 (2018): 2828–2855.

[9] Gama, João, Indrė Žliobaitė, Albert Bifet, Mykola Pechenizkiy, and Abdelhamid Bouchachia. "A survey on concept drift adaptation." *ACM Computing Surveys (CSUR)* 46, no. 4 (2014): 1–37.

[10] Gomes, Heitor Murilo, Jean Paul Barddal, Fabrício Enembreck, and Albert Bifet. "A survey on ensemble learning for data stream classification." *ACM Computing Surveys (CSUR)* 50, no. 2 (2017): 1–36.

[11] Branco, Paula, Luís Torgo, and Rita P. Ribeiro. "A survey of predictive modeling on imbalanced domains." *ACM Computing Surveys (CSUR)* 49, no. 2 (2016): 1–50.

[12] Wang, Shuo, Leandro L. Minku, and Xin Yao. "A systematic study of online class imbalance learning with concept drift." *IEEE Transactions on Neural Networks and Learning Systems* 29, no. 10 (2018): 4802–4821.

[13] Madakam, Somayya, Vihar Lake, Vihar Lake, and Vihar Lake. "Internet of Things (IoT): A literature review." *Journal of Computer and Communications* 3, no. 5 (2015): 164.

[14] Poirot, Valentin, Beshr Al Nahas, and Olaf Landsiedel. "Paxos made wireless: Consensus in the air." In *EWSN*, pp. 1–12, 2019.

[15] Chang, Jenghorng, and Fanpyn Liu. "A byzantine sensing network based on majority-consensus data aggregation mechanism." *Sensors* 21, no. 1 (2021): 248.

[16] Kolter, J. Zico, and Marcus A. Maloof. "Dynamic weighted majority: An ensemble method for drifting concepts." *The Journal of Machine Learning Research* 8 (2007): 2755–2790.

[17] Wang, Haixun, Wei Fan, Philip S. Yu, and Jiawei Han. "Mining concept-drifting data streams using ensemble classifiers." In *Proceedings of the Ninth ACM SIGKDD International Conference on Knowledge Discovery and Data Mining*, pp. 226–235, 2003.

[18] Antwi, Daniel K., Herna L. Viktor, and Nathalie Japkowicz. "The PerfSim algorithm for concept drift detection in imbalanced data." In *2012 IEEE 12th International Conference on Data Mining Workshops*, pp. 619–628. IEEE, 2012.

[19] Ho, Tin Kam, Jonathan J. Hull, and Sargur N. Srihari. "Decision combination in multiple classifier systems." *IEEE Transactions on Pattern Analysis and Machine Intelligence* 16, no. 1 (1994): 66–75.

[20] Rokach, Lior. "Ensemble-based classifiers." *Artificial Intelligence Review* 33 (2010): 1–39

[21] Brown, Gavin, Jeremy L. Wyatt, Peter Tino, and Yoshua Bengio. "Managing diversity in regression ensembles." *Journal of Machine Learning Research* 6, no. 9 (2005).

[22] Freund, Yoav, and Robert E. Schapire. "Experiments with a new boosting algorithm." In *ICML*, vol. 96, pp. 148–156, 1996.

[23] Wang, Shuo, Huanhuan Chen, and Xin Yao. "Negative correlation learning for classification ensembles." In *The 2010 International Joint Conference on Neural Networks (IJCNN)*, pp. 1–8. IEEE, 2010.

[24] Mehmood, Hassan, Panos Kostakos, Marta Cortes, Theodoros Anagnostopoulos, Susanna Pirttikangas, and Ekaterina Gilman. "Concept drift adaptation techniques in distributed environment for real-world data streams." *Smart Cities* 4, no. 1 (2021): 349–371

[25] Gonzalez, Carlos, Salim Mahamat Charfadine, Olivier Flauzac, and Florent Nolot. "SDN-based security framework for the IoT in distributed grid." In *2016 International Multidisciplinary Conference on Computer and Energy Science (SpliTech)*, pp. 1–5. IEEE, 2016.

[26] Boudi, Abderrahmane, Ivan Farris, Miloud Bagaa, and Tarik Taleb. "Assessing lightweight virtualization for security-as-a-service at the network edge." *IEICE Transactions on Communications* 102, no. 5 (2019): 970–977.

[27] Morabito, Roberto, Vittorio Cozzolino, Aaron Yi Ding, Nicklas Beijar, and Jorg Ott. "Consolidate IoT edge computing with lightweight virtualization." *IEEE Network* 32, no. 1 (2018): 102–111.

[28] Sultana, Nasrin, Naveen Chilamkurti, Wei Peng, and Rabei Alhadad. "Survey on SDN based network intrusion detection system using machine learning approaches." *Peer-to-Peer Networking and Applications* 12 (2019): 493–501.

[29] Zafar, Saniya, Sobia Jangsher, Ouns Bouachir, Moayad Aloqaily, and Jalel Ben Othman. "QoS enhancement with deep learning-based interference prediction in mobile IoT." *Computer Communications* 148 (2019): 86–97.

[30] Tseng, Lewis, Liwen Wong, Safa Otoum, Moayad Aloqaily, and Jalel Ben Othman. "Blockchain for managing heterogeneous internet of things: A perspective architecture." *IEEE Network* 34, no. 1 (2020): 16–23.

[31] Chang, Jenghorng, and Fanpyn Liu. "A byzantine sensing network based on majority-consensus data aggregation mechanism." *Sensors* 21, no. 1 (2021): 248

[32] Al Ridhawi, Ismaeel, Safa Otoum, Moayad Aloqaily, Yaser Jararweh, and Thar Baker. "Providing secure and reliable communication for next generation networks in smart cities." *Sustainable Cities and Society* 56 (2020): 102080.

[33] Wang, Xiaofei, Yiwen Han, Victor C.M. Leung, Dusit Niyato, Xueqiang Yan, and Xu Chen. "Convergence of edge computing and deep learning: A comprehensive survey." *IEEE Communications Surveys & Tutorials* 22, no. 2 (2020): 869–904.

[34] Sarker, Iqbal H. "Machine learning: Algorithms, real-world applications and research directions." *SN Computer Science* 2, no. 3 (2021): 160.

[35] Injadat, MohammadNoor, Abdallah Moubayed, and Abdallah Shami. "Detecting botnet attacks in IoT environments: An optimized machine learning approach." In *2020 32nd International Conference on Microelectronics (ICM)*, pp. 1–4. IEEE, 2020.

[36] Yang, Li, Abdallah Moubayed, Ismail Hamieh, and Abdallah Shami. "Tree-based intelligent intrusion detection system in internet of vehicles." In *2019 IEEE Global Communications Conference (GLOBECOM)*, pp. 1–6. IEEE, 2019.

[37] Cook, Andrew A., Göksel Mısırlı, and Zhong Fan. "Anomaly detection for IoT time-series data: A survey." *IEEE Internet of Things Journal* 7, no. 7 (2019): 6481–6494.

[38] Branco, Paula, Luís Torgo, and Rita P. Ribeiro. "A survey of predictive modeling on imbalanced domains." *ACM Computing Surveys (CSUR)* 49, no. 2 (2016): 1–50.

[39] Wang, Shuo, Leandro L. Minku, and Xin Yao. "A systematic study of online class imbalance learning with concept drift." *IEEE Transactions on Neural Networks and Learning Systems* 29, no. 10 (2018): 4802–4821.

[40] Wang, Shuo, Leandro L. Minku, and Xin Yao. "Resampling-based ensemble methods for online class imbalance learning." *IEEE Transactions on Knowledge and Data Engineering* 27, no. 5 (2014): 1356–1368.

[41] Yu, Shujian, and Zubin Abraham. "Concept drift detection with hierarchical hypothesis testing." In *Proceedings of the 2017 SIAM International Conference on Data Mining*, pp. 768–776. Society for Industrial and Applied Mathematics, 2017.

[42] Wu, Ke, Andrea Edwards, Wei Fan, Jing Gao, and Kun Zhang. "Classifying imbalanced data streams via dynamic feature group weighting with importance sampling." In *Proceedings of the 2014 SIAM International Conference on Data Mining*, pp. 722–730. Society for Industrial and Applied Mathematics, 2014.

[43] Lu, Yang, Yiu-ming Cheung, and Yuan Yan Tang. "Dynamic weighted majority for incremental learning of imbalanced data streams with concept drift." In *IJCAI*, pp. 2393–2399, 2017.

[44] Gomes, Heitor Murilo, Jean Paul Barddal, Fabrício Enembreck, and Albert Bifet. "A survey on ensemble learning for data stream classification." *ACM Computing Surveys (CSUR)* 50, no. 2 (2017): 1–36.

[45] Krawczyk, Bartosz, Leandro L. Minku, João Gama, Jerzy Stefanowski, and Michał Woźniak. "Ensemble learning for data stream analysis: A survey." *Information Fusion* 37 (2017): 132–156.

[46] Lughofer, Edwin, and Moamar Sayed-Mouchaweh. "Prologue: Predictive maintenance in dynamic systems." *Predictive Maintenance in Dynamic Systems: Advanced Methods, Decision Support Tools and Real-World Applications* (2019): 1–23.

[47] Bao, Yixin, Xiaoke Wang, Zhi Wang, Chuan Wu, and Francis C. M. Lau. "Online influence maximization in non-stationary social networks." In *2016 IEEE/ACM 24th International Symposium on Quality of Service (IWQoS)*, pp. 1–6. IEEE, 2016.

[48] Blanco, I. I. F., J. del Campo-Ávila, G. Ramos-Jiménez, R. M. Bueno, A. A. O. Díaz, and Y. C. Mota. "Online and non-parametric drift detection methods based on Hoeffding's bounds." *IEEE Transactions on Knowledge and Data Engineering* 27, no. 3 (2015): 810–823.

[49] Khamassi, Imen, Moamar Sayed-Mouchaweh, Moez Hammami, and Khaled Ghédira. "Discussion and review on evolving data streams and concept drift adapting." *Evolving Systems* 9 (2018): 1–23.

[50] Ditzler, Gregory, Manuel Roveri, Cesare Alippi, and Robi Polikar. "Learning in nonstationary environments: A survey." *IEEE Computational Intelligence Magazine* 10, no. 4 (2015): 12–25.

[51] Zhang, Jie, Zhi Wei, Zhenyu Yan, MengChu Zhou, and Abhishek Pani. "Online change-point detection in sparse time series with application to online advertising." *IEEE Transactions on Systems, Man, and Cybernetics: Systems* 49, no. 6 (2017): 1141–1151.

[52] Wang, Xuesong, Qi Kang, Jing An, and Mengchu Zhou. "Drifted Twitter spam classification using multiscale detection test on KL divergence." *IEEE Access* 7 (2019): 108384–108394.

[53] Alrubaian, Majed, Muhammad Al-Qurishi, Mabrook Al-Rakhami, Mohammad Mehedi Hassan, and Atif Alamri. "Reputation-based credibility analysis of Twitter social network users." *Concurrency and Computation: Practice and Experience* 29, no. 7 (2017): e3873.

[54] Lu, Yang, and Li Da Xu. "Internet of Things (IoT) cybersecurity research: A review of current research topics." *IEEE Internet of Things Journal* 6, no. 2 (2018): 2103–2115.

[55] Anthi, Eirini, Lowri Williams, Matilda Rhode, Pete Burnap, and Adam Wedgbury. "Adversarial attacks on machine learning cybersecurity defences in industrial control systems." *Journal of Information Security and Applications* 58 (2021): 102717.

[56] Zhou, Yuyang, Guang Cheng, Shanqing Jiang, and Mian Dai. "Building an efficient intrusion detection system based on feature selection and ensemble classifier." *Computer Networks* 174 (2020): 107247.

[57] Yang, Li, and Abdallah Shami. "A lightweight concept drift detection and adaptation framework for IoT data streams." *IEEE Internet of Things Magazine* 4, no. 2 (2021): 96–101.

[58] Abdul Wahab, Omar. "Sustaining the effectiveness of IoT-driven intrusion detection over time: Defeating concept and data drifts." Authorea Preprints (2023).

[59] Lu, Yang, and Li Da Xu. "Internet of Things (IoT) cybersecurity research: A review of current research topics." *IEEE Internet of Things Journal* 6, no. 2 (2018): 2103–2115.

[60] Færøy, Fartein Lemjan, Muhammad Mudassar Yamin, Ankur Shukla, and Basel Katt. "Automatic verification and execution of cyber attack on IoT devices." *Sensors* 23, no. 2 (2023): 733.

[61] Tan, Haowen. "An efficient IoT group association and data sharing mechanism in edge computing paradigm." *Cyber Security and Applications* 1 (2023): 100003.

11

A Study on Image Detection and Extraction to Estimate Distracted Drivers Using CNN and IoT

VENUGEETHA Y, HARSHITHA H,
HARSHITHA K AND KARAN KUMAR

11.1 Introduction

Up to 20% of serious accidents on motorways and boring roads in Great Britain are caused by driver weariness, which is a major factor in traffic accidents. According to the government's Road Safety Strategy, Tomorrow's Roads: safer for everyone, driver weariness is one of the key aspects of driver behaviour that must be addressed if the target of reducing the number of people killed and seriously injured in traffic accidents by 40% during 2023 is to be realised. The most accurate technique to gauge driver weariness is by observing the driver's level of drowsiness. The creation of a system for detecting sleepiness is the goal of this project. This technology works by analysing the driver's eye movement and notifying them when they are asleep by sounding the buzzer. A non-intrusive real-time monitoring system for eye detection has been put into place with this technology. The technology can determine whether the eyes are open or closed while being monitored. A signal to warn the driver is sent when the eyelids are detected as closed for an extended time. According to research by the AAA foundation for traffic safety, distracted driving causes six out of ten car accidents. Overall, 50 million road accidents and 1.35 billion fatalities worldwide are attributed to distracted driving, according to the World Health Organization (WHO). Nearly as many people are

DOI: 10.1201/9781003406716-11

killed by hepatitis and HIV as are killed in traffic accidents. If the driver really paid attention when driving, then the number of accidents could be cut in half by four. About 2,895 persons were killed in distracted driving incidents in the United States in 2019, according to the National Highway Transportation and Safety Administration, which was 8.7% of all fatalities in traffic accidents during the year. Many scientists have concentrated on studying the issues of traffic accidents and their solutions and definitions of distracted driving. Distracted driving is defined as driving behaviour that causes the driver to lose their concentration, such as using a cell phone, eating, drinking, or turning on the radio. According to another definition, distracted driving includes anything that prevents the driver from paying attention to the road. Martin et al. classify distraction into three categories: cognitive, manual, and visual. With the help of sensors, drivers' hand or foot movements on the gas and brake pedals are monitored during manual distraction. Cognitive tests predict the psycho-physiological state of drivers, such as their heart rate, blood pressure, and body temperature. According to Alexey Kashevnik, machine learning is concerned with the creation and application of models or algorithms that enable a system to research the required knowledge based on previous knowledge or datasets. Machine learning, which has drawn the attention of numerous researchers as an emerging option, can now be successfully used to monitor and analyse distracted driving behaviours, address issues,

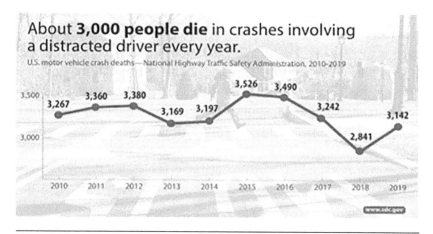

Figure 11.1   Statistics of distracted driving deaths within 10 years in the US.

The Figure 11.1 shows the statistics of distracted driving deaths within 10 years in the US.

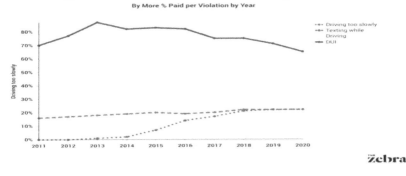

Figure 11.2 Average premium by distracted driving violations.

and identify an efficient solution. To address the issue of inattentive driving, the time to collision (TTC) standard has been implemented. Having automated longitudinal and lateral control, the driving system relieves the driver of some of their driving duties and provides emergency braking and turning. TTC is an important criterion for calculating the relative collision time based on the vehicle and its surroundings while ignoring the driver's behaviour.

In referring to numerous studies on distracted driving, the focus is on identifying the driver's actions and calculating alcohol consumption by using sensors and alerting the driver with a sound through the use of a convolutional neural network (CNN). The objective is to increase driver safety without impeding traffic as shown in Figure 11.2. People who are sleep-deprived or have sleep disturbances feel sleepy when they should be alert. Even one night of sleep deprivation can result in significant short-term fatigue, and repeated sleep interruptions can result in chronic drowsiness. The only way to successfully address exhaustion is to sleep. When sleep is less than four hours per night, performance diminishes. Losing one or two hours of sleep per night might have a cumulative effect that may lead to persistent sleepiness. Numerous factors, some of which are out of an individual's control but some are personal choices, can result in sleep loss and disruption, including long work hours and shift work, family responsibilities, social activities, illness including sleep disorders, medication, and stress. Without being intrusive, the goal is to increase driver safety. Using a webcam, visual cues were collected from eye blink rates, which normally indicate a person's level of attention. To determine the driver's state of weariness, these were systematically combined and extracted in real-time. The technology can monitor the driver's eyes to identify brief naps of three to four seconds. This approach's system operates at 8–15 frames per second. OpenCV was used to implement the application in a PC environment with a single camera view. This method was intended to prevent accidents on the road by detecting the driver's tiredness. The PC With OpenCV is a component of the suggested system. Facial recognition is mostly used to protect the sleepy driver. Due to the growing population, driving has become necessary, which has caused an alarming rise in accidents that have resulted in significant loss of life and property. The purpose of this initiative is to track down accidents and report their locations. Through SMS, the vehicle's position is communicated by using global system for mobile applications (GSM) technology in the form of latitude and longitude coordinates. The global positioning system (GPS), a navigational system utilising a network of satellites orbiting the earth, is used to retrieve the location.

11.2 Motivations

One of the major contributing factors to automobile accidents in recent years is driver error. The condition of the driver, such as drowsiness, can be directly estimated as a sign of driver weakness. Therefore, it is crucial to detect driver drowsiness to protect people and property.

- The goal of this endeavour is to provide a framework for to identify sleepiness. This framework continuously gathers images, analyses them to identify the eye, mouth, and head node rates in accordance with calculated parameters, and issues warnings as necessary.
- Several OpenCV libraries are used to implement this framework, including Haar-cascade.

11.3 Literature Survey or Related Work

A study by the National Highway and Traffic Safety Administration found that sleep deprivation was likely to be a factor in 56,000 car accidents that occurred in the United States in 1996. A 2007 survey found that fatigue was the main factor in 18% of accidents. In Britain, fatigue had a role in up to 20% of serious traffic incidents. Similarly, the Road and Traffic Authority found that weariness played a role in 20% of incidents on the road in 2007. Accidents caused by drowsy driving were controlled while the vehicle was out of control. The alcohol detector in a car can also be used to catch drunk drivers. Here, the expression "using the driver's eye blink" is used to denote driver fatigue.

These incidents happened because the driver was drowsy and could not control the car when he or she awoke. The driver's infrared sensor, which was attached to the frame of his glasses, used the pace at which his eyes closed to detect sleepiness. If the driver is drowsy, then the system will sound a buzzer, reduce the vehicle's speed, and use the obstacle sensor to detect any nearby vehicles to prevent collisions. If there are no nearby vehicles on the left side of the road, then the vehicle will automatically veer to the left side of the road and park with advance warning. Numerous academics have been working on these devices in recent years, although few methods have been published.

One of the methods suggested is to watch the car's motion to detect the driver's fatigue. This method, however, has limitations because the results depend on the type of vehicle and the condition of the road. Another approach involves processing the driver's electrocardiogram (ECG) signals. This approach has limitations as long as the ECG probes are attached to the driver's body. This is sure to annoy the driver. Few studies have tried to gauge the driver's level of fatigue by counting the number of times that their eyes blink. Many studies have developed approaches based on a combination of projection and the geometry characteristics of the iris and pupil for the successful identification of the eye blink rate.

[1] In order to recognise driver conduct, provide them with the appropriate alerting system, and lessen traffic illusions, the lightweight CNN architecture is deployed. With the benefits of typical convolutional layers, depth-wise separable convolution layers, average pooling layers, and feature maps that are derived by suggested adaptive connections, the network combines feature extraction and classifier modules. The global average pooling and softmax layer in the classifier module aid in determining the probability of each class. This method has limitations because it was created with a two-stage driver behaviour warning mechanism.

[2] To transfer learning to machines, four architectures, including CNN, VGG-16, ResNet50, and MobileNetV2, have been used. The system is trained by using a considerable number of photos from commonly accessible datasets that show various distracted driving postures, and the results are examined using a variety of factors to successfully validate it. However, it is ineffective when used in real time.

[3] The cutting-edge framework combines driver perception, vehicle condition, and behavioural identification to deliver pertinent notifications. Right decision and Error! Hyperlink reference not valid. compassionate and efficient warnings, various time-to-collision criteria are explored along with the behaviour. However, the 3D objects were not recognised, leading to an error scenario that is not more thorough and appropriate than real-world driving situations.

[4] Convolutional sleepiness detection methods based on driving performance and behaviour may not be available where automated driving system distractions are concentrated, so in this case, methods based on physiological measurements such as heart rate variability (HRV) become an effective solution. As a result, automated driving could potentially impair HRV when there is less work to be performed. For this reason, it is important to investigate the impact of automated driving by using real-world experimental datasets on HRV and sleepiness.

[5] The effective Det model extracts the zone of interest of the body parts and the distracting features from the photos so that the predictions can be made stronger and a legitimate outcome can be achieved. The most effective approach for identifying a distracted driver is Efficient Det D3, as seen by its MAP of a 99% learning rate of 3.50 epouch, which shows that it can successfully assist drivers in upholding and establishing safe driving practises.

[6] The information from physiological sensors, including breathing, heart rate, and optical sensors, and facial action units and emotional activation is used to detect distractions. Machine learning techniques may suffer from issues including label jitter, scenario overfitting, and poor generalisation performance.

[7] To address this issue, triplets are created by creating positive and negative samples of each input. The positive samples are produced by applying structure-aware illumination to the human body region of each input. For the networks to perform numerous jobs to investigate

the global information, triplets are used in the training process. However, it failed to evaluate the model's generalizability and obtain data from the researchers themselves.

[8] The main characteristic of this proposed work is using deep learning-based segmentation to extract movements of the driver's body parts from the onboard camera. The machine is trained with 10 activities, of which 1 is normal driving and 9 instances are distracted driving. According to the experimental findings, the segmentation module considerably enhances classification performance. Building an embedded system to deploy a driving warning system based on suggested distraction solutions can further improve it.

[9] By using trigger words for speech to text classification models, the driver's movements and head posture are monitored by using deep learning ideas, and the distraction is removed by voice commands. However, this is unrelated to the identification of retinal anomalies such as an open sleeping eye. The results from real-time testing indicate that the driver's behaviour classification and command have a response time of 0.080 seconds.

[10] The three basic types of driver distraction are physical, visual, and cognitive. This framework depicts the entire detection process, including the usage of sensors, measurements, computation of data, computation of events, inference of behaviour, and type of distraction. Additionally, it contains expanded developmental strategies for automatic driving.

11.4 Existing System

While driving, a lot of attentional impairment impacts drivers' reactions. Driving while fatigued puts the motorist at a substantially higher crash risk than when they are awake, making it one of the main factors in traffic accidents. Therefore, using an assistive system that checks a driver's state of alertness and warns them if they are getting sleepy can be very helpful in preventing accidents. The current system describes a method for detecting driver tiredness based on head movement and a yawning measurement. This system entails a number of processes such as the in-flight detection and tracking of the driver's face, the in-flight detection and tracking of the mouth contour, the in-flight detection of yawning based on measuring both the rate and the quantity of changes in the mouth contour area, and head movement monitoring.

In the past, MATLAB was used to develop sensor-operated equipment including eyewear for sleep detection, and drivers' conditions were manually assessed before each trip. Additionally, the driver's tiredness was not disclosed. Once lost, life cannot be recovered. There is a chance to partially prevent these types of accidents because of advanced technologies. Because of the higher speeds involved and the fact that the driver cannot take any action to prevent the disaster, not even to press the brakes, sleep-related accidents are more severe. An accident can occur if the driver falls asleep, veers off the road, or collides with another car. When street lights are out, especially on highways, accidents can also occur. Therefore, when a car approaches from the other side, the driver's failure to adjust the light's brightness plays a significant role in accidents.

Accidents result from the opposing driver missing judgement calls. Accidents can also be caused by someone abruptly entering the car from either side, which causes the driver to make a mistake and crash. When the driver is beyond the limit, the vehicle will automatically beep and transmit the owner information about the specific location of the vehicle at the same time.

Disadvantages

- As wearable devices were externally connected to the driver, this caused a distraction while driving.
- The driver's consumption of alcohol during the trip went undetected. Image processing was not exact because MATLAB was used.

11.5 Methodology and Objectives

We performed this work by dividing the entire project into three modules.

1. Device Initialisation Module
2. Drowsiness Detection Module
3. Alert Module

11.5.1 Device Initialisation Module

In this module, we initialise the webcam to detect the driver's drowsiness. A buzzer or beeper is the signaling device used to alert the driver.

11.5.2 Drowsiness Detection Module

OpenCV is employed in this module to acquire webcam photos and feed them into an intelligence model that categorises distracting behaviours. This uses a camera's image as input. The classifier classifies the things in the image and determines whether the driver is distracted and whether any risky intentions are present.

11.5.3 Alert Module

The Alert Module is used to alert not only the driver but also concerned people. This module will also send a request to a nearby police station if the driver needs emergency help.

11.6 Proposed System

The whole system is built upon PC, QT as an editor and the OpenCV image processing library. The quickest sleepiness detection and data processing are the main priorities. The system uses a Logitech camera, which has no external connections, to determine whether the eyes are open or closed in real time. It is exceedingly unlikely that the system will malfunction. Through the IoT, notification services are offered where eyeball detection is used to warn drivers. Although it can be applied to any object, its primary purpose is for predicting facial landmarks and form. The proposed design uses a camera to continuously record the driver's face to identify levels of hypo-vigilance. The motion of closing one's eyes is then recorded to indicate sleepiness as shown in Figure 11.3. The sign

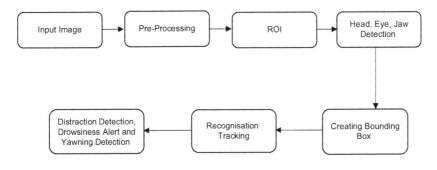

Figure 11.3 System architecture.

of weariness is an increase in the number of eye blinks compared to usual. Microsleep, which lasts for 3 to 4 seconds, is a reliable sign of exhaustion. OpenCV was used to implement the closed eye motion. A buzzer notifies the driver of their level of drowsiness. We have put out a technology that can recognise distracted driving and mobile phone use, among other driving behaviours. The camera identifies the distractions and warns the motorist to pay attention to the road.

We utilise the following modules to generally implement this system.

- Capturing Video: With the help of this module, we use the built-in OPENCV function named VideoCapture to connect the operation to a webcam.
- Frame Extraction: Using this module, we can capture webcam frames and the value of each image frame-by-frame and convert it to a two-dimensional array.
- Face Recognition and Facial Landmarking Detection: We identify faces in photos by using the SVM method, and we also extract facial expressions from the frames.
- Detection: We identify the mouth and eyes on the face with this module.
- Calculate: In this module, we use the Euclidean Distance formula to determine how far a particular face is from an eye blink or yawn. If the eyes blink for 20 consecutive frames and the mouth opens when yawning, then the driver will be warned.

11.7 Face Detection Using OpenCV

This initially appears difficult, but it is very simple as shown in Figure 11.4.

Step 1: Let us start with an image and consider the prerequisites. Finally, to give us the features of the face, we must build a waterfall classifier.

Step 2: In this stage, OpenCV is used to read the image and the features train. As a result, the main data points at this stage are NumPy arrays. Finding the row and column values of the face NumPy N-dimensional array is all that is required. The array in question has a face cell value.

Step 3: Displaying the picture with the blocky face box is the last action.

For eye tracking and monitoring, there are numerous different algorithms and techniques. Most of them are connected in some way to characteristics of the eye (usually eye reflections) in a video image of the driver. The initial goal of this study was to locate the eyes on a face by using the retinal reflection and to determine when the eyes are closed by using the absence of this reflection. Calculating the eye closure period can be made easier by using this algorithm on a series of video frames. Drivers who are fatigued tend to close their eyes for longer periods of time than usual. Additionally, even a very slight extension of time could lead to a serious accident. Therefore, the moment that we notice a closed eye, we alert the driver. Along with eye and head movements, the detection analysis of a person's eyes and face may also be able to indicate how sleepy they are. Making a real-time application with computer vision is a highly difficult endeavour that requires a robust processing machine. Computer vision is created with open source software called OpenCV. C, C++, Python, and Java programming language extensions all support OpenCV. The PC can be overclocked to a maximum of 1500 MHz with OpenCV and Raspbian, a lightweight Linux operating system. OpenCV and other programming tools are abundant in the Raspbian OS. When a driver is found to be tired or fatigued, a message is delivered via Twilio, and a buzzer is activated. The Haar Feature-based Cascade Classifier technique uses machine learning to create a cascade function from a large number of positive and negative images. This positive image is then used to update the region of interest (ROI) by identifying the face and eye regions. A detector and a trainer are both included in OpenCV. OpenCV is used to build a user-defined item classifier. The created object classifier is saved as an extension.xml file to be used later in the programming process. Additionally, in this study, we use deft operator edge detection to identify the precise coordinates of the region surrounding the eyes.

This study proposes a deep learning-based cell phone use behaviour detection system that can identify driving behaviours and issue an early warning quickly and in real time, eliminating this possible risk. To enhance the integrity of picture capture and to guarantee the detection accuracy of target recognition for the scheme design, a multi-angle arrangement of cameras is used. By maximising the size and quantity of the convolution kernels, two independent CNNs are trained, and they can then accurately identify hands and cell phones in real time. Then,

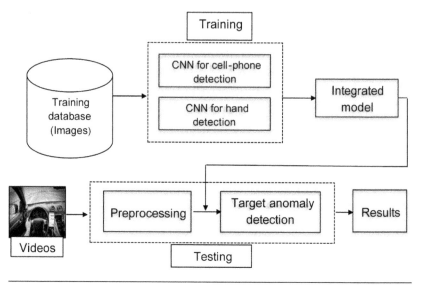

Figure 11.4 Cell phone detection.

based on the distance of the interaction between the cell phone and the hand, trained CNNs deliver the necessary early warning or forensics. The outcomes of numerous tests show that the suggested technique can accurately detect cell phone use while driving in real time.

11.8 Search Strategy

A software requirement is a detailed explanation of the behaviour of the system that is being developed, often known as a requirement specification. The SRS includes both functional and non-functional criteria in addition to a description of how the software works. Software requirements describe a branch of software engineering that focuses on gathering, analysing, specifying, and validating software needs.

software specifications
OPERATING SYSTEM: Raspbian OS
LIBRARY: OpenCV Library, Wiring PI library
EDITOR: QT
LANGUAGES: C and Python
WINDOW SERVER: Xming with Putty

OpenCV MODULES

cv: Primary OpenCV operations

cvaux is an acronym for auxiliary (experimental) OpenCV functions.

cxcore provides support for data structures and linear algebra.

highgui: GUI capabilities

Working with video capture in OpenCV

OpenCV allows for the capture of images from an AVI video file or a camera.

starting the camera's capture:

Capture from video device #0 with CvCapture* capture = cvCaptureFromCAM(0).

CvCapture* capture = cvCaptureFromAVI("infile.avi") is used to start the capture from a file.

Taking a picture: 0 for IplImage* img; If (!cvGrabFrame(capture)) is true, then a frame will be captured. Could not grab a frame, n, 7, printf; exit(0); // recover the captured frame; img=cvRetrieveFrame(capture);

Grab an image from each camera before grabbing images from many cameras at once. After the grabbing is finished, retrieve the pictures that were taken by releasing the source of the capture: cvReleaseCapture(&capture);

11.9 Conclusion

Based on real-time fatigue detection, a driver alertness detection system was suggested. The suggested method accurately picks up on tiredness and eye blinks. Image processing algorithms are used to determine the eyes' location. Drowsiness can be detected without any inconvenience or disturbance to the driver by using image processing. A face recognition algorithm is also used. It was discovered that this technique produces a reliable measurement of the blink rate. The suggested algorithm can detect the eyeballs at medium and high illumination, regardless of gender or age; nevertheless, for the best detection, the camera has to be placed as close to the subject as feasible. A night vision camera is put in place to prevent the consequences of poor detection caused by insufficient light so that better results, unaffected by a lack of brightness, are produced. By using a buzzer indicator, the motorist is signaled, ensuring safe driving.

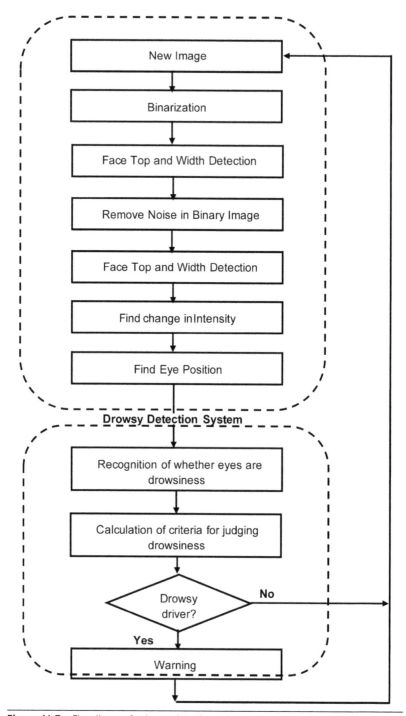

Figure 11.5 Flow diagram for drowsy detection system.

The Figure 11.5 shows the flow diagram for drowsy detection system.

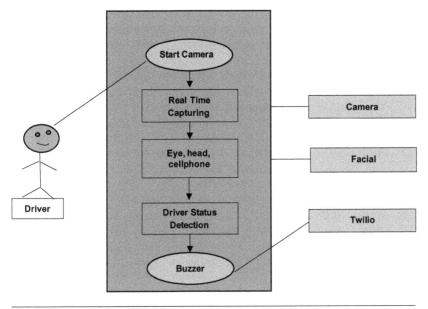

Figure 11.6 Chart for driver distraction detection.

The Figure 11.6 shows the graphical representation of chart for driver distraction detection.

11.10 Future Enhancement

The hybrid system solution makes it possible to detect cell phones more successfully because of machine learning for movement detection and additional features from optical flow, such as horizontal movement, the area of connected components, and the dimensions of the region movement seen, and the improvement in image resolution and processing frames per second.

References

[1] Duy-Linh Nguyen, Muhamad Dwisnanto Pwtro, and Kang-Hyun Jo, "Driver Behaviors Recognizer Based on Light Weight Convolutional Neural Network Architecture and Attention Mechanism", *IEEE Access* 10: 71019–71029, Date of publication 29 June 2022. DOI: 10.1109/ ACCESS.2022.3187185

[2] Md. Uzzol Hossain, Md. Ataur Rahman, Md. Monowarul Islam, Arnisha Akhter, Md. Ashraf Uddin, and Bikash Kumar Paul, "Automatic Driver Distraction Detection Using Deep Convolutional Neural Networks", published by Elsevier Ltd, in 2022.

[3] Peng-Wei Lin and CHIh-Ming HSU, "Innovative Framework for Distracted Driving Alert System Based on Deep Learning", *IEEE Access* 10: 77523–77536, Date of publication 27 June 2022. DOI: 10.1109/ ACCESS.2022.3186674

[4] Ke Lu, Johan Karlsson, Anna Sjors Dahlman, Bengt Arne Sjuquist, and Stefan Candefjord, "Detecting Driver Sleepiness Using Consumer Wearable Devices in Manual & Partial Automated Real-Road Driving", *IEEE Transactions on Intelligent Transportation Systems* 99: 1–10, Date of publication December 2021. DOI: 10.1109/TITS.2021.3127944

[5] Faiqa Sajid, Abdul Rehman Javed, Asma Basharat, Natalia Kryvinska, Adil Afzal, and Muhammod Rizwan, "An Efficient Deep Learning Framework for Distracted Driver Detection", *IEEE Access* 9: 169270– 169280, Date of publication 2021. DOI: 10.1109/ACCESS.2021.3138137

[6] Martin Gjoreski, Matja Z. Gams, Mitja Lustrek, Pelin Genc, Jens-U. Garbas, and Teena Hassan, "Machine Learning and End-to-End Deep Learning for Monitoring Driver Distractions from Physiological & Visual Signals", Date of publication 9 April 2020. DOI: 10.1109/ ACCESS.2020.2986810

[7] Dichao Liu, Tostihiko Yamasaki, Yu Wang, Kenji Mase, and Jein Kato, "TML: A Triple Wise Multi Task Learning Framework for Distracted Driver Recognition", *IEEE Access* 99: 1–1, Date of publication 2021. DOI: 10.1109/ACCESS.2021.3109815

[8] Amal Ezzouhri, Zakaria Charouh, Mounir GhoGho, and Zouhair Guennoun, "Robust Deep Learning-Based Driver Distraction Detection & Classification", *IEEE Access*, 9: 168080–168092, Date of published 2021. DOI: 10.1109/ACCESS.2021.3133797

[9] Abdul Rahman Abououf, Ibrahim Sobh, Mahammed Nasser, Omar Alsaqa, Omar Elezaby, and John F.W. Zaki, "Multimodel System for Driver Distraction Detection & Elimination", *IEEE Access*, 10: 72458–72469, Date of publication 5 July 2022. DOI: 10.1109/ACCESS.2022.3188715

[10] Alexey Kashevnik, Roman Shchedrin, Christian Kaiser, and Alexander Stocker, "Driver Distraction Detection Methods: A Literature Review & Framework", *IEEE Access*, 9: 60063–60076, Date of published 2021. DOI: 10.1109/ACCESS.2021.3073599

12

SOCIAL ENGINEERING

Cyberattacks, Countermeasures, and Conclusions

DR. KAMALAKSHI NAGANNA
AND CHETHANA R KARIGER

12.1 Introduction

With the increasing prevalence of digitalization, social engineering has emerged as a major cybersecurity threat for organizations. This practice involves exploiting human vulnerabilities by manipulating individuals to achieve malicious goals. Attackers use their victim's flaws as a basis for the attack and lure them into downloading harmful files or applications, clicking on malicious links, or revealing personal and sensitive information. Social engineering is a manipulation technique aimed at retrieving personal data, revealing sensitive information, and causing harm to individuals or organizations. Digitalization is a critical component of modern business operations, but it also presents complex challenges in terms of understanding and securing the technology infrastructure. This includes a combination of tools and technologies that may be stored on-premise, on the cloud, or a mix of both. Organizations must take proactive measures to protect their information and operations in the cyber world, including educating employees on the risks of social engineering, implementing strict security protocols, and employing advanced cybersecurity technologies. Regularly reviewing and updating security policies is also essential to stay ahead of emerging threats. With a multi-faceted approach and the right tools, organizations can protect their data and operations from social engineering attacks and prevent potentially disastrous data breaches that could harm both the organization and its customers [1–24].

The incidence of cybercrimes has increased due to the vulnerability of information systems, which makes it challenging to secure

DOI: 10.1201/9781003406716-12

information in the digital age. Attackers use various methods, including intrusion into computer networks and dissemination of computer viruses, to exploit the protected information of targeted organizations. These attacks involve analyzing the network infrastructure of the organization, identifying vulnerabilities, and attempting to gain unauthorized access to organizational resources. The risk of network-based attacks is significant, as they can further lead to the harm or embezzlement of crucial information. To mitigate this risk, organizations need to adopt a comprehensive approach to cybersecurity that includes regular security assessments, incident response protocols, and continuous monitoring of network activity to detect and respond to threats. The following Table 12.1 highlights several real-life incidents of social engineering attacks [26–40].

These incidents highlight the real-world risks posed by social engineering attacks, and the need for entities and establishments to be cautious and shield themselves after these threats. Figure 12.1 highlights the various real time attacks.

The social engineering conceptual model explains the mechanics of social engineering attacks. The model includes three main elements: effect mechanism, human vulnerability, and attack method. These elements work together to provide a comprehensive perspective

Table 12.1   Real-Life Incidents of Social Engineering Attacks

SLNO	NAME OF THE INCIDENT	YEAR	THEFT TYPE	LOSS
1	Target Data Breach	2013	Credit and debit card information	$40 Million
2	CEO Fraud	2016	Impersonating a high- level executive to trick an employee into making a wire transfer or divulging sensitive information	$100 Million
3	Social Media Hacks	2020	Twitter suffered a major security breach where attackers were able to compromise the accounts of high- profile individuals and companies, including Barack Obama and Elon Musk	
4	Watering Hole Attacks	2019	Asian mobile app store	
5	USB drops	2011		

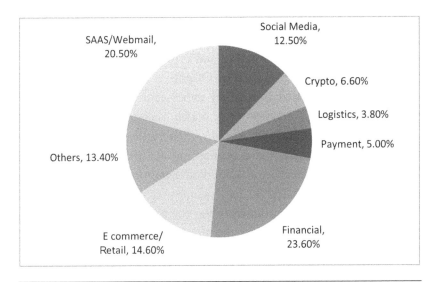

Figure 12.1 Most targeted industries.

Software as a service (SAAS) allows users to connect to and use cloud-based apps over the Internet.

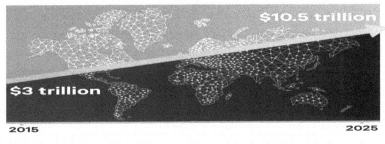

Figure 12.2 Growth of cybercrime costs.

It is also expected that in 2025, the growth of cybercrime may reach $10.5 trillion as depicted in Figure 12.2.

for understanding social engineering attacks. Various social engineering attack scenarios have been demonstrated mainly to showcase the implementation of these techniques, weaknesses, and methods of attack, providing insight into how social engineering attacks operate and succeed, as discussed by Zuoguang wang et al. [1]. Social engineering attacks are performed by using the Social Engineer Toolkit (SET), a pre-installed tool in Kali Linux, specifically, a Debian Linux-based operating system used for penetration testing. Kali Linux provides a range of tools designed to analyze and exploit system vulnerabilities, and it is maintained and funded by Offensive Security, a well-known open-source project that is used by cybersecurity professionals and enthusiasts. The SET framework is widely recognized as a standard tool for advanced technological attacks in social engineering settings, according to Breda F [2]. Social networking sites (SNSs) are a common target for social engineering attacks. The dynamics of social engineering in SNSs are impacted by four primary elements: the social networking service (the environment), the social engineer (the attacker), the strategy and tactics utilized (the attack method), and the SNS user (the target), as discussed by Abdullah Algarni [3].

To facilitate the detection of social engineering attacks, the Social Engineering Attack Detection Model (SEADM) employs a decision tree approach that divides the whole detection process into smaller, more manageable stages. In this way, SEADM provides decision-making guidelines that can help identify and prevent social engineering attacks. SEADM includes four stages, specifically, pre-contact, contact, information gathering, and exploitation, and each stage identifies specific indicators that can help detect social engineering attacks. For instance, in the pre-contact stage, unsolicited emails or phone calls can be used to recognize potential attackers, while in the contact stage, requests for sensitive information or unusual behavior can indicate a social engineering attack. The common social engineering tactics used by attackers are phishing, pretexting, baiting, and water holing. Organizations can employ SEADM to improve their information security defenses, as suggested by Monique Bezuidenhout [4]. A knowledge graph was utilized to gather threat data and new sets of training and testing data were created by varying the combinations of the features when investigating the effectiveness of the machine learning techniques in detecting social engineering attacks. Then, 9 machine learning models were created, and 27 threat detectors/classifiers were trained and tested. The results showed that machine learning techniques can effectively detect general social engineering attacks and that they complement graph-based approaches. The decision tree model performed the best, achieving an average precision, recall, and F1-score of 89.6%, 85.5%, and 87.6%, respectively. Other models such as MLP, SVM, AdaBoost, the Nearest Centroid, and integrated voting models also showed promising results, according to Zuoguang wang [5]. The shift of daily activities to online platforms due to the COVID-19 pandemic has resulted in an increase in the number of people online. However, the lack of cybersecurity education has left users vulnerable to various forms of online attacks. COVID-19-themed attacks, with phishing emails that had subject lines such as —2020 Corona virus Updates‖, —2019-n Cov: New confirmed cases in your City‖ were a common tactic used by attackers. These emails typically used subject lines that appealed to human curiosity and fear. These emails also had attachments that installed malware or directed users to fraudulent websites to obtain their login information, as explained by Venkatesha Sushruth in 2021 [6].

12.2 Case Study on Social Engg Attack—IBM Report [25]

12.2.1 The Cost of Average Social Engineering-Related Breach

As per the 2022 report released by IBM, the average price tag of a data breach with social engineering as the primary outbreak vector was $4 million. This is quite more than, for example, the Federal Emergency Management Agency (FEMA) funded the Massachusetts Department of Transportation for Winter Storm Kenan's road snow plowing and sanding expenses in January 2022 [25].

12.2.1.1. Data Breach Identification Time   The 2022 report also showed that data breaches with social engineering as the initial attack vector took nearly 9 months for the companies to

- Identify the breaches (201 mean time days), and
- Contain them (69 mean time days) [25] (Figure 12.3).

This means that social engineering-based breaches performed slightly better than the average data breach in 2022, which took 207 and 70 mean time days to identify and contain, respectively [25].

12.2.1.2 Data Breach Involvement: the Human Element (82%)   The company's expressed in their report that among the five causes of the investigated data breaches, four were due to human-related factors. This reflects the consideration that social engineering is the reprehensible

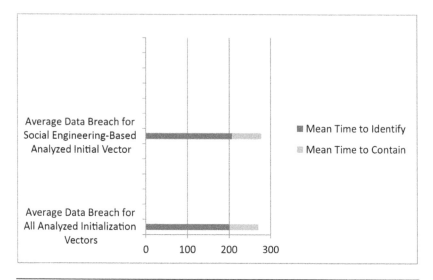

Figure 12.3 The difference between the time required to identify and the time required to contain social engineering-based data breaches.

knack of utilizing psychological diplomacies to dupe human employees. Cybercriminals can use social media and other publicly available information sources to learn about you and your company. After the collection of all of these data, they can couple this acquaintance with social engineering strategies to improve their position into your business [25].

12.2.1.3 Cyberattacks Are Targeting Organization Employees Rather than Technology (90%) Out of the 10 cyberattacks reported, 9 were in contradiction of organizations target employees, despite IT and cybersecurity fortifications. The reason behind this, as determined by Arctic Wolf Networks in their report [5], is because an organization's workforce is always a less risk-averse, which results in great benefits for attackers. Systems can be patched, and defenselessness can be diminished. Nevertheless, cybercriminals usually aim at the feeblest associations in the chain, as this may lead to major disbursement with very minimal effort. Cybercriminals are very aware that organization employees are human and that humans are assured to commit mistakes. Cybercriminals bank on these circumstances. Because of this, organizations should aim to empower and increase employees' cyber awareness education programmes via regular offline and online training [25].

12.2.1.4 Data Disclosure Issues (47%)   As per the report by Verizon, of the 2,249 reported incidents they analyzed involving social engineering, 1,063 resulted has been revealed. This signifies that only half of the incidents were explored, including personally identifiable information comprising 24% and login credentials comprising 63%. This signifies that nearly 2 out of 3 social engineering attacks target employees while they dispense login credentials, which occurs through various means such as pretending to be a member organization's IT team or by directing an employee to a phishing email that redirects to a website with a forged login portal. When the actual genuine credentials are entered, the attacker steals them [25].

As per the 2022 report, based on the complaints received in 2022, phishing, personal data breaches, and non-payment/non-delivery were the greatest number of cases, and the details are depicted in Table 12.2.

Illinois, for example, was in the 5th position for the highest number of victims at 14,786 and in the 7th position for the highest victim dollar loss at $266.7 million as shown in Table 12.3.

12.3 Methodology and Detection

12.3.1 Social Engineering Toolkit for SMS Spoofing

SET is a system that provides a menu-driven interface to tailor an attack to the targeted individual or organization. The menu system has various options, including social engineering attacks and

Table 12.2   Details of Social Engineering-Related Security Incidents [25]

SLNO	DETAILS	AMOUNT
1	Phishing	$52 million
2	Investment Fraud	$3.3 billion
3	Cryptocurrency Investment Fraud	$2.57 billion

Table 12.3   Details of the Illinois Social Engineering Attack in 2022 [25]

SLNO	COMPANY	AMOUNT
1	BEC	$83,883,493
2	Investment Fraud	$75,614,466
3	Tech Support	$31,413,362

direct exploitation tools. Our focus is on the social engineering attacks found under option 1. After launching the software, a main menu with 6 options and an option to exit the program appears (Figure 12.4).

In the context of social engineering attacks, a basic SMS spoofing attack is presented as an example; therefore, select the "SMS Spoofing Attack Vector" from the menu of social engineering attacks (as shown in Figure 12.5).

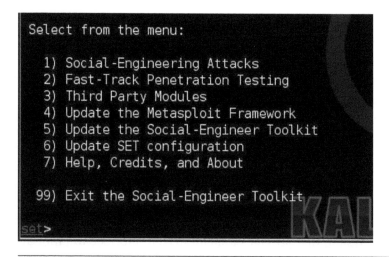

Figure 12.4 SET menu.

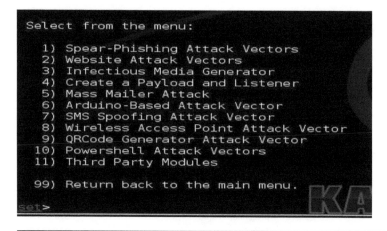

Figure 12.5 Social-Engineering Attacks menu.

To obtain the victim's credentials, the attacker proceeds to execute the steps outlined in SET. This involves selecting the SMS spoofing attack option, which is listed as option 7 in the toolkit's menu (Figure 12.6).

Next, choose option number 1 once more, which is the SMS attack option for targeting a single phone number, as depicted in Figure 12.7.

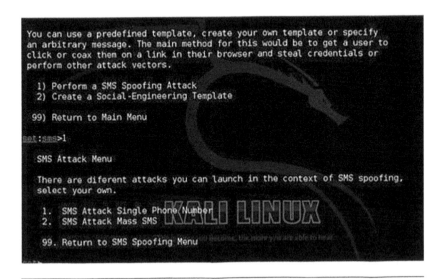

Figure 12.6   SMS Spoofing Attack Vector menu.

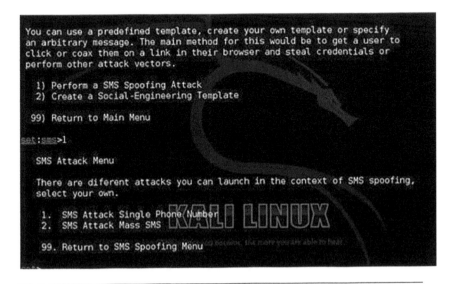

Figure 12.7   SMS Attack menu.

Input the phone number of the victim, including the country code, as illustrated in Figure 12.8.

Choose either a pre-made template or select from the templates provided in Figure 12.9.

The following figure displays the predefined templates menu. Choose any one to perform SMS spoofing (Figure 12.7). Finally, choose the service to send the SMS (Figures 12.10 and 12.11).

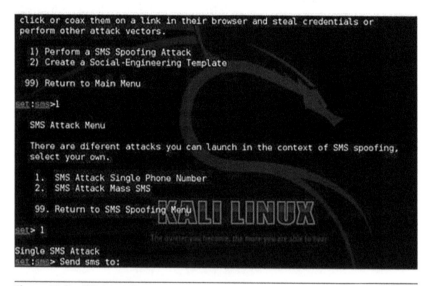

Figure 12.8 SMS Attack Menu.

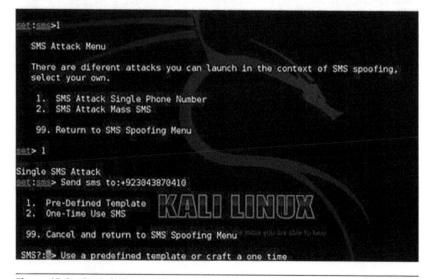

Figure 12.9 Single SMS Attack Menu.

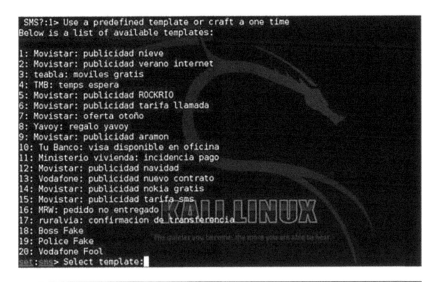

Figure 12.10   Predefined templates menu.

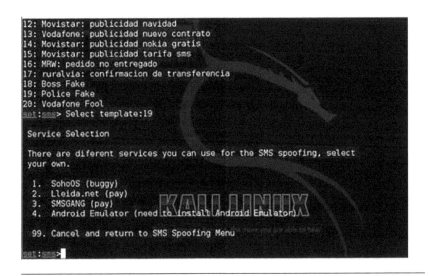

Figure 12.11   Service selection menu.

12.3.2 SMS Spam Message Detection with Term Frequency-Inverse Document Frequency (TF-IDF) and Random Forest Algorithm

The proposed study presented in Figure 12.12 aims to classify SMS text messages into two categories: ham or spam. The focus of this research is to develop a process that can accurately distinguish between the two types of messages.

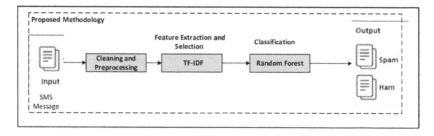

Figure 12.12 Process of SMS spam detection.

12.3.2.1 Phases of SMS Spam Detection The phases of spam detection involve preprocessing, feature extraction and selection, and classification.

12.3.2.1.1 Preprocessing The initial phase of message categorization involves pre-processing, which entails transforming unstructured data into more-structured data. Tokenization, stop word removal, and stemming are the three stages of pre-processing. In the first stage, tokenization removes symbols (@, #, %, and $), punctuation, and numbers. In the second stage, stop words, which are common words that provide no information, are removed. These include pronouns, prepositions, and conjunctions, such as "we," "are," "is," and others. In the final stage, stemming is performed. This involves identifying the roots of words and removing prefixes and suffixes. By performing stemming, different word forms, such as nouns, verbs, and adjectives, can be reduced to a common, similar word. For instance, "capturing" and "captured" can both be stemmed to "capture."

12.3.2.1.2 Feature Extraction and Selection The process of feature extraction and selection plays a crucial role in differentiating between ham and spam text messages. To accomplish this task, the TF-IDF method is utilized, which is a statistical technique frequently applied in the vector space model (Figure 12.13). This technique is widely used in the domains of information retrieval and text mining. TF-IDF is used to determine the importance of a word in a document by measuring its importance in relation to the entire corpus. The term frequency (TF) is measured by counting the number of times that a word appears in a document and is then normalized between 0 and 1.

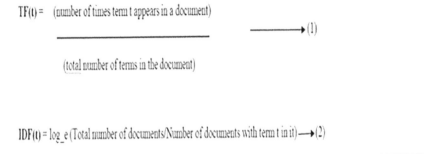

$$TF(t) = \frac{(\text{number of times term } t \text{ appears in a document})}{(\text{total number of terms in the document})} \longrightarrow (1)$$

$$IDF(t) = \log\_e (\text{Total number of documents/Number of documents with term } t \text{ in it}) \longrightarrow (2)$$

Figure 12.13   The equations of TF and IDF.

During tokenization, punctuation is removed, and all text is converted to lowercase to construct the index of terms in TF-IDF. TF reflects how important a term is if it occurs periodically in a document. Inverse document frequency (IDF) is also considered, which computes the informativeness of a term. While calculating TF, all terms are treated as equally important. However, certain terms such as "is," "of," and "that" may appear frequently but have little significance. Therefore, frequent terms are down-weighted, and rare ones are up-weighted. TF-IDF is a technique that measures the significance of words within individual documents and evaluates their overall importance in the entire document corpus.

12.3.2.1.3 SMS Message Spam Classification   During this phase, the classification of ham or spam is carried out by using the random forest (RF) algorithm. RF is a machine learning technique that employs ensemble learning to address the issue of overfitting that can occur with individual decision tree models. By averaging the results of multiple decision trees, RF creates a diverse set of predictions, with each tree producing its own unique performance. The average of these performances is then used to generalize the results. In the training stage, a group of decision trees is built, where features are chosen at random for their operation. RF can handle large datasets with various types of features, including binary, categorical, and numerical qualities. The algorithm works by selecting a bootstrap sample from S for each tree in the forest. To speed up the learning process of decision trees, a modified decision tree learning algorithm is employed in which only a random subset of features ($f \subseteq F$) is evaluated at each node of the tree.

This subset is significantly smaller than the full set of spam features (F), which reduces the computational cost of deciding on feature splits. As a result, the learning process of the tree is accelerated.

12.3.2.2 Pseudocode: Random Forest Method   Precondition: Training set $T=(x_i, y_i), \ldots, (x_n, y_n)$, feature F, and the number of trees in forest B

1. Function Random_Forest (T,F)
2. $L \leftarrow \emptyset$
3. For $i \in 1, \ldots, B$ do
4. $T^{(i)} \leftarrow$ A bootstrap sample from T
5. $L_i \leftarrow$ RandomizeTreeLearn ($T^{(i)}$,F)
6. $L \leftarrow L \cup \{l_i\}$
7. End for
8. Return L
9. End Function
10. Function RandomizeTreeLearn (T,F)
11. At each node:
12. $F \leftarrow$ very small subset of F
13. Split on best feature in f
14. Return the learned tree
15. End Function.

12.4 Results

To gauge the effectiveness of the employed algorithms, diverse performance evaluation metrics such as accuracy, precision, and the F-measure are employed. It was observed that the TF-IDF+RF algorithm performs the best compared to the other algorithms evaluated in terms of accuracy. It achieved an accuracy score of 97.50% with a precision of 0.98 and 0.97 for both recall and the F-measure. The next-best algorithm in terms of accuracy is TF-IDF with MNB, with a percentage of 97.06% and a precision result that differs only by 0.1 from the proposed method. Surprisingly, the F-measure result is the same as the proposed method at a rate of 0.97. To the contrary, the lowest performance was obtained by using the TF-IDF with the SVM algorithm, with an accuracy rate of 87.49%, a precision of 0.77, and an F-measure of 0.82. The reason for this outcome could be attributed to the

Table 12.4 Comparison of Algorithms

ALGORITHM	ACCURACY	PRECISION	F-MEASURE
+++TF-IDF+Multinomial Naive Bayes (MNB)	97.06	0.97	0.97
TF-IDF+K-Nearest Neighbor (KNN)	91.19	0.92	0.89
TF-IDF+Support Vector Machine (SVM)	87.49	0.77	0.82
TF-IDF+Decision Tree (DT)	96.57	0.96	0.97
TF-IDF+Random Forest	97.50	0.98	0.97

```
test4 = ['Hi sushil how are you doing?']
test5 = ['You won a car worth $1 million, to claim it call 626564']
test6 = ['How was your day?']

print(RFclassifier.predict(test4))
print(RFclassifier.predict(test5))
print(RFclassifier.predict(test6))

['ham']
['spam']
['ham']
```

Figure 12.14 Classifying messages as spam and ham.

fact that SVM is not very effective in handling imbalanced datasets. Imbalanced data can negatively affect the performance of the machine learning algorithms, including SVM, in various ways. Although SVM can face issues such as imbalances in the distribution of positive and negative support vectors and the possibility of positive points being distant from the optimal boundary, it still manages to attain an impressive performance level of over 75%. The results of various algorithms are shown in Figure 12.4.

12.5 Conclusion

The proliferation of SMS spam messages has become a major problem worldwide due to the increasing number of mobile users and cheap SMS rates. To combat this issue, this study presents a spam detection technique using various machine learning algorithms. The results indicate that the TF-IDF with the RF classification algorithm achieves the highest percentage of accuracy. However, accuracy alone is not sufficient to assess the performance since the dataset is imbalanced. Hence, other performance measures such as precision, recall, and the F-measure must also be considered. Despite the imbalanced dataset, the RF algorithm still achieves good precision and F-measure scores of 0.98 and 0.97. It is notable that the choice of algorithm and the features used can have a significant impact on the performance and results.

12.6 Acknowledgment

We wish to extend our heartfelt appreciation to the Management and Principal of Sapthagiri College of Engineering Bangalore for their support and the facilities provided to us.

References

[1] Zuoguang Wang, Hongsong Zhu, and Limin Sun. "Social Engineering in Cybersecurity: Effect Mechanisms, Human Vulnerabilities and Attack Methods." *IEEE Access* 9 (January 2021).

[2] Filipe Breda, Hugo Barbosa, and Telmo Morais. "Social Engineering and Cyber Security." In *INTED2017 Proceedings*. IATED, 2017, pp. 4204–4211.

[3] Abdullah Algarni, Yue Xu, Taizan Chan, and Yu-Chu Tian. "Social Engineering in Social Networking Sites: Affect-Based Model." In *8th International Conference for Internet Technology and Secured Transactions (ICITST-2013)*. IEEE, 2013, pp. 508–515.

[4] Monique Bezuidenhout, Francois Mouton, and Hein S. Venter. "Social Engineering Attack Detection Model: Seadm." In *2010 Information Security for South Africa*. IEEE, 2010, pp. 1–8.

[5] Zuoguang Wang, Yimo Ren, Hongsong Zhu, and Limin Sun. "Threat Detection for General Social Engineering Attack Using Machine Learning Techniques." *arXiv preprint arXiv:2203.07933* (2022).

[6] Sushruth Venkatesha, K. Rahul Reddy, and B. R. Chandavarkar. "Social Engineering Attacks During the COVID-19 Pandemic." *SN Computer Science* 2 (2021): 1–9.

[7] Kangfeng Zheng, Tong Wu, Xiujuan Wang, Bin Wu, and Chunhua Wu. "A Session and Dialogue-Based Social Engineering Framework." *IEEE Access* 7 (2019).

[8] Murtaza Ahmed Siddiqi, Wooguil Pak, and Moquddam A. Siddiqi. "A Study on the Psychology of Social Engineering-Based Cyberattacks and Existing Countermeasures." *Applied Sciences* 12, no. 12 (2022): 6042.

[9] A. S. Alazri. "The Awareness of Social Engineering in Information Revolution: Techniques and Challenges." In *2015 10th International Conference for Internet Technology and Secured Transactions (ICITST)*. IEEE, 2015, pp. 198–201.

[10] B. B. Gupta, A. Tewari, A. K. Jain, and D. P. Agrawal. "Fighting Against Phishing Attacks: State of the Art and Future Challenges." *Neural Computing and Applications* 28, no. 12 (1 December 2017): 3629–3654.

[11] B. B. Gupta, A. Tewari, A. K. Jain, and D. P. Agrawal. "Fighting Against Phishing Attacks: State of the Art and Future Challenges." *Neural Computing and Applications* 28, no. 12 (1 December 2017): 3629–3654.

[12] V. Sokolov and O. Korzhenko. "Analysis of Recent Attacks Based on Social Engineering Techniques." *arXiv preprint arXiv:1902.07965* (2019).

[13] H. Aldawood and G. Skinner. "A Taxonomy for Social Engineering Attacks via Personal Devices." *International Journal of Computer Applications* 975 (2019): 8887.

[14] K. Thomas, et al. "Data Breaches, Phishing, or Malware?: Understanding the Risks of Stolen Credentials." In *Proceedings of the 2017 ACM SIGSAC Conference on Computer and Communications Security.* ACM, 2017, pp. 1421–1434.

[15] R. Alavi, S. Islam, H. Mouratidis, and S. Lee. "Managing Social Engineering Attacks-Considering Human Factors and Security Investment." In *HAISA*, 2015, pp. 161–171.

[16] I. Ghafir, V. Prenosil, A. Alhejailan, and M. Hammoudeh. "Social Engineering Attack Strategies and Defence Approaches." In *2016 IEEE 4th International Conference on Future Internet of Things and Cloud (FiCloud)*, pp. 145–149. IEEE, 2016.

[17] D. D. Caputo, S. L. Pfleeger, J. D. Freeman, and M. E. Johnson. "Going Spear Phishing: Exploring Embedded Training and Awareness." *IEEE Security & Privacy* 12, no. 1 (2014): 28–38.

[18] Surbhi Gupta, Abhishek Singhal, and Akanksha Kapoor. "A Literature Survey on Social Engineering Attacks: Phishing Attack." In *2016 International Conference on Computing, Communication and Automation (ICCCA).* IEEE, 2016, pp. 537–540.

[19] Xin Luo, Richard Brody, Alessandro Seazzu, and Stephen Burd. "Social Engineering: The Neglected Human Factor for Information Security Management." *Information Resources Management Journal (IRMJ)* 24, no. 3 (2011): 1–8.

[20] Katharina Krombholz, Heidelinde Hobel, Markus Huber, and Edgar Weippl. "Advance Social Engineering Attacks." *Journal of Information Security and Applications* (2014) 3, no. 12 (December 2022): 343–349.

[21] Devika C.J. Nair and Teslin Jacob. "An Automated System for Detection of Social Engineering Phishing Attacks Using Machine Learning." *International Journal of Engineering and Technology* 7, no. 7 (2020).

[22] Sandhya Mishra and Devpriya Soni. "SMS Phishing and Mitigation Approaches." In *2019 Twelfth International Conference on Contemporary Computing (ic3).* IEEE, 2019, pp. 1–5.

[23] T. Subburaj and K. Suthendran. "DigitalWatering Hole Attack Detection Using Sequential Pattern." *Journal of Cyber Security and Mobility* (2018): 1–12.

[24] Abeer F. AL-Otaibi and Emad S. Alsuwat. "A Study on Social Engineering Attacks: Phishing Attack." *International Journal of Recent advances in Multidisciplinary Research* 7, no. 11 (2020): 6374–6380.

[25] www.thesslstore.com/blog/social-engineering-statistics/

[26] S. Venkatesha, K.R. Reddy, and B.R. Chandavarkar. "Social Engineering Attacks During the COVID-19 Pandemic." *SN Computer Science* 2 (2021): 78.

[27] F. Mouton, L. Leenen, and H. S. Venter. "Social Engineering Attack Examples, Templates and Scenarios." *Computers & Security* 59 (2016): 186–209. https://doi.org/10.1016/j.cose.2016.03.004.

[28] K. Krombholz, H. Hobel, M. Huber, and E. Weippl. "Advanced Social Engineering Attacks." *Journal of Information Security and Applications* 22 (2015): 113–122. https://doi.org/10.1016/j.jisa.2014.09.005.

[29] A. Yasin, R. Fatima, L. Liu, J. Wang, R. Ali, and Z. Wei. "Understanding and Deciphering of Socialengineering Attack Scenarios." *Security & Privacy* 4, no. 4 (2021): 1–17. https://doi.org/10.1002/spy2.161.

[30] D. Irani, M. Balduzzi, D. Balzarotti, E. Kirda, and C. Pu. "Reverse Social Engineering Attacks in Online Socialnetworks." *Lecture Notes in Computer Science* (including Subser. Lect. Notes Artif. Intell. Lect. Notes Bioinformatics) 6739 LNCS, no. March 2010 (2011): 55–74. https://doi.org/10.1007/978-3-642-22424-9_4.

[31] Y. S. Saini, L. Sharma, P. Chawla, and S. Parashar. "Social Engineering Attacks." *Lecture Notes in Networks and Systems* 491, no. 6 (2023): 497–509. https://doi.org/10.1007/978-981-19-4193-1_49.

[32] A. U. Zulkurnain, A. Kamal, B. Kamarun, A. Bin Husain, and H. Chizari. "Social Engineering AttackMitigation." *International Journal of Mathematics and Computer Science* 1, no. 4 (2015): 188–198. www.aiscience.org/journal/ijmcs

[33] I. Ghafir, V. Prenosil, A. Alhejailan, and M. Hammoudeh. "Social Engineering Attack Strategies and Defence Approaches." *Proceedings 2016 IEEE 4th International Conference Future Internet Things Cloud, FiCloud 2016*, 2016, pp. 145–149. https://doi.org/10.1109/FiCloud.2016.28.

[34] F. Salahdine and N. Kaabouch. "Social Engineering Attacks: A Survey." *Future Internet* 11, no. 4 (2019). https://doi.org/10.3390/FI11040089.

[35] R. Heartfield and G. Loukas. "A Taxonomy of Attacks and a Survey of Defence Mechanisms for Semanticsocial Engineering Attacks." *ACM Computing Surveys* 48, no. 3 (2015). https://doi.org/10.1145/2835375.

[36] P. N. Astya. "Galgotias University. School of Computing Science and Engineering, Institute of Electrical and Electronics Engineers." *Uttar Pradesh Section, Institute of Electrical and Electronics Engineers.* Uttar PradeshSection. SP/C Joint Chapter, and Institute of Electrical and Electronics Engineers, —Proceeding, International Conference on Computing, Communication and Automation (ICCCA 2016) : 29–30 April, 2016, pp. 1–4, 2016 (PDF) Social Engineering Attacks Techniques [accessed Sep 18 2023].

[37] F. Salahdine and N. Kaabouch. "Social Engineering Attacks: A Survey." *Future Internet* 11 (2019): 89. https://doi.org/10.3390/fi11040089

[38] N. Y. Conteh and P. J. Schmick. "Cybersecurity: Risks, Vulnerabilities and Countermeasures to Prevent Social Engineering Attacks." *International Journal Advanced Computer Research* 6 (2016): 1–31. [Google Scholar] [CrossRef].

[39] R. Heartfield and G. Loukas. "A Taxonomy of Attacks and a Survey of Defence Mechanisms for Semantic Social Engineering Attacks." *ACM Computing Surveys* 48 (2016): 1–37. [Google Scholar] [CrossRef].

[40] A. Madain, M.A. Ala, and R. Al-Sayyed. "Online Social Networks Security: Threats, Attacks, and Future Directions. In *Social Media Shaping e-Publishing and Academia*. Springer International Publishing: New York, NY, 2017, pp. 121–132. [Google Scholar].

Index

Milton Keynes UK
Ingram Content Group UK Ltd.
UKHW031131141024
449569UK00006B/280